# Marketing Metaphors and Metamorphosis

# Marketing Metaphors and Metamorphosis

Edited by

Philip J. Kitchen
*Chair and Professor of Strategic Marketing, University of Hull Business School, UK*

First published 2008 by
PALGRAVE MACMILLAN
Houndmills, Basingstoke, Hampshire RG21 6XS and
175 Fifth Avenue, New York, N.Y. 10010
Companies and representatives throughout the world

PALGRAVE MACMILLAN is the global academic imprint of the Palgrave Macmillan division of St. Martin's Press, LLC and of Palgrave Macmillan Ltd. Macmillan® is a registered trademark in the United States, United Kingdom and other countries. Palgrave is a registered trademark in the European Union and other countries.

ISBN-13: 978–1–4039–9861–3    hardback
ISBN-10: 1–4039–9861–2    hardback

This book is printed on paper suitable for recycling and made from fully managed and sustained forest sources. Logging, pulping and manufacturing processes are expected to conform to the environmental regulations of the country of origin.

A catalogue record for this book is available from the British Library.

Library of Congress Cataloging-in-Publication Data

Marketing : metaphors and metamorphosis / [edited by] Philip J. Kitchen.
    p. cm.
Includes bibliographical references and index.
ISBN 1–4039–9861–2 (alk. paper)
1. Marketing. 2. Marketing—Management. 3. Communication in marketing. I. Kitchen, Philip J.
HF5415.M2998 2008
658.8—dc22

2008016157

10  9  8  7  6  5  4  3  2  1
17  16  15  14  13  12  11  10  09  08

Printed and bound in Great Britain by
CPI Antony Rowe, Chippenham and Eastbourne

*To my wife Diane for her witty humour, and companionship,
during the development and editing of this book.
Thank you.*

# Contents

| | |
|---|---|
| *List of Figures* | ix |
| *List of Tables* | xi |
| *Acknowledgements* | xii |
| *Notes on the Contributors* | xiii |

1 **Marketing Metaphors and Metamorphosis: an Introduction**    1
 *Philip J. Kitchen*

2 **Metaphors and Marketing: Some Uses and Abuses**    10
 *Caroline Tynan*

3 **The Globalization of Markets and the Rule of Three**    26
 *Jagdish N. Sheth, Can Uslay and Rajendra S. Sisodia*

4 **Marketing Mix Metaphorosis: the Heavy Toll of too much Popularity**    42
 *Walter van Waterschoot and Joeri De Haes*

5 **Market Segmentation as a Metaphor: Whoever Heard of Alexander the Mediocre?**    62
 *Malcolm McDonald*

6 **It's a Kinda Magic: Adventures in Alchemy**    88
 *Stephen Brown*

7 **Viral Marketing**    102
 *Adam Lindgreen, Angela Dobele, Michael Beverland and Joëlle Vanhamme*

8 **Viral Marketing: How to Spread the Word via Mobile Device**    118
 *Shintaro Okazaki*

9  Brand Ambassadors: Strategic Diplomats or Tactical
   Promoters?                                                    132
   *Claudia Fisher-Buttinger and Christine Vallaster*

10 Negative Comparative Advertising: When
   Marketers Attack                                              146
   *Fred Beard*

11 Why Do They Lag and Why Should We Care?                       162
   *Jacob Goldenberg and Shaul Oreg*

12 Relationship Marketing as a Marriage                          172
   *Adam Lindgreen, Roger Palmer and Michael Beverland*

13 Products and the Life Cycle                                   183
   *Roger Palmer and Adam Lindgreen*

14 Don't Blame it on the Metaphor: Marketing, Metaphors
   and Metamorphosis in the Internal Market                      195
   *Ian Buckingham*

15 Marketing, Metaphors and Metamorphosis: Marketing
   Management as a Caring Profession                             206
   *Michael Thomas*

*Index*                                                          217

# List of Figures

| | | |
|---|---|---|
| 3.1 | The Rule of Three | 32 |
| 4.1 | The new exchange model | 43 |
| 5.1 | Non-cumulative diffusion pattern | 64 |
| 5.2 | A market life cycle and different managerial orientations | 66 |
| 5.3 | The shape of the car market | 67 |
| 5.4 | The shape of the lawn mower market | 67 |
| 5.5 | Early growth, rapid growth and a mature market | 68 |
| 5.6 | Personalizing segments | 70 |
| 5.7 | The photocopier market | 71 |
| 5.8 | The product/market life cycle and market characteristics | 72 |
| 5.9 | Fast moving consumer goods value chain | 73 |
| 5.10 | The relationship between market share and return on investment | 73 |
| 5.11 | A generic market map | 78 |
| 5.12 | Market map listing the different junction types | 79 |
| 5.13 | Market leverage points on a market map | 80 |
| 5.14 | The market segmentation process | 81 |
| 5.15 | Micro-segments | 82 |
| 5.16 | An undifferentiated market | 83 |
| 5.17 | Different needs in a market | 83 |
| 5.18 | Segments in a market | 83 |
| 5.19 | Summarizing the market segmentation process | 85 |
| 7.1 | Steps in order to create a viral marketing campaign | 114 |
| 8.1 | Internet connection terminals in Japan | 125 |
| 8.2 | Structure of the viral campaign | 126 |
| 8.3 | Illustrations of photos sent to the viral campaign site | 127 |
| 9.1 | Brand evangelists | 143 |
| 10.1 | Miller Brewing launches both evaluative and factual attacks on Anheuser-Busch | 153 |
| 10.2 | Diet Pepsi's evaluative attack on Diet Coke | 154 |
| 10.3 | Juniper Networks and an implied attack on Cisco | 155 |
| 11.1 | Rogers's (2003) 'Adopting Segments' | 165 |
| 13.1 | The Boston matrix | 185 |
| 14.1 | 'BS Bingo' matrix | 198 |

14.2   Profile of a 'chief engagement officer'                    205
15.1   Mutual determination with social trustee
       civic professionalism                                     212

# List of Tables

| | | |
|---|---|---|
| 4.1 | Denotations of the marketing mix metaphor | 49 |
| 5.1 | Key elements of world class marketing | 63 |
| 5.2 | Some market definitions (personal market) | 77 |
| 5.3 | Understand market segmentation | 84 |
| 7.1 | Emotions behind viral marketing | 105 |
| 7.2 | Online viewing of the Big Ad | 108 |
| 15.1 | What is it we need to do to become more professional? | 213 |

# Acknowledgements

With grateful thanks to the contributors for sharing their knowledge, expertise, wisdom and understanding of marketing and the ways in which the domain accesses and utilizes *metaphors* as constructs to explain or justify how marketing works. This bringing together of learned colleagues at a time when marketing is transitioning into new and more dynamic forms is likely without parallel. I am indebted to the contributors who have provided, discussed or clarified specific examples of metaphor constructs and critically engaged with the ways these have been applied in the field.

I acknowledge, with the contributors, the various individuals, companies, and research-oriented journals who have assisted us by allowing material to be cited and shared. In addition, we thank the myriad of marketing students who through their questions and comments have helped the contributors and editor sharpen and hone their critical faculties in relation to the marketing discipline. And we also acknowledge the many practitioners and colleagues who, through various means, have influenced development of the ideas herein expressed.

To all of you, thank you for your help, guidance, support and encouragement in the expression and critique of these metaphors and their relevance to theorists and practitioners of marketing in the twenty-first century.

PHILIP J. KITCHEN

The editor, contributors and publishers are grateful for permission to use or cite copyright material. Every effort has been made to trace all the copyright holders, but if any have been inadvertently overlooked the publishers will be pleased to make the necessary arrangements at the first opportunity.

# Notes on the Contributors

**Philip J. Kitchen** holds the Chair and is Professor of Strategic Marketing at the University of Hull Business School and Director, Research Centre for Marketing, Communications and International Strategy (CMCIS). He is also founder and editor of the *Journal of Marketing Communication*. He has published eleven books and over 100 academic papers in leading journals around the world. In 2003, he was listed as one of 'the top 50 gurus who have influenced the future of marketing' (*Marketing Business*). He is a Fellow of CIM, the RSA and Member of the Institute of Directors. A recent report for the Chartered Institute of Marketing, London, UK, was *A Marketing Communications Scenario for 2010* (2006). He serves on the editorial review boards of, among others, the *Journal of Advertising*, the *European Journal of Marketing*, the *Journal of Marketing Management*, and the *International Journal of Advertising*. His research interests lie in marketing theory, integrated marketing communications, corporate communications, branding, and global marketing.

**Fred Beard** is a professor of advertising in the Gaylord College of Journalism and Mass Communication, University of Oklahoma. He has published and presented nearly eighty articles and research papers on advertising humour, client–advertising agency relationships, and other topics. His work has been published in numerous US and international scholarly journals, including the *Journal of Advertising*, the *Journal of Advertising Research*, the *Journal of Business Ethics*, the *Journal of Business Research*, *Journalism History*, the *Journal of Macromarketing*, and the *Journal of Marketing Communications*. He is also the author of *Humor in the Advertising Business: Theory, Practice, and Wit* (2007).

**Stephen Brown** is Professor of Marketing Research at the University of Ulster. Best known for *Postmodern Marketing* (2005), he has written numerous books including *Fail Better!* (2008), *Free Gift Inside!!* (2003), *The Marketing Code* (2006) and *Wizard! Harry Potter's Brand Magic* (2005).

**Ian Buckingham** is an employee engagement specialist and much-published thought leader, with his own leadership career spanning financial services, people-centred consultancy and the communications agency worlds. As the founding MD of the Omnicom-owned Interbrand

Inside (arguably the original employee engagement agency), he created the methodology for bringing brands to life from within. His most recent work: *Brand Engagement – How Employees Make or Break Brands* was published by Palgrave Macmillan in late 2007 and is a provocative treatise on the power of employee engagement as a key driver of brand transformation.

**Joeri De Haes** is a senior research and teaching assistant in the Marketing Department of the University of Antwerp. He holds Masters and PhD degrees in applied economic sciences from the University of Antwerp. His research interests lie predominantly in the area of retailing and online consumer behaviour. Currently, his main focus is on (online) store environment research.

**Claudia Fisher-Buttinger** is the founder of boutique consulting firm Lemontree Brand Strategy, headquartered in Munich, Germany. For more than a decade, Claudia has designed and implemented brand and marketing strategies for many leading international companies across Europe and the US. Her speciality areas include brand portfolio strategy, brand identity development, business-driven brand strategy, marketing strategy and customer experience strategy.

**Jacob Goldenberg** is an associate professor of marketing at the School of Business Administration at the Hebrew University of Jerusalem. He received his PhD from the Hebrew University of Jerusalem in a joint programme of the School of Business Administration and Racach Institute of Physics. His research focuses on creativity, new product development, diffusion of innovation and complexity in market dynamics. He has published in leading journals such as the *Journal of Marketing*, the *Journal of Marketing Research*, *Management Science*, *Marketing Science*, *Nature* and *Science*. In addition, he is co-author with David Mazursky  of the book *Creativity in Product Innovation* (2002). His scientific work on creativity has been covered in the *New York Times*, the *Wall Street Journal*, the *Boston Globe*, BBC news and the *Herald Tribune*.

**Adam Lindgreen** is Professor of Strategic Marketing at Hull University Business School. Lindgreen received his PhD at Cranfield University. He has published in *Business Horizons*, *Industrial Marketing Management*, the *Journal of Business Ethics*, the *Journal of Business & Industrial Marketing*, and *Psychology & Marketing*, and has articles forthcoming in the *Journal of Product Innovation Management* and the *Journal of the*

*Academy of Marketing Science*, among others. His research interests include business and industrial marketing management, consumer behaviour, experiential marketing, and corporate social responsibility. He serves on the boards of many journals.

**Malcolm McDonald**, until recently, Professor of Marketing and Deputy Director Cranfield School of Management with special responsibility for E-Business, is a graduate in English Language and Literature from Oxford University, in Business Studies from Bradford University Management Centre, and has a PhD from Cranfield University. He also has an honorary doctorate from Bradford University. He has extensive industrial experience, including a number of years as marketing director of Canada Dry. He is chairman of six companies and spends much of his time working with the operating boards of the world's biggest multinational companies, such as IBM, Xerox, BP and the like, in most countries in the world, including Japan, USA, Europe, South America, ASEAN and Australasia. He has written forty-two books, including the best-seller *Marketing Plans: How to Prepare Them; How to Use Them* (2007) and many of his papers have been published. His current interests centre around the use of information technology in advanced marketing processes and global best practice key account management.

**Shintaro Okazaki**, PhD, is Associate Professor of Marketing at Universidad Autónoma de Madrid, Spain. He has published articles in, among others, the *Journal of Advertising*, the *Journal of Advertising Research*, the *International Journal of Advertising*, the *Journal of Marketing Communications*, the *Journal of International Marketing*, the *Journal of Business Research*, the *Journal of World Business*, the *European Journal of Marketing*, the *International Journal of Market Research*, *Psychology & Marketing*, and *International Marketing Review*. His primary research interests lie in marketing communications, online consumer behaviour, and global marketing. He serves on the editorial boards of a number of journals, including the *Journal of Advertising*, the *International Journal of Advertising*, the *Journal of Marketing Communications*, the *Journal of Public Policy & Marketing*, *Internet Research*, and the *Journal of International Consumer Marketing*.

**Shaul Oreg** is an assistant professor in the Department of Sociology and Anthropology at the University of Haifa, Israel. He received his PhD in organizational behaviour from Cornell University in 2003. His research focuses on individual differences in social and organizational contexts. A specific focus of his research is on the dispositional and contextual sources of resistance to organizational change. His other works on individual differences include the study of personal values, dispositional correlates of persuasiveness, and the interaction between personality and context in predicting effective leadership. Dr Oreg has published in journals such as the *Journal of Applied Psychology* and the *Journal of Organizational Behavior*, and he is a member of the Academy of Management, the Society of Industrial and Organizational Psychology, and the European Association of Personality Psychology.

**Roger Palmer** is Professor of Marketing and Management at Henley Management College, UK. He is also a visiting professor at the Brisbane Graduate School of Business, Australia. His primary interests are in the area of business to business marketing, technology and new product development, strategic marketing and marketing practice, and he is a leading member of an international research group. He has published numerous journal articles and a number of books, and teaches and consults around the world.

**Jagdish N. Sheth**, PhD, is Charles H. Kellstadt Professor of Marketing at Goizueta Business School, Emory University. He has published more than 200 research papers and books in different areas of marketing and business strategy. His book *The Theory of Buyer Behavior* (1969) with John A. Howard is a classic in the field. He is an American Psychological Association Fellow and past President of APA's Consumer Psychology Division and Association for Consumer Research (ACR). He was the recipient of the Viktor Mataja Medal from the Austrian Research Society in Vienna (1977) and the 1989 Outstanding Marketing Educator Award from the Academy of Marketing Science. In 1991 and 1999, Dr Sheth was also recognized as the Marketing Educator of the year by Sales and Marketing Executives International (SMEI). In 1992 the American Marketing Association awarded Dr Sheth the PD Converse Award for his life-long contribution to the discipline of marketing theory. In 1996, he was elected to be the Distinguished Fellow of the Academy of Marketing Science. In 2002, he was recognized with a Distinguished Scholar Award by the Marketing Management Association. In 2004, he was awarded both the prestigious Charles Cooldige Parlin Award and the title of Irwin/McGraw Hill Distinguished Marketing Educator by the American Marketing Association. He currently serves on the editorial boards of the *Journal of Strategic Marketing*, the *Journal of Service Research*, *Customer Relationship Management Journal*, the *Journal of Relationship*

*Marketing*, the *Journal of Marketing Theory*, the *Journal of International Marketing*, and the *Journal of Customer Behavior*.

**Rajendra S. Sisodia** is Professor of Marketing and founding director of the Center for Marketing Technology at Bentley College, Waltham, MA, USA. He has a PhD in marketing and business policy from Columbia University. He has published nearly 100 articles in many journals, including the *Harvard Business Review*, the *Journal of Marketing*, the *Journal of Business Strategy* and the *Journal of Business Research*. He also writes frequently for the *Wall Street Journal*. His research, teaching, and consulting expertise spans the areas of strategic marketing, marketing productivity, marketing ethics, and stakeholder-based marketing. In 2003, he was cited as one of '50 Leading Marketing Thinkers' by the UK-based Chartered Institute of Marketing. He consults with and provides executive seminars for companies in various industries. Clients have included Sprint, Volvo, and IBM, to name a few.

**Michael Thomas** OBE, OM (Poland) is Past President of the Market Research Society, past Chairman of the Chartered Institute of Marketing, and Emeritus Professor of Marketing at Strathclyde University. Author of several books, and many articles in leading journals, he is also founding editor of *Marketing Intelligence and Planning*. Currently he writes more about birds than about marketing.

**Caroline Tynan** is Professor of Marketing and Head of Marketing at Nottingham University Business School, Vice President of the Academy of Marketing and Dean of the Academic Senate of the Chartered Institute of Marketing. She has published in a number of journals including the *Journal of Business Research*, the *European Journal of Marketing*, the *Journal of Marketing Management*, the *Journal of Strategic Marketing*, and the *International Journal of Advertising and Managerial Decision Economics*. Her research interests include relationship marketing, particularly within business-to-consumer and cross-cultural contexts, consumption meanings and managerial marketing practice. She serves on the editorial boards of the *European Journal of Marketing*, the *Journal of Marketing Management* and the *Journal of Consumer Behaviour*.

**Can Uslay**, PhD, is Assistant Professor of Marketing at Argyros School of Business and Economics, Chapman University, Orange, CA, USA. He has published articles in the *European Business Review*, the *International Journal of Technology Management*, the *Journal of Business-to-Business*

*Marketing*, the *Journal of Public Policy and Marketing*, the *Journal of Research in Marketing and Entrepreneurship*, *Marketing Education Review*, and the *Review of Marketing Research*. He currently serves as a Vice-Chair of Research for the Entrepreneurship SIG of the American Marketing Association. His research interests lie broadly within marketing strategy, policy, and theory construction.

**Christine Vallaster** is a research fellow in the Marketing Department, University of Giessen, Germany, sponsored by the German Scientific Community (DFG). Her publications have appeared in scholarly journals such as the *Journal of Marketing Management*, the *International Journal of Cross-Cultural Management*, *Qualitative Market Research: an International Journal*, and the *European Journal of Marketing*. Her focus of research interest is brand management processes, culture, identity, and leadership. Additionally, she works as a consultant.

**Joëlle Vanhamme** is in the Department of Marketing, RSM Erasmus University, Rotterdam, The Netherlands. She received her PhD at the Catholic University of Louvain. She has published in *Business Horizons*, *Industrial Marketing Management*, the *Journal of Economic Psychology*, the *Journal of Marketing Management*, *Psychology & Marketing*, and *Recherche et Applications en Marketing*, among others. Her research interests include the influence of emotions on marketing variables including customer satisfaction, children advertising, corporate social responsibility, gift giving, word-of-mouth marketing, and senior marketing.

**Walter van Waterschoot**, PhD, is Professor of Marketing and Channel Management at the University of Antwerp. He is a vested author of marketing textbooks written in Dutch. The general marketing management textbook he co-authored is currently in its eleventh edition. He has also contributed numerous chapters in international monographs, including the *Oxford Textbook of Marketing* (2000). He prepared entries for several encyclopaedias, including the *International Encyclopaedia of Marketing* (2000). He has published papers in leading academic journals including the *Journal of Marketing*, the *Journal of Retailing*, the *Journal of Retailing and Consumer Services*, the *International Journal of Research in Marketing*, and *Health Marketing Quarterly*. His paper on the classification of the marketing mix ('The 4P classification of the marketing mix revisited', with Christophe Van den Bulte, *Journal of Marketing*, 56(4) (October): 83–93) was included in the compilation of the most influential articles in the history of marketing published by Routledge (2000).

# 1

# Marketing Metaphors and Metamorphosis: an Introduction

*Philip J. Kitchen*

This book is an extension to a trilogy beginning with *The Future of Marketing* (2003), followed by *The Rhetoric and Reality of Marketing: an International Managerial Approach* (2003), and then *Marketing Mind Prints* (2005). Each of these edited volumes dealt with the subject and discipline of marketing and were favoured by contributions from some of the leading theorists in the discipline. As was stated in a previous volume, marketing as a theory, practice, and discipline has now been under fire or under criticism for some time. Certainly the received wisdom associated with the managerial school of marketing and indeed the value of the school is under serious scrutiny by practitioners, and not least by theorists and students.

The first book concluded with the rather conservative solution that the future of marketing was indeed valuable and important but that change needed to be gradual, perhaps incremental. Change in such a fundamental discipline could not be undertaken rapidly, and the timing did not seem right in 2003 for a radical overhaul of theory or practice. This type of thinking was exemplified by the Academy of Marketing's approach at the Cardiff Business School (2003) where 'new directions in marketing' were diligently sought for, but not necessarily found.

The case perhaps for more radical adjustment was presented in the second edited book where marketing in eight nation-states was examined via sixteen case studies or vignettes. For some firms, marketing as a managerial philosophy and business practice seemed to be deeply embedded in the organizational psyche and extended outwards to delivering need satisfactions. For other firms, marketing was a form of idea or concept more akin to 'window dressing', or 'dressing up' marketing in a form which appeared to be customer and consumer-oriented, but wherein these vital groups received lip-service. By the time this book was published, the American guardian of marketing, the American Marketing Association, had decided that perhaps marketing was 'in need of reform'. A two-day conference (2005) held in Bentley College, Boston to discuss this topic, achieved the consensus that marketing was in fact in need of serious remedial attention. The real questions of whether this concerned wholesale reformation or a full renaissance were not tackled. Of course, this was the *American* Marketing Association and 99 per cent of all topics tackled concerned, unsurprisingly, marketing in North America. I thought then of how many other nations, business schools, and marketing faculties, not to mention marketing practitioners, looked to America for leadership. And, in a golden age of 'global marketing' perhaps expectations could be raised for a widening of the reform issue to include the Pacific Rim nations, perhaps to include the expanding European Union, or maybe even reach toward the burgeoning economies of China or India. However, these minor issues remained unaddressed and unconsidered.

In the third book of the marketing trilogy, contributors were asked to address specific subjects within the managerial school where managers could easily access these *mind prints* as occasion required. These *mind prints* included:

- marketing due diligence
- innovation and sustainable competitive advantage
- why new products fail
- landmarks in international marketing
- integrated marketing
- beyond relationship marketing

This book was reasonably well received in 2005 and its purpose amply fulfilled. By 2007, however, the firestorms raging around marketing had not been put out, and indeed seemed to be gaining in intensity. The paradigmatical problems with which the managerial school had been identified as early as the 1980s had to some degree been augmented by such subjects as relationship or network marketing or customer experience marketing. However, the extent of radical change required was not necessarily envisioned initially. Perhaps one of the most powerful advocates of radical change over the past thirty years has been Christian Gronroos. His significant contribution is extended in his latest book, *In Search of a New Logic for Marketing* (2006), which cogently argues that the old logic is now out of date, and not as relevant as it used to be. His new logic, which is firmly anchored in a services marketing orientation and relationship marketing, argues powerfully for a radical adjustment of marketing in favour of continually delivering on customer-focused prom-ises, before, during, and after purchase decisions have been made.

Perhaps much of the furore revolves around the significant issue of how marketing is done. All managerial disciplines progress in terms of 'received beliefs' which form the basis for managerial practice and for knowledge transference to students. Until around 1980, these beliefs were largely rigorous, intact, and related predominately to the elegance and simplicity associated with the 'managerial school' and the 'buyer behaviour school'. However – from that time – markets became much more complex, buyers more discerning, and consumers more critical, and these trends were further accelerated with the development of the internet and the world wide web. Suddenly, consumers and customers were empowered with knowledge and information and market *places* were transformed into market *spaces*. Transactions were no longer con-strained by time, physical location, or full market control by manufac-turers and retailers. Control over information was passing to the final element of the value chain, which meant that consumers and customers could – if they desired – shop the world for products and services. Schultz and Schultz referred to this in an early paper (1998: 19) as a 'transition-ing process'.

> The argument is developed that marketing and marketing communi-cation are in transition, moving from the historical marketing approaches of the 1960s, which focused on the 4Ps to a new, interac-tive marketplace in the twenty-first century. A structural model of three marketplaces is presented based on the location and control of information technology. The premise is developed that as informa-tion technology shifts from one market player to the next, definitive changes in the need for communication develop. A description of the development of the Integrated Marketing Communication concept is furnished. Based on that, a four level transition process is proposed as organizations move from one stage of integrated marketing commu-nication development to another, generally based on their ability to capture and manage information technology.

There are many other references that could be cited, but this is sufficient for purpose. The idea that 'marketing' itself was somehow 'in transition' was not new by 1998, but it was expressed cogently at that time. Another way of putting this is that some of the basic ideas, models, systems and processes of marketing were apparently being modified or adjusted in the face of market realities. The old-style paradigm or paradigms of marketing were changing. It is important to recall that these paradigms are plural in nature. The last count was that there are approximately 40 different paradigms (see Achrol, 1997; Ambler, 1994; Baker, 2005; Combe, 1999; David, 1998; Godin, 2001; Palmer and Ponsoby, 2002; Peppers and Rogers, 1995; Reddy, 1999; Sheth, 2005), which are dominated theoretically by logical positivism which emphasizes measurability and intersubjective certification (Arndt, 1985; Hunt, 2002). However, having said this, there is no strict interpretation of any marketing paradigm, just a generalized acceptance of a concept that is 'perceived to be appropriate' and a set of tools (that is, the marketing mix) which can be applied differentially based on the underlying dynamics of served markets. If this generalized concept and related tools no longer works, it might be because

(a) *of the failure of marketing practitioners to implement marketing properly.*
    There is already a widespread acceptance of this worldwide failure, with some countries – such as the United Kingdom – being particularly poor. However, it could be argued that with such a poorly defined generalized concept and a mixed bag of tools, it was perhaps inevitable that many businesses would take the line of least resistance and move toward a more rhetorical approach.

Or

(b) *of the need for marketing to be redefined.*
    Under (b) there seems little doubt that marketing, or its theorists, has to adopt this course of action, for if this does not happen, marketing's stated ideal of being customer or consumer-oriented cannot be achieved, and morever, marketing has to move toward a future by providing measurable contributions that are *strategic* as well as tactical in nature.

Jagdish Sheth in a keynote address on this topic in 2005 (Post-IMA Workshop) stated that the underlying dynamics of marketing include the facts that

- the driving force is now the global economy wherein economic growth engines are switching
- traditional (marketing) paradigms may no longer work
- customer needs are changing more rapidly than ever before
- there are many gaps to be filled and issues to be tackled

One could argue that in this dynamic context where marketing productivity is declining, activism is growing and expectations are rising consumers do seem to need a form of marketing that is better synchronized, and more focused on their needs. Some (not all) customers and consumers seek for better marketing processes and closer relationships with suppliers (note the relationship sought should be driven by consumer needs, not organizational needs). Marketing research should be focused on insight, not revamping processes; and in an earlier text Thomas (2003) has argued for the need to defeat or redirect marketing away from epistemopathology or a shortsighted narrow view of marketing and markets which are inevitably focused on organizational or competitive and not customer needs.

## Toward the metaphor construct

The major issue or problem to be explored in the text and via its chapters is traceable to the use and practice of metaphors within marketing. These are widespread in nature, yet their use is not acknowledged nor widely recognized nor indeed commented upon in any marketing textbook (see, for example, latest editions by any major marketing author). While these metaphors may include the following, such a list is by no means complete.

- viral marketing
- product life cycle
- marketing as 'warfare'
- steps or stages to successful marketing
- portfolio matrices
- globalization of markets
- customer relationship management and marketing
- integrated marketing communications
- integrated marketing
- orientations of marketing
- strategic planning outcomes
- marketing planning models
- market segmentation
- buyer behaviour models
- stages in the buying process
- hierarchy of effects models
- the marketing mix

For example:

- The concept of marketing as 'warfare' is an illustrative attempt of how business practitioners can be enthused and/or misled by a simplified metaphor. Plainly managers do not 'control troops', 'inflict casualties', 'deploy guerrilla warfare' or 'recover from defeats' in the way an armed force might do (Luzon et al., 2004).
- The 'product life cycle' is a biological metaphor that suggests products pass through similar stages to biological entities (that is, birth, growth, maturity, decline). Yet over several decades it has proven extremely difficult to assess which stage of the life cycle a product may be in, or to identify when movement is made from one stage to another. The product life cycle cannot be seen as an independent variable, as it is dependent on managerial decision-making.
- The use of portfolio matrices such as the Boston Consulting Group share-growth matrix and the General Electric business screen are plainly metaphorical in nature. If their recommended and simplistic strategic outcomes are seen as prescriptive rather than descriptive in nature, they often lead to disaster or less than optimal business performance.
- The globalization of markets concept popularized by Levitt in 1983 was again metaphorical in nature. Firms who adopted the over-simplified recommendations were firms that rapidly lost sales and market share in the then emergent global markets of that time.

In this text major authors tackle many metaphors in the discipline of marketing. These are briefly outlined below.

Chapters 1, 2, and 3 can be considered as overarching contributions to this topic.

- Chapter 2 (Tynan) describes the uses and abuses of metaphors in marketing.
- Chapter 3 (Sheth, Uslay, and Sisodia) tackles the metaphor of the globalization of markets and the rule of three.

Chapters 4 to 13 consider specific sub-areas of marketing, where it may be relatively easy to mistake what is plainly metaphorical in nature for the realities encountered by companies.

- Chapter 4 (van Waterschoot and de Haes) questions the over-popularity and general messiness of the marketing mix.

- Chapter 5 (McDonald) acknowledges that much of market segmentation, without rigour, is metaphorical in nature.
- Chapter 6 (Brown) explores the relationship between alchemy and marketing, unsurprisingly both are rich in metaphorical constructs.
- Chapters 7 (Lindgreen, Dobele, Beverland and Vanhamme) and 8 (Okazaki) explore the popular metaphor of viral marketing. Chapter 7 from a general perspective and Chapter 8 specifically via mobile devices.
- Chapter 9 (Fischer-Buttinger and Vallaster) considers brand ambassadorialism, another popular metaphor, previously discussed by Brown in Chapter 6 as 'brandacadabra'.
- Chapter 10 (Beard) concerns negative comparative advertising and whether this is really a form of attack or use of yet another metaphor.
- Chapter 11 (Goldenberg and Oreg) refers to the diffusion of innovation metaphor and to the last group, that is, 'laggards' and why this may be of interest to avid readers.
- Chapter 12 (Lindgreen, Palmer and Beverland) brings the marketing wheel full circle by exploring the marriage metaphor in relationship marketing.
- Chapter 13 (Palmer and Lindgreen) resurrects the life cycle construct particularly from a product perspective.

Chapters 14 and 15 bring the text to a conclusion with a consideration of the full subject of the contemplative text. In Chapter 14, Buckingham considers marketing, metaphors and metamorphosis in the internal market (a recent extension of marketing), and in Chapter 15, Thomas tackles metaphors and metamorphosis in their broadest dimensionality.

## Toward marketing metamorphosis

Originally, I intended to add a concluding chapter on marketing metamorphosis. I have decided against this, given the rate of change and the criticisms targeted toward what could be called the 'old school of marketing'. Plainly, much of this school – the tools, techniques, processes, systems and descriptions – is metaphorical in nature. The exact nature of the ways in which each metaphor is used will be explored in the following chapters. However, one thing seems evident and that is that marketing itself may be seen as a metaphor, used in established textbooks as a broad template to attempt to describe how marketing works. It is almost never used as a simile. It is almost never stated as a metaphor. The idea of an underlying and widely held philosophy or belief held by practitioners that marketing is in some way related to consumers or customers and the satisfying of their needs is evidently a mistaken trope. The actual reality of this metaphor can easily be tested in a person's everyday experience. All a student of marketing needs to do is step outside the lecture theatre to experience the reality of marketing.

Yet, marketing is ubiquitous, all-embracing, and all-pervading. We are immersed or bathed in marketing from birth to death whether we care for it or not. Our parents, grandparents, social institutions, commercial institutions, political bodies, religious organizations, and virtually any institution in our societies vie continuously for our attention, make promises all the time, and deliver rarely, or only occasionally.

Now, a few years into the twenty-first century, marketing is under fire as never before. Its character as metaphor seems self-evident. Yet, consumers and businesses do need some type of construct to describe how exchange for goods or financial return takes place. For over half a century, 'marketing' has been a roughly acceptable term. Now, there is a great need for redefinition and better elucidation. Such redefinition and greater explanatory power has to be generated by the global community of scholars and practitioners. Perhaps we will find that marketing itself has been in fact a useful metaphor for its time, but the time has moved on. Maybe the world of marketing is metamorphosizing into something else – nascent, undefined, yet inexorably demanded by the new millennium.

## References

Achrol, R.S. (1997), 'Changes in the theory of interorganisational relations in marketing paradigm', *Journal of the Academy of Marketing Science*, 25(1): 72–5.

Ambler, T. (1994), 'Marketing's third paradigm: guanxi', *Business Strategy Review*, 5(4): 69–80.

Arndt, J. (1985), 'Making marketing science more scientific: role of orientations, paradigms, metaphors, and puzzle solving', *Journal of Marketing*, 49(3): 11–23.

Baker, M.J. (2005), 'Marketing is marketing everywhere', Seminar Compendium, International Conference on Marketing Paradigms for Emerging Economies, Indian Institute of Management, Ahmedabad, India, pp. 8–12.

Combe, A.I. (1999), 'Multiple strategy paradigms – an international framework', *Journal of Marketing Management*, 15: 341–59.

David, W.C. (1998), 'Examining the impact of market-based strategy paradigms on marketing strategy', *Journal of Strategic Marketing*, 6: 197–208.

Godin, S. (2001), 'Paradigm pillager', *Sales and Marketing Management*, 153(7): 32–5.

Gronroos, C. (2007), *In Search of a New Logic for Marketing: Contemporary Marketing Theory*, London: Wiley (see especially chapters 1, 10, and 11).

Hunt, S.D. (2002), *Foundations of Marketing Theory*, Boston: M.E. Sharpe.

Kitchen, P.J. (ed.) (2003), *The Future of Marketing*, Basingstoke: Palgrave Macmillan.

Kitchen, P.J. (ed.) (2003), *The Rhetoric and Reality of Marketing: an International Managerial Approach*, Basingstoke: Palgrave Macmillan.

Kitchen, P.J. (ed.) (2005) *Marketing Mind Prints*, Basingstoke: Palgrave Macmillan.

Levitt, T. (1983), 'The globalisation of markets', *Harvard Business Review*, 61(3): 91–102.

Luzon, Yoram, Jacob Goldenberg, Barak Libai, David Mazursky and Sorin Solomon (2004), 'Inevitably reborn: the reawakening of extinct innovations', forthcoming in *Technological Forecasting and Social Change*.

Palmer, A. and S. Ponsonby (2002), 'The social construction of new marketing paradigms: the influence of personal perspectives', *Journal of Marketing Management*, 18: 173–92.

Peppers, D. and M. Rogers (1995), 'A new marketing paradigm: share of customer, not market share', *Planning Review*, 23(2): 14–20.

Reddy, C.A. (1999), 'Towards a new services marketing paradigm for developing countries', *International Journal of Management*, 16(3): 366–73.

Schultz, D.E. and H. Schultz (1998), 'Transitioning marketing communications into the 21st century', *Journal of Marketing Communications*, 4(1): 19–26.

Sheth, J. (2005), Keynote address at the International Conference on Marketing Paradigms for Emerging Economies, 12–13 January, India, available online at http://www.iimaalumni.org/scripts/reading/archives/feb2005/marketing.asp?link=lnk3.

Sheth, J. (2005), 'Building new partnerships in the global food chain: experiences from North Africa, the Near East, and Asia', 2005 Post-IMA Workshop, Chicago, 29–30 June.

Thomas, M. (2003), 'Professionalism in marketing: an oxymoron?' in P.J. Kitchen (ed.), *The Future of Marketing* (Basingstoke: Palgrave Macmillan), p. 83.

# 2
# Metaphors and Marketing: Some Uses and Abuses

*Caroline Tynan*

## Introduction

Metaphors shape and structure our thoughts and thus govern our accepted view of the world. They are one of a number of tropes (figurative uses of a word) which allow us to view a problem in a new way through the juxtaposition of ideas, a process which can be enabling and generate creativity in conceptualizing and theorizing. Metaphors also allow us to clearly communicate ideas in an interesting fashion. This chapter reflects upon the nature and role of metaphors and offers guidance upon their use. The use of metaphors in marketing is then critically examined, finally the metaphor of marriage in relationship marketing is considered. It is argued that marriage has become a dormant metaphor which has artificially constrained our conceptualizing in this field and has become a substitute for thinking.

Metaphors are important in both our every day and our academic life. They are pervasive in that they shape our thoughts, our view of the world and therefore our actions. Our everyday conversations are riddled with metaphor as we 'spill the beans', avoid 'looking a gift horse in the mouth', aim to get our career into the 'fast lane', 'shed crocodile tears', 'let the cat out of the bag', drift 'into the doldrums', take a report 'with a grain of salt', 'polish off' our bottle of wine and become 'wound up as tight as a spring'. Zaltman (1996: 14) maintains that we use 'on average, nearly six metaphors per minute of speech'. This extensive use of metaphor extends to marketing when we 'launch' a new offering, describe a product as a 'cash cow', or watch the adoption of our innovative new service 'diffuse' across a market. We also use them as an aid to thinking, as a way of creatively visioning, to help us conceptualize a research problem in a new way. This helpful device also allows us to communicate ideas with clarity, and in a manner that contrives to add interest through the juxtaposition of ideas. According to Hirschman (2007), metaphor is a language game. Stern (1988) notes that the language of metaphor has long been valued, as the philosopher Aristotle's postulation of a link between literary genius and a command of metaphor indicates. 'But the greatest thing by far is to have a command of metaphors ... it is the mark of genius' (Fergusson, 1961: 104). Subsequently Winston Churchill noted: 'How infinite ... is the debt owed to metaphors by politicians who wish to speak strongly but are not sure what they are going to say' (cited in Fowler, 1968: 359), and as Fowler adds, 'Hardly less ... is the debt owed to metaphors by those who, knowing what they are going to say, wish to illumine and vivify it' (ibid.)

As Churchill the wily politician implicitly recognized, 'there is true power behind metaphors to shape reality and structure the thoughts of people' (Kendall and Kendall, 1993: 149). And it is the potential to 'illumine and vivify' the subject that is the great advantage that the use of metaphors can confer upon an author and that perhaps accounts for their continuing popularity.

According to Zaltman et al. (1982: 170) 'there are probably few areas of inquiry in the social sciences that rely on metaphor to the degree marketing does'. They are widely used and widespread. However in spite of their extensive adoption within the discipline of marketing there is little in the marketing literature that promotes an understanding of their nature, use and inherent limitations. In the words of Rindfleisch (1996: 9) 'Marketing theorists have paid too little attention to the metaphorical assumptions that underlie their standard world views.' The metaphor of marriage is one of the key metaphors in marketing according to Hunt and Menon (1995). Its seductive and pervasive nature has persuaded the academy of its universal applicability in relationship marketing, to the extent that the use of language and examples drawn from close interpersonal relationships are barely questioned. The marriage metaphor has become so pervasive in marketing thought that it is scarcely recognized as a metaphor. Van den Bulte has admonished the marketing academy for its uncritical use of metaphor. 'Since marketing is replete with metaphors taken from other spheres, and unexamined metaphors are a substitute for thinking and a threat to science, we can improve our field by being more critical of our existing metaphors and more conscious in picking up new metaphors' (1994: 419). In an attempt to address some of these issues, this chapter explores the metaphorical assumptions that underpin what has become a standard worldview of relationship marketing.

In order to address this issue this chapter aims to: (1) reflect upon the nature and role of metaphor, (2) offer guidance on the use of metaphors and (3) critically examine the use of metaphors in marketing, particularly the use of relationship and marriage metaphors in relationship marketing. It has been written with a number of readers in mind. These include theoreticians within the wider field of marketing who will want to utilize and to evaluate metaphors in their studies. Second, it applies to practitioners who may wish to consider the use of metaphor, particularly that of marriage in relationship marketing, as a method of communication within their business and the extended business community. Finally, it addresses students who need to be in a position to recognize and assess the multiple metaphors currently in use within our discipline.

## Understanding metaphors

Lakoff and Johnson (1980: 1) conclude that, 'the metaphor is pervasive in everyday life, not just in language but in thought and action'. That is, the human conceptual system is innately metaphorical. We use metaphors in everyday life to structure and define our conceptual system and thus our daily realities: to structure 'less concrete and inherently vague concepts' (Van den Bulte, 1994: 408) in terms of those of which we have a clear understanding that is based upon our own experience (Johnson, 1987; Lakoff and Johnson, 1980). For example, we commonly hear universities described as 'ivory towers', consider that 'time is money' or that a poor presentation 'sank without trace', we 'run out of steam' at the end of a busy day, 'brush up' a second language or plan to 'push the boat out' for a birthday celebration

### The nature of metaphor

A metaphor is one of a number of tropes, or figurative uses of a word, which include metonymy, irony and synecdoche (Burke, 1969). According to the *Concise Oxford Dictionary* (1995) metaphor is 'the application of a name or descriptive term or phrase to an object or action to which it is imaginatively but not literally applicable'. It derives from the Greek word *'metapherein'* which means to transfer or to carry over (Hunt and Menon, 1995). Hence metaphorical reasoning involves *'the transfer of relational information from a domain that already exists in memory (usually referred to as source or base domain) to the domain to be explained (referred to as the target domain)'* (Van den Bulte, 1994: 408; italics in original). That is, we use something with which we are all familiar to portray something which is less familiar. In contrasting these two objects, the dissimilarities and differences are illuminated while – paradoxically – the considerable similarities are also highlighted (Weaver in Kendall and Kendall, 1993). Interestingly, the power of the metaphor relies on the meaning supplied by the receiver to the inherent contradiction of the metaphor. While the general comparison is set by the author's choice of metaphor, it is the insight and experience that the receiver brings to bear on this comparison that fleshes it out. It is the interaction of the receiver and metaphor that brings the comparison to life. Lakoff (1987: 51) has noted that metaphors are not pre-defined objects but rather that they depend on the way in which receivers 'perceive them, image them, organize information about them, and behave toward them'.

## How metaphors work

The essence of a metaphor is experiencing and contemplating one thing in terms of another. So, for example, if we consider 'developing an argument' (the target domain) in terms of 'waging war' (the source domain) then that constrains the language we use to describe the argument, the way we conceive its likely progress and the form of the argument. We speak of 'marshalling' our argument, holding 'our position', 'attacking' every point, being right 'on target' or being 'wiped out' by 'our opponent's onslaught'. Thus the whole debate is coloured by aggression, notions of strategy and the necessity to 'fight to the bitter end' normally associated with war. Contrast this with the perspective we would hold if we considered 'argument' in terms of 'dance'. This would require entirely different language to indicate participation, cooperation, skill and balance employed to achieve an aesthetically pleasing outcome (Lakoff and Johnson, 1980). This pleasant and timely negotiation to build a symmetrical outcome for those involved conjures an entirely different picture of the argument, its likely progress and final determination. Additionally we could further conjecture the differences in argument conveyed when comparing it to different styles of dance, for example a stately minuet, a seductive tango or even a 'wicked' rave.

## Classifying metaphors

A useful summation of the characteristics of metaphors is offered by Rindfleisch (1996: 4) who indicates that they are 'fundamental, instrumental, systematic, partial, experiential, and able to shape both thought and action'. They are *fundamental* in that our language and much of our conceptual system is 'metaphorically structured and defined' (Lakoff and Johnson, 1980: 6). Thus our thinking and actions are affected by the metaphor. Metaphors are *instrumental* in that they lead to enhanced understanding and improved communication, especially in portraying difficult and abstract concepts. They are easier and quicker than literal explanation and can frequently offer surprising insights. Metaphors are *systematic*, transferring whole domains of experience from a source to a target rather than merely representing individual or isolated concepts. Metaphors are *partial* because they highlight some facets of the similarity between the source and domain while hiding others. If it were not for this partiality then one concept would be the other and a comparison would lead to no fresh understanding or insight. Metaphors are *grounded in experience* so that the author and receiver can share a broadly common understanding of the source domain. Metaphors *shape our thoughts and actions* in that they create a new reality. Thus those who accept that 'time is money' may respond by espousing time-management practices, while ignoring the problem that, inevitably, they have no more of this scarce resource than do other less well-organized individuals.

Van den Bulte (1994) usefully classifies metaphors into four different types:

- *Core metaphors* are 'basic presuppositional insights' which structure an entire school of thought. In marketing, an example of this might be the *markets as networks* perspective of the Industrial Marketing and Purchasing (IMP) Group (see, for example, Ford, 2002 and Ford et al., 2003 for overviews).
- *Theory-constitutive metaphors* (Boyd, 1979) at the level of individual models or theories serve as 'fundamental presuppositions underlying specific theories of attempts to theorise'. We could include the product life cycle and the family life cycle metaphors within this category.
- *Literary metaphors* are used to convey a message vividly and memorably as with 'marketing myopia', 'price skimming' or 'viral marketing' but do not have the theoretical scope of core or theory-constitutive metaphors.
- *Conveyance metaphors* (MacCormac, 1985) similarly do not have the theoretical scope of the first two types, nor are they as visible as are literary metaphors as part of the everyday language we use about marketing. These are the 'metaphors marketers live by' which have become so commonplace that we have forgotten that they are metaphors at all. In this category we could include the marketing 'mix', the 'world wide web' or the 'launch' of a new product.

## Using metaphors

There is little agreement in the literature on the 'rules' guiding metaphor use. Doving (1994) identified three errors that should be avoided in using metaphors. These concern the choice of an inappropriate metaphor because of the lack of commonality between the source and target domain, the over-extension of a metaphor when applied to the target domain, and finally the error of redundancy which occurs when the source and target domain are so similar that the metaphor has limited utility. Additionally Palmer and Dunford (1996) warn against the adoption of metaphors which are internally inconsistent, as such metaphors confuse and mislead the receiver. Finally it is important not to mix metaphors. Consider for example 'the parachute candidate won the election by a landslide', here two commonly used political metaphors leave the voter confusingly undecided whether the comparison is related to flying or geology. These five 'rules' probably represent a minimalist approach to avoiding some of the worst difficulties in the employment of metaphor, but they in no way constitute a comprehensive practitioners' code.

Guidance on the use of metaphors within the marketing literature is sparse. However the important issues to be considered in using metaphor effectively include the selection of an appropriate metaphor, understanding the limitations of metaphors and the ability to recognize a dormant metaphor. These are considered in order below.

### Selecting an appropriate metaphor

Metaphors are important to academics in that they allow us to reconsider and recast a research puzzle in an entirely new way. The ability to contemplate creatively, without the constraining straitjacket of pre-existing dogma, leads to new insights. 'Since observation presupposes conceptualisation and what we see depends to some extent on what we expect to see, it is extremely difficult to develop fundamentally new concepts. In order to escape this Catch 22, we all grow up using metaphors, *thinking of one thing in terms of something else'* (Van den Bulte, 1994: 407; italics in original). These 'useful fictions' (Whitehead, 1925) are a form of creative and constructive falsehood which facilitates the liberation of the imagination (Morgan, 1980). They offer a way of creatively communicating complex and abstract information concisely and memorably (Weinrauch, 2005). According to Brown and Turley (1997: 8) metaphors are 'now considered central to creativity, innovation and outstanding human accomplishment, in both scientific and artistic arenas'. Consideration of the research problem through metaphor develops a 'field of secondary and tertiary resonances, contrasts, and comparisons that do not merely describe, but also reconstruct and transform the original material' (Mirowski, 1988: 136). It allows us, as researchers, creatively to conceptualize the area of study and evolve a new and insightful understanding. It allows us to extend beyond the 'ordinary literal ways of thinking and talking into the range of what is called figurative, poetic, colourful or fanciful thought and language. Thus if ideas are objects, we can *dress them up in fancy clothes, juggle them, line them up nice and neat*' (Lakoff and Johnson, 1980: 13; italics in original). In short, we can use them as 'mind stretchers' (Van den Bulte, 1994: 408).

## Some limitations of metaphors

Metaphorical reasoning involves the transfer of information from one domain in our memory (the source domain) to the domain we are attempting to explain (the target domain). Van den Bulte (citing Vosniadou and Ortony, 1989: pp. 6–7) advises that for the metaphor to be effective it is essential 'that the domains be conceptually different. That is, a metaphor is a between-domain analogy in contrast to a literal or within-domain analogy' (1994: 408). Thus, it seems that the choice of metaphor is crucial in that it represents a judgement as to which are the most important features that are demonstrated by its application to the situation under study.

However, we should also recognize that the use of metaphor is subject to certain limitations. By its very nature, a metaphor illuminates some aspects of a phenomenon and conceals others. To be effective, the choice of metaphor for the subject under consideration must therefore be apposite. Domains that are completely dissimilar will generate nonsensical or weak imagery, while those with some overlap, but which maintain a significant degree of difference between domains, will generate the most illuminating comparisons. The creative potential depends on the degree of difference between the source and target domains. An example will serve to illustrate this quite powerfully. With the metaphor 'that child is an angel' the impression is created of an extraordinarily good, obedient and gentle child who endeavours to help others. The use of this metaphor requires that other assumed attributes of an angel, including its proximity to God, white feathered wings and dazzling radiance, be ignored in order to emphasize the characteristics which the child and angel share. Similarly, other features of the child may be completely obscured by the use of this metaphor. For example, we may never 'see' her torn jeans, untidy hair, and permanently worn MP3 headphones, or consider her irritating habits of singing to herself and tripping over things. Therefore, it is evident that any metaphor represents a partial truth as it 'always emphasises some aspects, de-emphasises others, and hides still others' (Van den Bulte, 1994: 413).

### Identifying and rejuvenating the dormant metaphor

Byron wrote that 'I hate to hunt down a tired metaphor' (*Don Juan*, canto XIII, stanza 36), thus the metaphor which has been absorbed into the language so that it is no longer recognized as a metaphor has ceased to make a contribution: it merely causes confusion. According to Van den Bulte (1994: 417) 'After long and repeated use, a metaphor may become so hackneyed that people forget it is a metaphor, and sublimate its relationship with reality.' This means that the use of an extinct or dormant metaphor serves to close our minds to the creative paradox inherent within it, rather than acting as a mental stimulus. In effect the dormant metaphor no longer challenges or provokes the reader to think.

However, once a dormant metaphor has been recognized it may be possible to revive and revitalize it. One approach is to flex the metaphor and ensure that all the implications embedded in a metaphor are fully explored. Thus the 'dogs' and 'cash cows' in the Boston Consulting Group's share-growth matrix do not just provide dogs to be 'kicked out' and cows to be 'milked' as was originally postulated. If we think more thoroughly about the metaphor we could see dogs as man's best friend giving unquestioning and loyal service and cows as the generators of many offspring. Thus we would be less likely to have 'shot' the loyal dog in markets where they were cash generators, or simply milked the cows rather than used them to 'breed' brand extensions in low-growth markets (Van den Bulte, 1994).

## Metaphors in marketing

Within the field of marketing our history as a discipline offers a further reason for re-evaluating the metaphors we adopt, in that metaphors play a 'pervasive and essential role in marketing' (Van den Bulte, 1994: 406). As Arndt (1985) outlines, various paradigmatic perspectives within marketing are riddled with metaphors, among them warfare, the organism and 'spaceship earth'. Key conceptual developments in the discipline are associated with particular metaphors. For example, in service marketing, Fisk et al.'s (1993) powerful use of the evolutionary metaphor to clarify and interpret the development of the discipline, and Bitner's (1992) use of the 'servicescape' metaphor to explore the impact of physical surroundings on customers and employees in service delivery have substantially impacted upon the way the field is conceptualized by the academy. Zaltman (1996) has even developed a patented consumer research process to help elicit deep thoughts and feelings, which is predicated upon the use of metaphors (Christensen and Olson, 2002). Furthermore, an examination of the current marketing literature confirms the continuing popularity of the metaphor across the discipline. Recently metaphor has been utilized by Cornelissen (2003) and Cornelissen et al. (2005) in the context of corporate identity and relationship marketing; by Dennis and Macaulay (2003) in their work on marketing planning through the application of the jazz improvisation metaphor; by Weinrauch (2005) as a tool for marketing education; by Celuch et al. (2006) in examining buyer–seller relationships; by Story and Hess (2006) in their work on customer-brand relationships; and finally by Hirschman (2007) in an exploration of marketplace meaning through anthropological metaphors.

Advertising practitioners are expert in the use of metaphor, and advertising images and copy are redolent with metaphor. As consumers, we have no difficulty in understanding the literary and visual metaphors implicit in the 'Innocent' Drinks Company smoothie brand name and logo, or the visual metaphor of Nicole Kidman as the personification of Chanel No 5 perfume.

It is clear that metaphors are important and widely used in marketing and that we, as members of the marketing academy, should develop a fuller understanding of the way in which this device shapes our thoughts and view of the world. Given the importance of the marriage metaphor within the new paradigm of relationship marketing it seems appropriate to consider its continued utility.

## The relationship and marriage metaphors in marketing

Relationship marketing has become an accepted part of the discipline. It is no longer the 'new paradigm' but is finally part of the orthodoxy, as confirmed by its presence in all the major undergraduate textbooks (see, for example, Baines et al., 2008; Jobber, 2007). Its position has been endorsed by the latest services dominant logic thinking where relationship marketing is core to producing and sustaining value with and among customers and partners (Vargo and Lusch, 2004). Whatever its future may prove to be, this new worldview of marketing is worthy of further study to enable its development and utilization by academics and practitioners.

Each individual's store of experiences of relationships means that this metaphor can be all things to all people. We all can, and do, identify with it. Unfortunately there is little evidence that we are experiencing the same thing or ascribing the same attributes to the relationship. One of the cornerstones of this flexible view of relationships is the use of Levitt's (1983) marriage metaphor (Tynan, 1997; O'Malley and Tynan, 1999) to conceptualize relationship marketing. In introducing the marriage metaphor, Levitt (1983: 111) comments that the 'sale merely consummates the courtship', after which 'the marriage begins'. Since its introduction, the marriage analogy has been widely cited in the relationship marketing literature (compare Dwyer et al., 1987; Perrien et al., 1993; Buttle, 1996; Celuch et al., 2006), with respected authors such as Leonard Berry, Barbara Jackson and A. Parasuraman recommending 'that marketers treat their long-standing relationships with key customers as "marriages"' (Hunt and Morgan, 1995). Hunt and Menon (1995) describe the marriage metaphor as one of the 'key metaphors in marketing' in their examination of competitive advantage. However, there has been a widespread acceptance that 'transfer from the marriage metaphor to buyer–seller relationships has not been fully explored' (Celuch et al., 2006: 579). Further, as this metaphor underpins the academy's 'standard worldview' of relationship marketing it is important to understand the metaphorical assumptions that underlie it. Therefore, this chapter critically reviews this important and influential metaphor and explores the implications of its widespread adoption and the excessive familiarity that has resulted in its status as an 'unquestioned truth'. It will also raise the question of whether marriage in relationship marketing is a metaphor which has been confounded with reality.

## Discussion

The marriage metaphor in marketing is a theoretical metaphor according to Hunt and Menon (1995). It is not a literary metaphor because it lacks visibility, nor a conveyance metaphor because of its extensive theoretical scope. Within the more detailed classification of theoretical metaphors offered by Van den Bulte (1994: 406; citing Boyd, 1979, italics in original) it is a *'theory-constitutive metaphor'* rather than a core metaphor, that is, one of those metaphors that serve as 'fundamental presuppositions underlying specific theories or attempts to theorise'. Therefore, this is an important metaphor for the marketing academy. Its widespread acceptance and promulgation has substantial impact in that it affects the way in which we conceptualize and operationalize relationship marketing.

Hunt and Menon (1995) examined the source, ontology, concepts, theories and values associated with the marriage metaphor. It offers a rich and heterogeneous list of foundational associations for the transfer of ideas and meaning. Thus by applying the metaphor of marriage to a commercial exchange relationship there is the metaphoric assumption that the values associated with marriage are shared by the exchange partners. Within a marriage there is the assumption of attendant relationships with spouse, family members, connected households, children, other relatives and step-relatives, fathers, mothers, sisters, brothers, neighbours, perhaps marriage counsellors, together with associated values of commitment, love, harmony, financial security and procreation (Hunt and Menon, 1995). Marriage partners are understood to live (ideally) in love and harmony, sharing affection and emotional support, through commitment, mutuality, trust, empathy, intimacy, and the ownership in common of all assets. While these implied values offer some notion of the values shared between relationship partners in an exchange relationship, they are generally – and paradoxically – far in excess of those that are manifest in a business to consumer relationship (O'Malley and Tynan, 2000).

As the discussion above established, the use of any metaphor emphasizes some issues, de-emphasizes others and hides still more. Addressing first those issues that are emphasized, or perhaps over-emphasized, while marriage stresses the role of love and faithfulness between partners this does not help us better understand relationship marketing, as these attributes are not paralleled in any relationship founded on a commercial exchange; here relationships rarely last beyond a stage when they are no longer mutually beneficial. This concentration on the long-term nature of (ideal) marriage relationships (until death) to some extent mirrors the long-term nature of many business to business relationships (Ford, 2002, 1990) and some service relationships, but any connection is harder to identify in business–consumer relationships. Thus the use of the marriage metaphor in relationship marketing serves to over-emphasize commitment, trust, fidelity, affection and closeness in a durable relationship.

At the same time, the marriage metaphor de-emphasizes the lack of consumer consent in many consumer–market relationships, the lack of equity in benefits accruing, the disparity in power between partners and hence the inability of the weaker partner to change the behaviour of the stronger partner, the recognition that such relationships are not necessarily public, and also the problem of unexpected burdens placed on one partner by the other (Blois, 1997). In marriage, total commitment is given to a spouse 'for better, for worse, for richer for poorer, in sickness and in health' whereas that in exchange relationships represents a far more qualified and bounded commitment which protects the interest of owners and shareholders. Thus, trust is offered within set boundaries, offering only limited vulnerability to the future actions of a relationship partner, and not in the all-encompassing way trust ideally operates within marriage. Issues which are de-emphasized by the use of the marriage metaphor also include the issue of consent, which is not always freely given by commercial partners when, for example, customer lists are bought and sold (Tynan, 1997).

Finally, we address those issues which are hidden by the use of the marriage metaphor. In marriage the couple have only one relationship of this kind (at any one time) whereas in relationship marketing there may be several, or in business–consumer relationships, millions at any one time. This leads to questions about the appropriate responses in the case of failure of the relationship, and finally the crucial issue that in consumer markets at least, the relationship in question is not an interpersonal relationship (O'Malley and Tynan, 2000, 2001).

The crucial difference between the metaphor and the reality is that an interpersonal relationship frequently exists in business to business and in service markets (Celuch et al., 2006) but rarely exists in consumer markets. In conceptualizing the general theoretical nature of relationships, Iacobucci and Ostrom (1996) identified four robust, underlying dimensions of interpersonal relationships. These are power symmetry-asymmetry, cooperative versus competitive, intensity of interdependence, and finally whether relationships were connected with work or social-life. In examining the marriage metaphor against the marketing relationship in each of these categories there is a very variable fit. Whereas modern marriage partners are seen as fairly equal in their roles, relationship partners are rarely so. In business to business, service and business to consumer markets there is frequently a size inequality between the partners, leading to power asymmetry. Even where size is not an issue, inequality of access to information and resource disparities can lead to similar asymmetry. Marriages exhibit intense, positive and cooperative relationships with compatible goals, but even the most intense commercial relationship is unlikely to display similar emotional bonding and nurturing behaviour. The intensity of interdependence is thought to be reflected in the perceived commitment of the parties to the relationship. Perhaps it is the final category that most firmly separates the metaphor from the commercial reality. Husbands and wives experience a social relationship whereas those in marketing-exchange relationships experience primarily a work-related relationship but one which may be managed into something with some social nuances and overtones. Individuals cannot and do not have interpersonal relationships with organizations.

## Conclusion

The metaphor is an enormously powerful tool for the marketing theoretician to develop new conceptualizations and theory. However, the processes by which metaphors work have not been fully explored in the marketing literature to date and it is timely to review the processes by which they should be developed and utilized. Attention has also been drawn to the limitations inherent in the use of metaphors. Namely the issues which are de-emphasized and those which remain hidden because of the use of a metaphor, and also the problems associated with the continued use of dormant metaphors.

When considering the application of these issues to the popular marriage metaphor in the relationship-marketing literature some questions emerge. Marriage no longer fits the situation witnessed in many marketing relationships. It offers most to the business to business and service relationship marketer but even there it badly overstates issues of affection, commitment, fidelity, power symmetry, intensity, compatibility of goals and the social aspects of the relationship. However its use in business–consumer relationships has served to build unreal expectations on the part of both partners in the exchange relationship, in terms of trust, commitment, closeness, mutuality, power symmetry, intensity, and, particularly, social aspects of the relationship. The metaphor promulgates a highly idealized, romanticized and interpersonally-based notion of the type of relationship that can develop and the degree of commitment that consumers can offer to their partners.

This metaphor, once lively and enabling is now dormant, or worse still it may already be extinct. Rather than facilitating creative thought and conceptualization in the field, it has constrained and limited our understanding, inventiveness and creativity in theorizing . It is no longer the window through which to see and interpret the new world of relationship marketing, but has become a steel door which marks the end of this avenue of investigation. In the light of Van den Bulte's admonition this chapter has sought to critically examine our existing metaphor of marriage in the field of relationship marketing on the basis that it has become an unquestioned truth and a 'substitute for thinking'. The way forward is now to develop new and appropriate metaphors to reduce confusion and stimulate creative and innovative theorizing in this area of study.

## Acknowledgements

The author would like to express her thanks to Dr Aidan O'Driscoll, the editor of *Irish Marketing Review*, for his kind permission to base this chapter on an earlier work published in the *IMR* (Tynan, 1999).

Thanks also to Lisa O'Malley and Maurice Patterson who were kind enough to review the original work and offer helpful insights.

## References

Arndt, J. (1985), 'On making marketing science more scientific: role of orienta- tions, paradigms, metaphors, and puzzle solving', *Journal of Marketing*, 49 (Summer): 11–23.

Baines, P., C. Fill and K. Page (2008), *Marketing*, Oxford: Oxford University Press.

Barnes, J.G. (1994), 'Close to the customer: but is it a relationship?' *Journal of Marketing Management*, 10: 561–70.

Bitner, M.J. (1992), 'Servicescapes: the impact of physical surroundings on customers and employees', *Journal of Marketing*, 56(2): 557–71.

Blois, K., (1997) 'Are business-to-business relationships inherently unstable?', *Journal of Marketing Management*, 13(5): 367–82.

Boyd, R. (1979), 'Metaphor and theory change: what is "metaphor" a metaphor for?' in Andrew Ortony (ed.), *Metaphor and Thought*, Cambridge: Cambridge University Press, pp. 356–408.

Brown, S. and D. Turley (eds) (1997), *Consumer Research: Postcards from the Edge*, London: Routledge.

Burke, K. (1969), *A Grammar of Motives*, Berkeley: University of California Press.

Buttle, F. (1996), *Relationship Marketing, Theory and Practice*, London: Paul Chapman Publishing.

Celuch, K.G., J.H. Bantham and C.J. Kasouf (2006), 'An extension of the marriage metaphor in buyer–seller relationships: an exploration of individual level process dynamics', *Journal of Business Research*, 59: 573–81.

Christensen, G.L. and J.C. Olson (2002), 'Mapping consumers' mental models with ZMET', *Psychology and Marketing*, 19(6): 477–502.

*The Concise Oxford Dictionary* (1995) (9th edition), Oxford: Clarendon Press.

Cornelissen, J.P. (2003), 'Metaphor as a method in the domain of marketing', *Psychology and Marketing*, 20(3): 209–25.

Cornelissen, J.P., M. Kafouros and A.R. Lock (2005), 'Metaphorical images of organization: how organizational researchers develop and select organizational metaphors', *Human Relations*, 58(12): 1545–78.

Dennis, N. and M. Macaulay (2003), 'Jazz and marketing planning', *Journal of Strategic Marketing*, 11 (September): 177–85.

Doving, E. (1994), 'Using anthropomorphistic metaphors: organisational action, knowledge, and learning', paper presented at the Conference on Metaphors in Organisational Theory and Behaviour, Kings College, University of London.

Dwyer, F.R., P.H. Schurr and S. Oh (1987), 'Developing buyer–seller relationships', *Journal of Marketing*, 51(April): 11–27.

Fergusson, F. (1961), *Aristotle's Poetics*, trans. S.H. Butcher, New York: Hill and Wang.

Fisk, R.P., S. Brown and M.J. Bitner (1993), 'Tracking the evolution of the services marketing literature', *Journal of Retailing*, 69(1): 61–103.

Ford, D. (2002), *Understanding Business Marketing and Purchasing*, 3rd edition, London: Thomson Learning.

Ford, D., L.E. Gadde, H. Håkansson and I. Snehota (2003), *Managing Business Relationships*, 3rd edition, Chichester, West Sussex: John Wiley and Sons.

Fowler, H.W. (1968), *Fowler's Modern English Usage*, Oxford: Oxford University Press.

Hirschman, E.C. (2007), 'Metaphor in the marketplace', *Marketing Theory*, 7(3): 227–48.

Hunt, S.D. and A. Menon (1995), 'Metaphors and competitive advantage: evaluating the use of metaphors in theories of competitive strategy', *Journal of Business Research*, 33(2): 81–90.

Hunt, S.D. and R.M. Morgan (1995), 'Relationship marketing in the era of network competition', *Marketing Management*, 3(1): 19–28.

Iacobucci, D. and A. Ostrom (1996), 'Commercial and interpersonal relationships: using the structure of interpersonal relationships to understand individual-to-individual, individual-to-firm, and firm-to-firm relationships in commerce', *International Journal of Research in Marketing*, 13: 53–72.

Jobber, D. (2007), *Principles and Practice of Marketing*, 5th edition, Maidenhead: McGraw Hill.

Johnson, M. (1987), *The Body in the Mind: the Bodily Basis of Meaning, Imagination, and Reasoning*, Chicago: University of Chicago Press.

Kendall, J.E. and K.E. Kendall (1993), 'Metaphors and methodologies: living beyond the systems machine', *MIS Quarterly*, 17 (June): 149–71.

Lakoff, G. (1987) *Women, Fire and Dangerous Things: What Categories Reveal about the Mind*, Chicago: University of Chicago Press.

Lakoff, G. and M. Johnson (1980), *Metaphors We Live By*, Chicago: University of Chicago Press.

Levitt, T. (1983), *The Marketing Imagination*, New York: The Free Press.

MacCormac, E.R. (1985), *A Cognitive Theory of Metaphor*, Cambridge, MA: MIT Press.

Mirowski, P. (1988), 'Shall I compare thee to a Minkowski-Ricardo-Leontief Matzler matrix of the Mosak-Hicks type?' in A. Klamer, D.M. McClosky and R.M. Solow (eds), *The Consequences of Economic Rhetoric*, Cambridge: Cambridge University Press, pp. 117–45.

Morgan, G. (1980), 'Paradigms, metaphors, and puzzle solving in organization theory', *Administrative Science Quarterly*, 25 (December): 605–22.

O'Malley, L. and A.C. Tynan (2001), 'Reframing relationship marketing for consumer markets', *Interactive Marketing*, 2(3): 240–6.

O'Malley, L. and A.C. Tynan (2000), 'Relationship marketing in consumer markets: rhetoric or reality?' *European Journal of Marketing*, 34(7): 797–815.

O'Malley, L. and A.C. Tynan (1999), 'The utility of relationship marketing in consumer markets: a critical evaluation', *Journal of Marketing Management*, 15(7): 587–602.

Palmer, I. and R. Dunford (1996), 'Conflicting uses of metaphors: reconceptualising their use in the field of organisational change', *Academy of Management Review*, 21(3): 691–717.

Perrien, J., P. Filiatrault and L. Ricard (1993), 'The implementation of relationship marketing in commercial banking', *Industrial Marketing Management*, 22: 141–8.

Rindfleisch, A. (1996), 'Marketing as warfare: reassessing a dominant metaphor', *Business Horizons*, 39(5) (September/October): 3–10.

Stern, B. B. (1988), 'Medieval allegory: roots of advertising strategy for the mass market', *Journal of Marketing*, 52(July): 84–94.

Story, J. and J. Hess (2006), 'Segmenting customer-brand relations: beyond the personal metaphor', *Journal of Consumer Marketing*, 23(7): 406–13.

Tynan, A.C. (1999), 'Metaphor, marketing and marriage', *Irish Marketing Review*, 12(1): 17–26.

Tynan, C. (1997) 'A review of the marriage analogy in relationship marketing', *Journal of Marketing Management*, 13: 695–703.

Van den Bulte, C. (1994), 'Metaphor at work', in G. Laurent, G.L. Lillien and B. Pras (eds), *Research Traditions in Marketing*, Boston: Kluwer Academic.

Vargo, S.L. and R.F. Lush (2004), 'Evolving a services dominant logic for marketing', *Journal of Marketing*, 68: 1–17.

Vosniadou, Stella and Andrew Ortony (eds) (1989), *Similarity and Analogical Reasoning*, Cambridge: Cambridge University Press, pp. 6–7.

Weinrauch, J.D. (2005), 'An exploratory use of musical metaphors to enhance student learning', *Journal of Marketing Education*, 27(2): 109–21.

Whitehead, A.N. (1925), *Science and the Modern World*, New York: Macmillan.

Zaltman, G. (1996), 'Metaphorically speaking', *Marketing Research: a Magazine of Management and Applications*, 8(2): 13–20.

Zaltman, G., K. Lemasters and M. Heffring (1982), *Theory Construction in Marketing: Some Thoughts on Thinking*, New York: John Wiley & Sons.

# 3
# The Globalization of Markets and the Rule of Three

*Jagdish N. Sheth, Can Uslay and Rajendra S. Sisodia*

Metaphors come in many forms: absolute, active, complex, compound, implicit, mixed, root and submerged... They are insightful, and enable us to make uncanny connections. They are powerful tools of rhetoric. Geniuses use them. The rest of us love them. However, a metaphor can also be 'dead', that is, so widely used that it can be dangerously misleading. Globalization is one such dead metaphor. Merriam-Webster defines it rather paradoxically:

> the development of an increasingly integrated *global* economy marked especially by free trade, free flow of capital, and the tapping of cheaper foreign labor markets. (Italics added)

Globalization is often attributed to Theodore Levitt and his seminal article 'The Globalization of Markets' (*Harvard Business Review*, 1983); however this is incorrect, the word entered the Merriam-Webster dictionary in 1951. The true origin of the phrase is unknown but its beginnings can be traced all the way to Genghis Khan and his Mongolian empire of the thirteenth century. In the modern management era, it was certainly covered by Peter Drucker earlier in his exploration of multinational (non-national) corporations.[1] The reason why globalization is a dead metaphor is because it has proven so successful: it simplified a very complex phenomenon for the masses. For the consumer, it has come to mean a unified world, one (consumer) culture, one language (English), one glorious brand for all, one alluring way of life: McDonaldization. For business, it has come to mean vast new consumer markets, savings in manufacturing, distribution, and promotion, one glorious brand for all (enter your brand here), and one strategy: aggressive acquisition.

It is as if globalization has single-handedly transformed the rules of competition and marketing. But the fact of the matter is that globalization does not benefit every firm, and a global brand should not be the be-all and end-all of marketing. There is a structure through which the forces of competition are organized. In this chapter, we deal with two key aspects of globalization: first, we describe why globalization must be understood better and why it is such a prevalent drive, especially at this point in time. We present our views on the pending social responsibilities of global corporations. Second, we introduce the 'Rule of Three' theory to enhance this understanding, provide our views on the future of global markets, and exemplify which brands are likely to be the surviving global brands at the end of the century. This part deals with the managerial realities that firms intent on succeeding in an inevitably global world must consider.

## Globalization: a social and economic imperative

In order to supplement our views on globalization, we undertook an exploratory examination of the construct using 'netnography'. In doing so, we examined hundreds of quotes regarding globalization available on the Internet.[2] Our analysis revealed that the quotes tend to fall under three main categories.

The first category of quotes emphasizes the positive influence and benefits of globalization:

> This is a very exciting time in the world of information. It's not just that the personal computer has come along as a great tool. The whole pace of business is moving faster. Globalization is forcing companies to do things in new ways.
>
> Bill Gates
> American entrepreneur, software executive, philanthropist

> Globalization has changed us into a company that searches the world, not just to sell or to source, but to find intellectual capital – the world's best talents and greatest ideas.
>
> Jack Welch
> Chairman and CEO of General Electric (1981–2001)

> Outsourcing and globalization of manufacturing allows companies to reduce costs, benefits consumers with lower cost goods and services,

causes economic expansion that reduces unemployment, and increases productivity and job creation.

Larry Elder
American radio and former TV talk show host and author

It is noteworthy that the claimed benefits of globalization go beyond trade and reach deep into the social fabric through innovation, human resource mobility, and cultural influence. Thus, globalization is beneficial to more than developed nations and multinational corporations. For example, the marketing of Vietnamese textile products in the US generates employment and economic growth for Vietnam. On the other hand, there are many who do not agree with this assessment. In this second category, anti-globalization sentiment appears to be even stronger, at least on the internet:

The essence of globalization is a subordination of human rights, of labor rights, consumer, environmental rights, democracy rights, to the imperatives of global trade and investment.

Ralph Nader
American attorney, author, lecturer, political activist

The standardization of world culture, with local popular or traditional forms driven out or dumbed down to make way for American television, American music, food, clothes and films, has been seen by many as the very heart of globalization ... So is it always nationalist to resist US globalization? The US thinks it is, and wants you to agree; and, moreover, to consider US interests as being universal ones ... For when we talk about the spreading power and influence of globalization, aren't we really referring to the spreading economic and military might of the US?

Fredric Jameson
American literary critic

Globalization, as defined by rich people like us, is a very nice thing ... you are talking about the Internet, you are talking about cell phones, you are talking about computers. This doesn't affect two-thirds of the people of the world ... If you're totally illiterate and living on one dollar a day, the benefits of globalization never come to you.

Jimmy Carter
39th President of the United States (1977–1981)

These views seem to equate globalization to American/corporate imperialism. However, they also rightly point out that it is important to pay attention to the distribution of the benefits of globalization more evenly. Global firms cannot simply benefit from cheap labour through outsourcing but ignore the poor working conditions or corruption in developing nations. Finally, there are those who point out that globalization is inevitable:

> Globalization is not something we can hold off or turn off ... it is the economic equivalent of a force of nature – like wind or water ... To realize the full possibilities of this economy, we must reach beyond our own borders, to shape the revolution that is tearing down barriers and building new networks among nations and individuals, and economies and cultures: globalization. It's the central reality of our time.
>
> Bill Clinton
> 42nd President of the United States (1993–2001)

> It has been said that arguing against globalization is like arguing against the laws of gravity ... Globalization is a fact of life. But I believe we have underestimated its fragility ... We must ensure that the global market is embedded in broadly shared values and practices that reflect global social needs, and that all the world's people share the benefits of globalization.
>
> Kofi Annan
> Secretary-General of the United Nations (1997–2007)

> People have accused me of being in favour of globalization. This is equivalent to accusing me of being in favour of the sun rising in the morning.
>
> Clare Short
> British politician and a member of the British Labour Party

The quotes in this third category are pragmatic in the sense that they argue that globalization, with its virtues and flaws, is a fact of life, and is a major process that must (be attempted to) be managed globally. In that respect, both the American and European consumers and the Vietnamese assembly line workers are better off because of globalization. However, globalization also has cultural, social and humane implications. The primary focus of globalization to date has been on the benefits to shareholders. Global firms will simply have to learn to treat their stakeholders (for example, employees, customers, distributors, and suppliers) the way they do in their home countries. It would be naive to think that this can simply be achieved through standardization. Cultures are unique and diversity is essential to our human heritage. Historically, trade between different nations (with different resource advantages) has been the single most important source of human development. However, nations do not trade, merchants do. These merchants not only generated financial wealth, but also served as a bridge for new inventions, social innovations, and culture. For example, both pasta and gunpowder found their way to Europe through trade. When it comes to development, trade works much better than direct foreign aid. Merchants of today are increasingly global corporations. Waiting for the world government to set the rules is a terrible way to build relationship and brand equity in a global world. Lobbying just for the interests of shareholders is even worse. The global corporation will be much better off in the long run if it starts to live up to its social responsibility. This means bringing quality of life to all of its stakeholders in planned, systematic ways.

## Why globalization now?

During the late nineteenth century, there was a great deal of openness and trade between nations across the globe. However, nationalism movements and two world wars greatly deterred the evolution of free trade in the first half of the twentieth century. After these wars, several world leaders across the globe became preoccupied with self-sufficiency through tariff and non-tariff barriers rather than building upon sustainable competitive advantages. However, it became increasingly apparent that their approaches were not working and globalization resumed its inevitable rise. Communism collapsed, economic pragmatism took over, and privatization of public firms accelerated the process, creating value for investors as well as consumers. Decreased tariffs, increased movement of people, adoption of new innovations in telecommunications, the internet, and marketing communications also contributed to cultural acceptance of foreign goods. Consumers came to appreciate diversity and variety in the marketplace. Turkish doner became the most consumed fast-food in Germany. Indian curry became the flavour of choice in England. Salsa sells more than ketchup in the US. As a result of trade liberalization, particularly after 1987, the level of trade between and among NAFTA, EU, and ASEAN has been increasing. Overall, there is a great deal of evidence that the economic growth engines of the global markets of tomorrow will be large emerging nations such as China, India, and Brazil rather than the historical US or European power bases.[3] These emerging nations are already moving away from being exporters of raw materials and inexpensive mass-produced goods to manufacturing of high value-added goods and services by importing more machinery, equipment and know-how from their developed counterparts. Their next phase in globalization will be to create global brands. Transforming a regional brand to a global brand is a particularly challenging strategy with very high stakes. Putting a company's faith simply in anecdotal lessons from others' success and failures is not wise. Managers need to have a grasp of the underlying structure and the big picture to put the risks and rewards into perspective. The Rule of Three theory provides precisely such insight.

## The Rule of Three

The Rule of Three theory suggests that cyclical and systematic market forces make it possible to predict the evolution of competitive industries.[4] During the early growth stage, there are many competitors. For example, there were close to three hundred automobile manufacturers in the US alone by 1915. As the industry matures, the three firms that adapt best survive and thrive, and typically command 70–90 per cent of the market share (that is, General Motors, Ford, and Chrysler). These become the three generalists (that each have more than 10 per cent market share) and coexist with numerous product/market/niche specialists (that each have between 1–5 per cent market share). The Rule of Three structure is optimal because the big three act as the tripod that stabilizes the industry against hyper-competition or collusion. In other words, it offers optimal mix of competition (innovation, quality), collaboration (efficiency, profitability), customer satisfaction (variety, affordability, accessibility, value co-creation). Those firms with 5–10 per cent market share (that is, 'ditch dwellers') can neither benefit from the economies of scale and efficiency of being a generalist, nor can they gain from the effectiveness and focus of serving a niche market. They are expected to perform worse than their generalist or specialist counterparts. Figure 3.1 illustrates the Rule of Three theory.

There are plenty of US industries where the Rule of Three structure has already emerged: burger chains (McDonald's, Burger King, Wendy's), pizza chains (Pizza Hut, Domino's, Papa John's), television networks (NBC, ABC, CBS), beer companies (Anheuser-Busch, Miller, Coors/Stroh), batteries (Duracell, Energizer, Rayovac), consumer reporting agencies

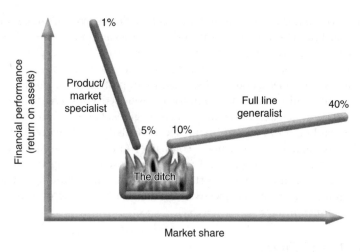

*Figure 3.1*   The Rule of Three
Note: Figure adopted from *The Rule of Three* (Sheth and Sisodia, 2002: 4; see note 4).

(Equifax, TransUnion, Experian), credit card networks (Visa, Mastercard, American Express), banks (Bank of America, Chase Manhattan, Banc One), cereal makers (General Mills, Kellogg, Post), jeans makers (Levi Strauss, Lee, Wrangler), pharmaceutical companies (Merck, Johnson & Johnson, Bristol-Myers Squibb), and the list goes on.

The application of the Rule of Three is not limited to the US markets. International examples include French automakers (Renault, Peugeot, Citroen), Japanese automakers (Toyota, Honda, Nissan), Japanese brewers (Kirin, Asahi, Sapporo), South Korean automakers (Hyundai, Daewoo, Kia), German banks (Deutsche Bank, Dresdner Bank, Commerzbank), UK banks (HSBC, Barclays, Lloyd's TSB), Australian banks (Westpac, National Australia bank, St George Bank), Japanese electronic manufacturers (Matsushita, Sony, Toshiba), and the list goes on. Obviously there are also exceptions to the Rule of Three. However, most of these can be explained by the role of regulation (for example, the US Department of Justice's blocking of airline mergers or monopoly power of utility companies), or the maturity stage of the industry (for example, online retailers).

## The global Rule of Three

The Rule of Three has fundamental corporate, marketing and investment implications. However, the interest in these implications has been predominately at the national level to date. It is illustrative to examine the following cases to contemplate the global implications.

## Aviation industry

Boeing, McDonnell Douglas and Lockheed Martin have been the traditional three generalists in the US aviation industry. However, the intensive competition between the top two players pushed Lockheed Martin into the ditch in the 1970s with less than 10 per cent market share (and it was ultimately acquired by Boeing), leaving two major players. Building upon the financial strength and know-how of its investing European government partners, Airbus capitalized on this gap in the market and became the number two player during the 1980s. This development effectively created a global triad. During the 1990s, the intensive competition between Boeing and Airbus pushed McDonnell Douglas into the ditch. McDonnell Douglas attempted to get out of the ditch by establishing a presence in Asian markets with an alliance with Taiwan Aerospace. When this effort was blocked by the Clinton administration, it was also forced to merge with Boeing. The gap in this strategic industry remains to this day, with Taiwan, Spain, and potentially Russia competing for the third spot globally.

## Tyre industry

The automobile tyre industry did not begin its journey toward globalization until the 1970s. Goodyear, Firestone, and Goodrich in the US, Michelin, Pirelli, Continental, and Dunlop in Europe, Bridgestone, Sumimoto, Toyo, and Yokohama in Japan were the respective generalists. Michelin, building upon the success of the radial tyres that it invented, began its journey towards globalization by opening a manufacturing plant in the US in 1975. It took several years for the US manufacturers to face the Michelin threat competitively. Several players, including the US number three, Goodrich, decided to exit or diversify. Michelin acquired Goodrich in 1989, and with subsequent acquisitions in Poland, Hungary and Colombia catapulted itself to the global number one position. In the meantime, Bridgestone of Japan also announced that it had global leadership in mind. It outbid Pirelli to acquire US number two, Firestone (which also had a European presence) and is currently the number two global player after Michelin. Goodyear is not far behind as the global number three after its acquisition of Dunlop operations in Japan. Amidst all this, specialists remained highly successful. For example, Cooper Tire and Rubber of the US retained its focus as a product specialist (of bias-ply tyres) and thrived with its 2 per cent global market share. Cooper spends little on R&D and uses independent retailers instead of costly company-owned stores. Other international players (for example, Continental and Pirelli) have ongoing merger discussions to enable them to get out of the ditch.

## Home appliance industry

The globalization of the home appliance industry can be dated back to world leader AB Electrolux's (Sweden) acquisition of White Consolidated (US) in 1986. White was the number three generalist in the US behind GE and Whirlpool. Whirlpool retaliated by purchasing the appliance division of Philips to become the number two European player over Bosch-Siemens (Germany) and Merloni (Italy). Whirlpool also acquired Maytag for $1.7 billion in 2006 to reinforce its US position. However, we fully expect Qingdao Heier (already the most valuable brand in China) to challenge both Whirlpool and Electrolux for global leadership. It is conceivable for Heier to purchase GE's appliance business in the process given GE's 'number one or number two or out' strategy. It should not be surprising to see Heier (1), Electrolux (2), and Whirlpool (3) as the top three global players by 2020.

These three industry cases clearly indicate a shift from a national Rule of Three (that is, three/four generalists in each of the triads, North America, Europe and the Far East) toward a global Rule of Three. Because of the fragmentation in Europe (UK *versus* EU) and historical regulatory intervention against consolidation, we tend to observe four generalists in Europe. In the Far East, Japanese firms have historically taken the lead with strong competition from South Korea and China. For example, it can be said that three Japanese firms, Citizen, Seiko, and Casio dominate the global market for watches while the Swiss have retired to a high margin niche position. During the convergence to the Rule of Three, several corollaries apply. Next, we summarize the process:

1. The number one player in each of the triads is best positioned to become one of the global three players since each can build upon their dominance in their home markets.
2. The number three domestic player is typically forced into the ditch during foreign entry.
3. To become a successful global player, a firm must establish itself in at least two of three triads as a major generalist.
4. The management has to make a decision on whether or not they want to become a generalist in their respective industry. There is typically room for only three generalists in a mature industry. This

tends to be four in Europe where regulatory forces have slowed down the consolidation process and the convergence to three.

5. The financial performance of the market leader benefits from increases in market share. However, diseconomies of scale and additional antitrust scrutiny play a role and hinder performance beyond 40 per cent market share.

6. Specialists' performance is enhanced when they grow their market share in their speciality but not necessarily when they grow their overall market share. As such, successful niche players can be considered to be monopolists in their niche while maintaining a miniscule market share of the overall industry.

7. If the number one generalist dominates the industry with more than 70 per cent market share, there may not be room for a third generalist. This is typically a temporary condition however; another player makes room for itself to become the number three player either via innovation or after the patent protection of the incumbent expires.

8. If the number one generalist possesses less than 40 per cent market share there may be room for a fourth generalist (typical phenomenon for Europe). Convergence to three is usually slowed down when industry consolidation/M&A activity is blocked.

9. When a generalist falls into the ditch, it should either attempt to regain over 10 per cent share (organic growth or growth through merger) or divest to become a specialist. Both are tough propositions.

10. The Rule of Three theory suggests that when the top two firms engage in intensive price competition, the third player usually ends up in the ditch. For example, Chrysler has historically been forced into this precarious position more than once. Lee Iacocca salvaged the situation with the minivan innovation in the 1980s, and the Daimler-Chrysler merger in the 1990s was the more recent but ultimately unsuccessful solution to an ongoing strategic problem. On the other hand, specialists do not suffer from price competition due to their dedication to serving their niches.

11. Generalists that acquire and try to manage specialists separately typically fail.

12. The number one generalist may have the biggest R&D budget but tends to be the least innovative of the top three players. Fast-follower strategy seems to work best for them.

13. The number three generalist tends to be the most innovative. However, these innovations are quickly adopted by the top two when possible.

14. Firms in the ditch display the worst financial performance and are candidates for bankruptcy or acquisition.
15. The top three generalists are typically valued at a premium in the stock market. This can be observed by their price:earning ratios, which have higher multiples than their smaller rivals.

There are several rules of engagement for firms that want to become a global top three player:

1. These firms have to conquer the domestic market first: a weak domestic base hinders international expansion.
2. They need to craft the right attack strategy: a better product at a lower price, rather than a better product at a premium price seems to increase adoption.
3. They need to time their market entry right: it is best if the industry is preoccupied with issues such as regulation or undergoing a major investment period.
4. They should not go to foreign markets alone: you can benefit from your traditional suppliers, distributors and even your competitors entering about the same time. This helps the entrant trigger a paradigm shift in the industry's landscape and carve a piece for itself.

### Exception to the Rule of Three

As mentioned before, patent protection or regulatory forces sometimes slow down the progression toward the Rule of Three. In addition, the Rule of Three appears to take place at the product category/brand level for consumer goods. For example, Coca Cola Classic is number 1, Pepsi is number two and Diet Coca Cola is number 3 for carbonated beverages globally. However, Nestlé is the global leader in bottled water. The reason for this phenomenon is because packaged consumer goods firms are highly diversified. For every product category they have a different set of competitors, even though their products may utilize the same distribution channels.

### Prospecting the future

It is possible to predict the global future of industries by applying the principles summarized above. We end with three industry predictions.

### IT services

We believe that the US will continue to dominate the high-value-added IT services industry with (1) IBM and (2) Accenture. TCS of India will occupy the third spot. Recognized names of today (for example, Wipro) will become specialists.

## Television sets

We expect the Far Eastern bloc to continue to dominate this industry globally. The US has no leading brands left and European powerhouses such as Philips and Thomson are either shifting to outsourcing or are for sale. Drastic consolidation is to be expected across the globe. Predicted winners: (1) LG, (2) Samsung, (3) TTE China. Others, such as Sharp and Sony, will be better off by focusing on the high-end LCD segment of the market.

## Telecommunications industry

(a) Cellular phones: (1) Nokia, (2) Motorola, (3) Samsung. Siemens, Ericsson, and Lucent have already become ditch dwellers.
(b) Service operators: (1) China mobile, (2) Vodafone, (3) will be fought out between Telefonica and AT&T Wireless.

## Conclusion

While its virtues and limits are being contemplated by governments, managers must realize that globalization is an inevitable phenomenon. As such, all corporate/marketing strategy must be re-evaluated and reconstructed with global, long-term objectives in mind. The Rule of Three provides profound guidance for crafting strategy and positioning in a global world. However, execution of strategy is just as important: firms must equitably share the economic and humane wealth of their countries with developing parts of the globe. This requires going beyond debating corporate social responsibility and engages the firm in global social responsibility. In this way, globalization can be raised from the 'dead metaphor' jargon it is today, and become the dominant business paradigm of the century.

## Appendix 3A: additional quotes on globalization

### Positives

What I've been trying to say ... is that this image of globalization that is all about push – what the United States and these global multilateral institutions are pushing onto the developing world – really misses the whole new platform, which is increasingly about pull.

Thomas Friedman,
American journalist, op-ed contributor to the *New York Times*

NAFTA recognizes the reality of today's economy – globalization and technology. Our future is not in competing at the low-level wage job; it is in creating high-wage, new technology jobs based on our skills and our productivity.

John F. Kerry
American Politician, Former Democratic Presidential Nominee

As often as I listen to the worries about China eating the jobs of the West, I hear the concern about the influence of the American way of life in the East. The question is: 'Does globalization mean Americanization?' My short answer is no. In measuring globalization, we can count telephone calls, currency flows, trade sums, and so on, but the spread of culture and ideas cannot be so easily measured. Embedded in the present is the unrecognized paradox that culturally, America itself is changing more dramatically than America is changing the world. It is the world that is changing the world. Immigration is reshaping America more profoundly than America's influence around the world.

John Naisbitt
Author of *New York Times* no. 1 best-selling book *Megatrends*

Globalization and free trade do spur economic growth, and they lead to lower prices on many goods.

Robert Reich
American politician, academic, and political commentator

We also have a cultural phenomenon: the emergence of a global culture, or of cultural globalization.

Peter L. Berger
American sociologist and Lutheran theologian

Globalization could be the answer to many of the world's seemingly intractable problems. But this requires strong democratic foundations based on a political will to ensure equity and justice.

Sharan Burrow
President of the Australian Council of Trade Unions

People now realize that globalization is not only for the multinationals and the circulation of money.

Lakhdar Brahimi
Veteran United Nations envoy and adviser

## Negatives

The threat to globalization is not the wasted American dollars but Washington's readiness to mix US commercial interests with its self-appointed role as global protector.

The great, unreported story in globalization is about power, not ideology. It's about how finance and business regularly, continuously insert their own self-interested deals and exceptions into rules and agreements that are then announced to the public as 'free trade'.

William Greider
American author of *The Soul of Capitalism: Opening Paths to a Moral Economy*

We are in a struggle against a globalization that has no place for principles, values and standards.

Bill Jordan
American lawman, marine and writer

Globalization presumes sustained economic growth. Otherwise, the process loses its economic benefits and political support.

Paul A. Samuelson
American neoclassical economist

The negative side to globalization is that it wipes out entire economic systems and in doing so wipes out the accompanying culture.

Peter L. Berger
American sociologist and Lutheran theologian

We must take care that globalization does not become something people become afraid of.

Gerhard Schroeder
German politician, Chancellor of Germany (1998–2005)

Globalization is also playing a role helping drugs trafficking and terrorism which now circulate in a global network.

Lakhdar Brahimi
Veteran United Nations envoy and adviser

Globalization, far from putting an end to power diplomacy between States, has, on the contrary, intensified it.

Omar Bongo
President of Gabon in 1967

There is a huge shift taking place in the global awareness in the last 5 years with strong views about globalization and the power structures of major corporations.

David Korten
Author and a leader in the global resistance against corporate
globalization

In its current form, globalization cannot be sustained. Democratic societies will not support it. Authoritarian leaders will fear to impose it ... Our task is not to make societies safe for globalization, but to make the global system safe for decent societies ... From the suites of Davos to the streets of Seattle, there is a growing consensus that globalization must now be reshaped to reflect values broader than simply the freedom of capital.

John J. Sweeney
President of the AFL-CIO

## Inevitable

Accordingly, globalization is not only something that will concern and threaten us in the future, but something that is taking place in the present and to which we must first open our eyes.

Ulrich Beck
German sociologist

Instead of saying that globalization is a fact, that it's inevitable, we've also got to demonstrate that while the growing interdependence of the world economy is indeed a fact, it's not uncontrollable.

Peter Mandelson
British Commissioner of the European Union for Trade

Globalization is a bottom-up phenomenon with all actions initiated by millions of individuals, the sum total of which is 'globalization.' No one is in charge, and no one can anticipate what the sum of all the individual initiatives will be before the result manifest. A global economy can only be the result of 'spontaneous order.'

John Naisbitt
Author of *New York Times* no. 1 best-selling book *Megatrends*

This is a basic requirement the meaning of globalization is that we should admit that the economy of each country is dependent on the economy of all the others.

Richard Grasso
Chairman and Chief Executive of New York Stock Exchange
(1995–2003)

It is people who are the objects of globalization and at the same time its subjects. What also follows logically from this is that globalization is not a law of nature, but rather a process set in train by people.

Tarja Halonen
President of Finland

## Notes

1. For example, see Peter F. Drucker (1973), *Management: Tasks, Responsibilities, Practices*, New York: Harper & Row.
2. Netnography is basically described as ethnography research on the internet, and is becoming a widely used method for marketing research. The quotes come from the following web links: http://thinkexist.com/quotations/globalization/; http://www.brainyquote.com/quotes/keywords/globalization.html; http://www.cultureofpeace.org/quotes/globalization-quotes.htm. Additional quotes are provided in Appendix A.
3. For more on the force and magnitude of globalization see Jagdish N. Sheth and Rajendra S. Sisodia (2006), *Tectonic Shift: the Geoeconomic Realignment of Globalizing Markets*, Thousands Oaks, CA: Sage.
4. For more on this theory see Jagdish N. Sheth and Rajendra S. Sisodia (2002), *The Rule of Three: Surviving and Thriving in Competitive Markets*, New York: Free Press. Our discussion of the Rule of Three also draws heavily from this book.

# 4

# Marketing Mix Metaphorosis: the Heavy Toll of too much Popularity

*Walter van Waterschoot and Joeri De Haes*

## Introduction: the conceptual marketing mix background

The marketing mix concept is quintessential to marketing. It follows directly from and expresses the very nature of marketing. It is inherent to any marketing situation – even if this is more obvious in some situations than in others. Logically therefore its origin and traces are intertwined with those of the marketing discipline. The antecedents of marketing go way back into the history of many economies, even if these show different time patterns (Fullerton, 1988). Taken together a study of marketing history reveals that marketing theory and managerial practice resulted from fundamentally and substantially changing market circumstances in the Western world, mainly around the end of the nineteenth and during the first half of the twentieth century. An increasing divide between production and consumption implied the structural presence of supply as well as of demand in diverse product and service areas. Over the course of history, both supply and demand potential tended to become increasingly substantial as well as heterogeneous and consequently also more or less non-transparent. Importantly also, even if potential demand typically increased (for example, because of rising incomes) potential supply was or became typically even larger in relative terms (for example, because of innovations). The emergence of these buyers' markets forced marketers to engage in all sorts of marketing efforts to attract the attention, interest and preference of potential customers. These developments did not occur in a completely identical, parallel, linear or isolated way. They took place instead in a more or less irregular and interactive but anyway substantial fashion – according to a 'complex flux model' (Fullerton, 1988).

The result of these developments was the emergence of a new exchange model fundamentally different from the one traditionally assumed by economists (see Figure 4.1). This new model gave rise to a new discipline for the first time given the formal course title of 'marketing' at Harvard Business School in 1902 (Bartels, 1962). The subject matter of the new discipline consisted of exchanges, the core conditions of which were later generically defined by Philip Kotler (1972). For exchanges to occur, the following conditions are necessary: '(1) (the presence of) two or more parties; (2) a scarcity of goods (in the generic sense of the latter term); (3) concept of private property; (4) one party must want a good held by another; (5) the "wanting" party must be able to offer some kind of payment for it; and (6) the "owning" party must be willing to forgo the good for the payment' (Kotler, 1972: 47). On top of these exchange conditions there are some typical properties explaining the distinct character of the new exchange model: heterogeneity and non-transparency of demand and supply as well as buyers' markets (represented in Figure 4.1 by dots, question marks and inequality signs respectively). Importantly, what is also of interest in the new exchange model as opposed to the traditional microeconomic model is the implied type of buyer response. Whereas the outcome of the traditional economic exchange model is to buy or not to buy, the outcomes of the new exchange model are far more differentiated. Not only do other types of visible responses become important, for example, visits to stores or active information gathering, but non-visible reactions and delayed reactions also become of importance. This is closely related to the idea that the new exchange model leaves room for subjective and even non-rational behaviour. The latter

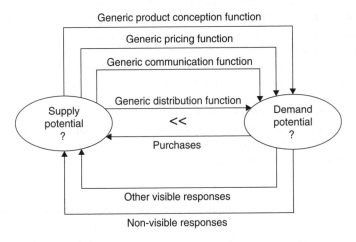

*Figure 4.1*   The new exchange model
*Source*: Van Waterschoot et al. (2006).

was not yet very prominent during the early decades of marketing devel-opment as a formal body of thought. This period is often referred to as a period of 'marketing economics', meaning that the rationality idea of economics was still very much present (Alderson, 1954; van Waterschoot et al., 2004). Multidisciplinary marketing arose foremost during the second half of the twentieth century, in an era when the marketing mix concept and marketing mix metaphor were coined.

This new exchange model is the inherent basis of marketing theory and practice. It structurally implies four unavoidable and therefore generic marketing exchange functions, which are in spectacular contrast with the absence of such functions in the traditional model of microeconom-ics of pure, transparent markets ruled by rationality (van Waterschoot and Van den Bulte, 1992; van Waterschoot, 2000; van Waterschoot et al., 2006). In Figure 4.1 these four generic marketing exchange func-tions are represented by arrows originating from the marketer(s) toward the market(s). In 'reciprocal marketing' they go both ways.

1. *A generic product conception function.* Instead of products and services being homogeneous and not posing any significant strategic choice in terms of product composition, they have now typically become heterogeneous, implying a passive or active product conception by marketers. A choice has to be made between the many imaginable alternative product concepts to determine which specific product composition would be marketed.
2. *A generic pricing function.* Instead of having to take or leave a market price, market participants enjoy more or less price freedom. They can actively or passively follow a pricing strategy – in fact they are even forced to.
3. *A generic communication function.* In the described setting, communi-cation with an eye on information and persuasion has become inevitable.
4. *A generic distribution function.* In the described setting production and consumption are separated by different types of gaps – geographic, choice, time and amount (Bucklin, 1966, 1972) – which market par-ticipants have to bridge in order to make their products or services available.

The four generic exchange functions of the new exchange model materialize via actual choices in terms of instruments – so by definition controllable elements – influencing demand to a greater or lesser extent: these include all sorts of product and/or service attributes, product ranges, price schemes, communication vehicles and schedules, compensation schemes for intermediaries and so on. This multitude of instruments can theoretically be combined in myriads of ways and can also be spread out over time and targeted in numerous ways. It is this concept of a controllable mixture of instruments that impinge on demand which is described by the coinage of the suggestive, figurative label of 'marketing mix' (or marketing concept). This concept is indissolubly inherent to marketing activity. But even if the reality of a large number and variety of instruments that impinge on demand is structurally inherent to the new exchange model, this idea was not clearly identified and described for a long period. It was not only a hardly identified concept; for a long period it was also an implicit concept without a name. The term 'marketing mix' was only coined in 1953 by Neil Borden in his presidential address to the American Marketing Association. He had been inspired by James Culliton (1948), who in the preceding decade had pictured the marketing executive as somebody combining different ingredients. The term 'marketing mix' from that point on referred not only to a picture or metaphor, but also to the corresponding concept (Borden, 1964) and also to the corresponding instruments.

## The rise and survival of the marketing mix metaphor

After an interpretation of the metaphor, we will compare its specific denotations with the traits of the corresponding concept, as well as with those of the overall marketing discipline. Next we discuss the nature and consequences of the so-called 4P-mnemonic which may arguably be considered a metaphor twinned to the marketing mix metaphor.

### The nature of the marketing mix metaphor

In line with Van den Bulte (1994a, 1994b) this section will interpret the marketing mix metaphor from a relatively operational point of view. It will not discuss this metaphor from a strictly linguistic point of view. First, we will assess the grounds on which it can be argued that the marketing mix term is a metaphor. We will then interpret its specific type. Next we will discern which specific denotations the marketing mix metaphor entails in comparison with the marketing mix concept and the marketing discipline.

In their review paper of metaphors in marketing Bremer and Lee (1997: 419) define a metaphor as 'a form of figurative or non-literal language. Figurative language expresses one thing in terms normally denoting another with which it may be regarded as analogous. We reason analogically when we make the inference that if two or more things agree with one another in some respects they will probably agree in others.' This definition essentially matches the definitions of Arndt (1985), Van den Bulte (1994a), Hunt and Menon (1994, 1995). It also corresponds with the views of Cornelissen (2003) in his review paper of the metaphor as a method in the domain of marketing.

The marketing mix – next to being a concept carrying the same label – arguably is a metaphor. The marketing 'mix' term or picture is, literally, false. The marketing manager is not literally a baker or a bartender mixing ingredients or alcohol to arrive at one or other bakery product or cocktail. There is some similarity though or 'existential equivalence' (Hunt and Menon, 1994, 1995). The property of the 'primary concept' – the literal cake or alcohol mix – is transferred to the 'secondary concept' of instruments that impinge upon demand by stating that the one concept is the other (Hunt and Menon, 1994, 1995). So, based on standard definitions the marketing mix picture is indeed a metaphor.

To determine what type of metaphor the marketing mix metaphor is, we refer to Van den Bulte (1994a: 406) who, based on literature research, distinguishes between four types of metaphors.

- *Core metaphors* are 'basic presuppositional insights or intuitions undergirding entire schools of thought, research traditions, or Lakatosian scientific research program[s]'. Consumer researchers and theorists in microeconomics for example see consumers essentially as utility maximizers.
- *Theory-constitutive metaphors* serve as fundamental presuppositions underlying specific theories or attempts to theorize. An example is the product life cycle.
- *Literary metaphors* are aesthetically pleasing and as a result relatively vivid and memorable. An example would be the marketing myopia metaphor.
- *Conveyance metaphors* 'do not have the theoretical scope of core and theory-constitutive metaphors, but they pervade the way we talk and think about marketing. Less visible than literary metaphors but as commonplace, they are the metaphors marketers live by. They are so familiar and plain that we often forget that they are metaphors at all: a company ... "fights" the competition and "defends its position" (an arena or battlefield?), and so on.'

The marketing mix metaphor is arguably a 'core metaphor' in terms of scope. As explained in the introduction the marketing mix concept is indissolubly intertwined with the generic marketing exchange functions, which in turn determine the boundaries of the discipline. So intrinsically the application field of the mix metaphor matches that of the marketing discipline. However, to interpret the mix metaphor in terms of how literally it does or does not apply to the marketing discipline, it needs to be interpreted in terms of the denotations it does and does not contain. More particularly, we need to investigate which specific denotations the marketing mix metaphor entails, in comparison with the marketing mix concept and the marketing discipline. We should indeed be very much aware of the fact that metaphors are by definition partial and selective. 'Indeed, by metaphorical reasoning, one always selects certain aspects of the subject under investigation to compare with another and leaves out the other aspects' (Van den Bulte, 1994a: 412); 'A metaphor always emphasizes some aspects, deemphasizes others, and hides still others' (ibid.: 413). As a result of the magnified focus on particular aspects, together with the ignorance concerning other aspects, a metaphor implies exaggeration by its very nature. In the same train of thought it is logical that the narrower the primary concept of the metaphor is in comparison to its secondary concept, the stronger this exaggeration becomes. The properties of the metaphor play a part in this respect, as do the reactions of its users. 'Just as we can inadvertently overextend the used part of the metaphor, we can myopically leave interesting relations unused' (ibid.: 414). Moreover, metaphor acceptance shows the properties of a process. Over time metaphors may become accepted as every-day language and their oversimplification may also become accepted as truth. They sound less figurative and are considered plain truth (Cornelissen et al., 2006). As the following sections will show, the marketing mix metaphor is a literary metaphor in the sense that it is aesthetically pleasing, relatively vivid and memorable. However, over time it has become a conveyance metaphor, meaning that it has become so familiar and plain that we forget that it actually is a metaphor.

## Metaphor, concept and marketing discipline compared

This section discusses the denotations which are specifically inherent to the mix metaphor. The denotations of a metaphor are by definition partial in comparison to the concept they represent, even if the metaphor would apply to the overall discipline. Also, the implied denotations may be right or wrong, desired or undesired. They may be used more or less frequently in theory and practice or perhaps remain completely unused (Van den Bulte, 1994a). Moreover, from the point of view of the corresponding concept (and discipline) some denotations may be missing. The more denotations that are wrong, undesired, unused and/or missing, the more twisted the metaphor is in comparison to its secondary concept and the more problematic it may be or become, from the point of view of the discipline to which the secondary concept belongs.

With an eye on distinguishing the associations which could logically or factually be made concerning the metaphor, this section also checks the criticisms which have been expressed over time concerning the mix concept. These sometimes prove to concern the metaphor or the discipline in the first place rather than the mix concept. On the other hand, it turns out that what is raised as criticism of the metaphor is sometimes criticism of the marketing mix concept and/or of the marketing discipline and/or of marketing practice (Arndt, 1985; Van den Bulte, 1991, 1992, 1994a, 1994b; van Waterschoot and De Haes, 2001). Table 4.1 summarizes the specific denotations of the mix metaphor as compared to the mix concept and the marketing discipline, by grouping them into four classes. Following Van den Bulte's division (1991, 1994a), the table and corresponding text distinguish between compatible and non-compatible denotations and used and unused denotations. We also discuss missing denotations, referring to the remarkable properties of the mix concept and/or of (particular subfields of) the marketing discipline which make up no part of the metaphor.

The first group of denotations in Table 4.1 is essentially compatible with both the marketing mix concept and the marketing discipline – even if the metaphor is not literally true:

- The metaphor suggests the availability of an endless set of combinations leading to a range of possible outcomes – both evident and less evident ones, both positive and negative ones, both immediate and longer-term effects as listed in Table 4.1. These very direct metaphorical suggestions are completely in line with the marketing mix concept. As a result they also match the overall discipline, even if the relevance to some subfields is less obvious or prominent as, for example, in the case of relationship marketing (see below).
- The metaphor suggests a cake or alcohol mixer who has control over a number of elements which s/he can self-reliantly mix as s/he pleases. This denotation is basically compatible – even if not completely true – in the sense that exchange situations are subject to constraints. An example would be programmed channels, where market participants can only mix demand-impinging instruments within the boundaries of accepted arrangements. So, this denotation implies more or less exaggeration.

*Table 4.1* Denotations of the marketing mix metaphor

| Denotations of the marketing mix metaphor | | Compared with the nature of | |
| --- | --- | --- | --- |
| | | The marketing mix concept | The marketing discipline |
| Compatible and actually used | Instrumental man<br>Large set of possible ingredients/elements/instruments<br>Large set of possible combinations<br>Wide range of effects<br>Positive and/or negative effects<br>Primary and secondary effects<br>Postponed effects<br>(Dis-)synergistic effects<br>Mixed effects | These metaphor denotations are completely in line with essential properties of the marketing mix concept. The metaphor helps by emphasizing and recalling those important characteristics. These metaphor denotations are compatible, but may imply too much exaggeration and risk to be interpreted too one-sidedly and literally. | These metaphor denotations are completely in line with the marketing discipline. In some situations or applications the mix concept is less exclusively or evidently prominent in comparison to other concepts, even if it still holds and even deserves careful attention and analysis. In those situations the metaphor is less helpful, even if the corresponding concept is structurally unavoidably. |
| Compatible but actually unused (or not used enough) | Secondary effects<br>Creativeness | The mix concept leaves room for carefully studying secondary effects and calls for creativeness next to critical analysis. However, these denotations have been somewhat neglected in the past. | The marketing discipline – even when concentrating much on analysis – does not always study enough secondary mix effects thoroughly. Also creativeness aspects of the marketing mix are understudied. |

*(Continued)*

*Table 4.1* (Continued)

| Denotations of the marketing mix metaphor | | Compared with the nature of | |
| --- | --- | --- | --- |
| | | The marketing mix concept | The marketing discipline |
| Non-compatible | One-time-operation/ concentrated in time Tangible elements only | Contrary to the metaphor the marketing mix concept is not confined to one-time operations or tangible elements only. | The discipline covers operations spread out over time, and also non-tangible elements. The mix concept is in any case structurally unavoidable. The metaphor, however, suggests more or less the opposite. |
| Lacking | Purposeful decision-making Interactiveness Repetitiveness Relationship | The marketing mix concept is unavoidably present in interactive settings, as it is in relationships. | Discipline covers interactive, repetitive as well as relationship situations. The mix concept is in any case structurally unavoidable. |

The second group consists of those denotations which have not been translated systematically enough into marketing theory, research and practice – even if they match both the basic nature of the mix concept and of the discipline. For example, the discipline does not use enough the suggestion of the secondary effects and functionality of mix instruments. Following the same train of thought it looks as though the creativeness aspect is not studied as much as it should be.

The third set groups suggestions that neither perfectly mirror the marketing mix concept nor the discipline. They are in smaller or larger conflict with the mix concept and with the discipline, and are therefore less desirable or even undesirable.

- One-time operation (as in mixing a cocktail) is not completely in line (thus, undesired) with the marketing mix concept and the marketing discipline where, for example, advertising money is allocated over time and not concentrated at one particular moment.
- The metaphor of the cocktail or cake mixer also suggests the use of tangible ingredients. This is in contrast with the marketing mix concept and the marketing discipline, where non-tangible elements such as brand and store image may play an essential role.

The fourth set consists of the allegedly missing denotations from the point of view of the discipline and/or of the mix concept. This group concerns suggestions which are not made by the metaphor and as a result make the metaphor particularly partial. The importance of this group has increased over time, as new subfields in marketing, for example, service marketing, have become more prominent.

- The suggestion of the cake or alcohol mixer is essentially non-interactive. If one thinks of a bartender, s/he may be interacting with a customer whilst making a show out of cocktail mixing. But this seems to be an exception. The metaphor does not suggest much interaction, which is undesirable to some extent. The marketing discipline leaves room for interaction – to say the least – and so does the marketing mix concept. Interactions may lead to further market responses, which in turn cause further marketing mix adaptations and so on.
- The metaphor does not suggest repetition. The possibility that the cocktail mixer might repeat his/her operation should not be excluded, but the metaphor is essentially non-repetitive. This (absent) feature too is in partial contradiction with the marketing discipline, as well as with the marketing mix concept, which both leave room

for repetitiveness. The marketing discipline even has a long educational tradition – including in so-called transaction marketing – of stressing the desirability of aiming at repetitiveness, for example, via retention marketing, which would stress such notions as customer loyalty schemes.

- The metaphor does not suggest relationships, but rather seems to suggest complete independence via the self-reliance of the alcohol mixer. Indeed, it seems logical to conclude that the mix metaphor does not suggest any relationship between the mixer and his target. In some instances this is warranted, in other instances it is not. So, at least to some extent, this is not desirable (see above). The marketing mix concept on the other hand – as well as the marketing discipline – does leave room for relationships (see below).
- The marketing mix concept has been accused of provoking rational reactions only. This is an unwarranted criticism as far as the concept (and discipline) is concerned. As far as the metaphor is concerned, the rational/non-rational dichotomy seems to be equally irrelevant. The mix concept (and discipline) in any case may apply – depending on the setting – to either rational or irrational reactions or to both. The metaphor has no particular denotation in this respect and therefore is surely neither in conflict with the marketing concept, nor with the marketing discipline.
- The mix concept would lead to myopic concentration on customers and dealers at the expense of other publics. This criticism is clearly neither relevant for the mix concept nor for the metaphor, because on principle mixes can be developed towards any public.
- Some sources suggest that the metaphor implies purposeful decision-making only. Contrary to that interpretation we feel that the metaphor does not exclude 'wild' mixing or 'thoughtless' mixing and the like. So, according to our judgement, the metaphor certainly does not suggest purposeful decision-making. The same goes more or less for the mix concept. The discipline so far as it is descriptive – it is to a large extent – leaves room for non-purposeful decision-making. To the extent that the discipline is normative, purposeful decision-making from the point of view of the marketer is implied, including purposeful marketing mix choices. In brief, we think that there is no problem whatsoever in terms of compatibility – only that the metaphor does not strongly suggest purposeful decision-making, but leaves the issue more or less open. In other words, we think that the critics here raise an irrelevant point.

## The clash of metaphors: unwarranted subfield polarization

Major communication qualities explaining the acceptance of a metaphor, as distinguished by Bremer and Lee (1997), are comprehensibility, aptness and memorability. The mix metaphor presumably gained currency at a spectacular speed in particular as a result of its expressiveness, liveliness, compactness and therefore memorability (Van den Bulte, 1991; van Waterschoot and Van den Bulte, 1992). The metaphor apparently scored so well on these criteria that it became immensely popular in no time – even amongst educators and researchers. The metaphor acceptance was so overwhelming that it could be compared with love at first sight. This immediate and uncritical love was not just a blessing though. It has caused an unwarranted concept and subfield polarization at the level of the discipline. Relationship marketing as well as e-marketing are cases in point.

In the case of relationship marketing, scholars, surprisingly and erroneously, contrast the existence of relationships with the marketing mix (Rust and Chung, 2006). This illustrates how strongly metaphors dominate thoughts, to the extent that they cause scholars to exaggerate the meaning of concepts and lose sight of instances where and degrees to which concepts are compatible. Metaphors are partial suggestions and therefore exaggerations. They make the underlying concepts appear contradictory, even if the concepts themselves leave room for differentiated combined applications.

The conceptual basis of marketing is exchange – under typical circumstances such as buyers' markets. The parties involved in such an exchange process – and in the first place the initiator who by definition is called the marketer – naturally try to increase their level of control over it. The level of control is increased by means of manipulating marketing mix instruments and/or by taking all sorts of programming measures. The other party is tied up to the initiator – and to some extent vice versa – by organizational, contractual and physical arrangements and even by emotional ties. Relationship marketing is the most widely-used embracing metaphorical term for this type of situation (Cornelissen, 2003).

At the limit of the relationship – by definition the most extreme situation – the distinction between the two parties disappears. The two exchange parties become one. In that extreme situation marketing ceases to exist because there are no longer any exchange parties. The generic exchange functions cease to exist and so does the marketing mix. This is the ultimate situation suggested by the relationship metaphor. The marriage between the parties is in contradiction with negotiation about exchange conditions. If husband and wife start exchanging domestic jobs like dishwashing or lawn-mowing for not pretending a headache in the evening, this haggling would throw a shadow over their marriage. A true marriage is in contrast with that sort of bargaining.

The concepts of the marketing mix and of relationships are not necessarily in conflict though, as long as the relationship is not particularly strong. Even in programmed marketing channels, product and service offerings are conceived, prices are determined, persuasive communication is taking place and so on. Even if there is a relationship between exchange parties in terms of knowledge, interest, affection, organizational arrangements and the like, the generic exchange functions still hold. The exchange effects may become more difficult to identify, as the contacts and exchanges have a more continuous nature. The marketing mix instruments may – and probably will – develop a different composition, for example, in the form of loyalty schemes. As long as the relationship is not so strong that there would no longer be any voluntary exchanges, there is still a marketing situation at stake; and therefore also need of marketing exchange functions and marketing mix instruments. Only in the extreme situation – suggested by the marriage metaphor but exceptional in practice – where separate parties no longer exist, because they are completely tied up in a relationship, would there no longer be any marketing. In the case of such complete integration there would be grounds neither for exchange functions, nor for marketing mix instruments. So, the *concepts* of the marketing mix and of relationships do not necessarily exclude each other as long as the relationships are partial. Because the marriage *metaphor* suggests an extremely intimate relationship, however, it is indeed in conflict with the marketing mix *metaphor*. The metaphor of relationship marketing – the wedding picture – even represents a contradiction in terms, as the relationship suggests the absence of distinct parties, whereas marketing by definition presupposes essentially distinct parties. In other words, if scholars polarize relationship marketing with traditional marketing based on the marketing mix, they are intuitively following metaphorical suggestions, instead of thinking logically according to the premises of their own discipline.

## The 4P-mnemonic: a Siamese twin metaphor

While the marketing mix metaphor is in conflict with some other metaphors, there are further metaphors and communication vehicles to which it is related in a convergent and even synergistic fashion, for example, to the metaphors of instrumental man and to the metaphor of captain of industry. It is particularly strongly related to the

4P-mnemonic, which was formulated by McCarthy (1960) shortly after Neil H. Borden had coined the figurative marketing mix label in his 1953 AMA Presidential Address (Borden, 1964). McCarthy pragmatically grouped mix instruments into four categories: product, price, place and promotion (van Waterschoot, 1995). This 4P-mnemonic possesses the properties of a metaphor in the sense that a primary concept – namely a classification summarized as a mnemonic – is transferred to the secondary concept of demand-impinging instruments (see metaphor definitions of Arndt, 1985; Bremer and Lee, 1997; Hunt and Menon, 1994, 1995; Van den Bulte, 1994a). It generally suggests, in a non-literal fashion, that the marketing mix is the 4Ps and vice versa. More particularly, the linguistic memory aid suggests that instrument category labels should begin with the same character – 'P'. It suggests that – at the present stage of knowledge and science – the marketing mix is confined to four such categories. It implicitly suggests that this categorization is a proper one, namely that it would meet the basic classificatory requirements put forward by Hunt (1976, 2002), such as collective exhaustiveness and mutual exclusiveness. It suggests that if new scientific developments were to take place, these would lead to the identification of even more Ps. Some of these suggestions are correct, for example, that the marketing mix contains several elements which can broadly be categorized in a limited number of classes. Most of the suggestions are strongly exaggerated though and should not be taken literally. Marketing literature, however, is replete with exaggerated and unwarranted reliance on the 4 – or more – Ps metaphor – indeed, by P-mania.

The marketing mix metaphor and the 4P-mnemonic and metaphor have become so closely related in everyday usage – not just by practitioners but also by scholars – that they are often used as synonyms. That is to say, the two metaphors are used interchangeably. The one metaphor – and even the underlying concept – is perceived as being equal to the other. They are so closely twinned that they could be considered 'Siamese' twin metaphors. This expression is relevant because while each metaphor – however closely related they are – does have its own individual meaning and identity, albeit in practice they can hardly be separated. In perceptual terms they have become more or less identical.

Both the marketing mix metaphor and the 4P-metaphor possess strong communication qualities. When it comes to liveliness the marketing mix metaphor will probably score higher, whereas the 4P-metaphor would – by its very nature – probably score highest in terms of memorability. Both have a very strong spontaneous appeal. As a result, both communicate some crude essentials of marketing quickly and easily in a mutually enforcing way – explaining the immense popularity of the combination. At the level of the discipline, the spectacular popularity of the twin metaphor is a mixed blessing. On the one hand, the communication process of knowledge, as well as related conceptualization and empirical research within the traditional application fields suffers from P-mania. On the other hand, new subfields tend to contrast, and even polarize, their conceptual base model with the traditional marketing mix model. This is an unjustified and superficial polarization, partly explained by the abundant presence of Ps and P-jargon in traditional settings, making it easy – and tempting – to deny the more subtle and unavoidable presence of the marketing mix concept in newer settings.

### P-mania: service marketing as a conceptual case in point

Some subfields of the marketing discipline are very illustrative of P-mania; one such is service marketing where a number of alternative marketing mix classifications have been formulated. Instead of challenging McCarthy's pragmatic P-mnemonic it was extended with additional P-classes in order to highlight the importance of particular service marketing aspects (van Waterschoot, 1997, 1999). However, these additional classes were typically only further submixes of the four broad instrument categories, corresponding primarily with the four generic exchange functions discussed earlier (van Waterschoot and Van den Bulte, 1992). In other cases, they suggested elements that did not belong to the marketing mix at all. In other words, instead of playing a subordinate role, the aid of memory began playing an obligatory, dominant and therefore unjustified role. The aim of memorability led logical thinking instead of the other way around, as illustrated by the following example (van Waterschoot and De Haes, 2001).

In the context of services marketing, Booms and Bitner (1981) have suggested three extra P's to denote people, physical evidence and process.

1. 'People' was added to recognize the importance of the human element – such as employees or customers – in all aspects of the marketing of services. The people involved in a service marketing situation can indeed significantly improve or harm the quality of service provision (van Waterschoot, 1999). However, the conception of the service activities that personnel need to carry out belongs – already – to the product conception mix (van Waterschoot and Van den Bulte, 1992). Insofar as customers are meant by 'people', the extra P is conceptually incorrect, since the marketing mix groups, by definition, only demand impinging elements that are under the control of the marketer.

2. 'Physical evidence' was added to stress the importance of physical surroundings in service settings; and of tangible elements that help communicating and performing the service. However, there is no conceptual necessity to include these elements in a separate class. Physical surroundings belong to the distribution mix; and the tangible elements that help communicate and perform the service typically belong to the communication mix and the product conception mix respectively (van Waterschoot and Van den Bulte, 1992).
3. Finally, 'Process' includes the procedures, mechanisms and flow of activities by which services are consumed. Again, although process decisions indeed radically affect how a service is delivered to customers, there is no need to include them in a separate class, since they belong to the product conception mix (van Waterschoot and Van den Bulte, 1992).

## P-mania: the frightening idiosyncrasy of empirical research

These examples illustrate clearly how the 4P-metaphor dominates conceptualization instead of the other way around. This phenomenon is so marked, and also so misplaced, that it is well typified by a term like 'P-mania'. The flip-side of this P-mania is that more recent subdisciplines – instead of joining the P-chorus – like to emphasize their newness by stressing that they are bringing a completely new type of approach, completely differing from marketing mix thinking, as in the case of relationship marketing (see above).

Another phenomenon arising from P-mania is the way in which it fuels the overly empirical nature of the discipline. More than two decades ago, Arndt (1985) rightly complained about the one-sided character of empirical positivism of the marketing discipline; and of the enormous opportunities that were consequently lost or not enjoyed. 'Marketing has been dominated by the logical empiricist paradigm stressing rationality, objectivity, and measurement. While leading to many breakthroughs, this domination has contributed to a neglect of important aspects of marketing and a lack of attention to alternative research approaches' (Arndt, 1985: 11). Today, Arndt's criticism seems just as relevant (van Waterschoot, 2007). P-mania plays a part in this sad picture, because the mnemonic metaphorically suggests that marketing mix instruments represent an endless set that can hardly be categorized. It suggests that marketing mix research comes down to investigating the effects of any marketing mix combination without any limitation or priority, since, a priori, any one marketing mix combination is as relevant and as unpredictable as any other. In other words it sustains the cause of idiosyncratic research as opposed to inte-grated research, that is, research that would explicitly try to compare itself with other empirical research, that would aim at a confrontation with deductive research and ultimately at harmony between inductive and deductive research.

## Conclusion: the heavy toll of too much popularity

The term 'marketing mix' was coined in 1953, at a moment when the facts representing and fuelling the concept were becoming increasingly manifest in the market circumstances and marketing practice of various advanced Western economies. Even if the metaphor of the manager as a cake mixer of demand-impinging instruments had already been intro-duced several years before, the concept itself had barely yet been explic-itly defined and named by marketing scholars. The marketing discipline was developing fast, but it was not, at that time, actively and systemati-cally seeking its identity, in the sense of trying to pinpoint its true nature and define its conceptual boundaries. An authoritative consensus in this respect would only be reached two decades later. The new expression 'marketing mix' not only indicated a metaphor, but was also used to refer to the corresponding concept of controllable demand-impinging instruments.

In 1960 McCarthy devised the 4P-mnemonic, with the aim of easily summarizing and memorizing the pragmatic grouping of marketing mix instruments into four crude categories. In the communication proc-ess to users, this mnemonic has proven to possess characteristics meta-phorically transferred to the marketing mix concept. As a result the marketing mix metaphor has become so closely intertwined with the 4P-mnemonic and metaphor that they could be called Siamese twin metaphors. Each metaphor possesses strong communication properties, the impact of which has only increased synergistically through their mutual linkage.

Half a century after their introduction the twin metaphors are cer-tainly not dead. On the contrary, they are alive and kicking – and appa-rently kicking far too hard. As such they are no exception to the marketing discipline, which more than any other discipline is replete with metaphors – as markedly so as formal, a priori, assumptions are missing. Metaphors do have a role to play in the development of a discipline – perhaps even a lasting one. But a discipline cannot be ruled by metaphors, which to some extent seems to be the case with marketing.

If metaphors start dominating logical thinking; if metaphors dictate the development of concepts; if clashing metaphors cause unwarranted polarization of compatible concepts and schools of thought; if metaphors fuel idiosyncratic empirical research and thereby block more integrated research, something is fundamentally wrong. The role of metaphors has become exaggerated, misplaced and even pathological. Metaphors risk causing over-dominance, too strong contrasts, oversimplification, superficiality, over-inspiration and over-suggestion instead of stimulating differentiated, logical thinking. In its mature stage the discipline is no longer blessed by the richness of its metaphors, but suffers from metaphorosis.

Metaphorosis is a phenomenon which does far more than marginally affect managerial practice. On the contrary, marketing management pays a heavy toll for it. Admittedly the marketing mix twin-metaphors did, and still do, contribute immensely to the quick intuitive understanding of some key aspects of marketing. At the same time, however, they directly and indirectly block more profound conceptual and empirical learning. Unwarranted conceptual subfield polarization is not what managers need. A continuous reinvention of the wheel by empirical research is not what they need either. These ongoing phenomena in marketing, for which managers bear much of the opportunity costs, hamper the generation and dissemination of knowledge to end users, as does the striking emphasis of the discipline on high-brow academic journals aimed at specialists, to the detriment of communication vehicles aimed at end users. In conclusion, the story of the marketing mix metaphor underscores the fact that, in the much needed reflection on the communication process of knowledge to end users (van Waterschoot and Gijsbrechts, 2003), a thorough assessment of the role of metaphors is a major aspect.

## Acknowledgements

The authors thank Thomas Foscht (California State University) and Christophe Van den Bulte (Wharton School/University of Pennsylvania) for their comments on an earlier draft.

## References

Alderson, W. (1954), 'Factors governing the development of marketing channels', in R.M. Clewitt (ed.), *Marketing Channels for Manufactured Products*, Homewood, IL: Richard D. Irwin.

Arndt, Johan (1985), 'On making marketing science more scientific. The role of orientations, paradigms, metaphors, and puzzle solving', *Journal of Marketing*, 49(3) (Summer): 11–23.

Bartels, R. (1962), *The Development of Marketing Thought*, Homewood, IL: R.D. Irwin.

Booms, B.H. and M.J. Bitner (1981), 'Marketing strategies and organization structures for service firms', in J.H. Donnelly and W.R. George (eds), *Marketing of Services*, Chicago, IL: American Marketing Association, pp. 47–51.

Borden, N. (1964), 'The concept of the marketing mix', *Journal of Advertising Research*, 4: 2–7.

Bremer, Kristine and Moonkyu Lee (1997), 'Metaphors in marketing: review and implications for marketers', *Advances in Consumer Research*, 24: 419–24.

Bucklin, L.P. (1966), *A Theory of Distribution Channel Structure*, Berkeley, CA: IBER Special Publications.

Bucklin, L.P. (1972), *Competition and Evolution in the Distributive Trades*, Englewood Cliffs, NJ: Prentice-Hall.

Cornelissen, Joep P. (2003), 'Metaphor as a method in the domain of marketing', *Psychology & Marketing*, 20(3): 209–25.

Cornelissen, Joep P., Lars Thöger Christensen and Pieter Vijn (2006), 'Understanding the development and diffusion of integrated marketing communications – a metaphorical perspective', NRG Working Paper no. 06-02.

Culliton, J.W. (1948), 'The management of marketing costs', Division of Research, Graduate School of Business Administration, Harvard University, Boston, MA.

Fullerton, Ronald A. (1988), 'How modern is modern marketing? Marketing's evolution and the myth of the "production era"', *Journal of Marketing*, 52(1) (January): 108–25.

Hunt, Shelby D. (1976), *Marketing Theory*, Columbus, OH: Grid.

Hunt, Shelby D. (2002), *Foundations of Marketing Theory: Toward a General Theory of Marketing*, Armonk, NY: M.E. Sharpe.

Hunt, Shelby D. and Anil Menon (1994), 'Is it "metaphor at work" or is it "metaphors, theories, and models at work"?', in G. Laurent, G. Lilien and B. Bras (eds), *Research Traditions in Marketing*, Norwell, MA: Kluwer Academic Publications, pp. 426–32.

Hunt, Shelby D. and Anil Menon (1995), 'Metaphors and competitive advantage: evaluating the use of metaphors in theories of competitive strategy', *Journal of Business Research*, 33: 81–90.

Kotler, P. (1972), 'A generic concept of marketing', *Journal of Marketing*, 36: 46–54.

McCarthy, Jerome (1960), *Basic Marketing: a Managerial Approach*, Homewood, IL: Richard D. Irwin.

Rust, Roland T. and Tuck Siong Chung (2006), 'Marketing models of service and relationships', *Marketing Science*, 25(6) (November-December): 560–80.

Van den Bulte, Christophe (1991), 'The concept of the marketing mix revisited – a case analysis of metaphor in marketing theory and management', the Vlerick School of Management, University of Ghent, Belgium.

Van den Bulte, Christophe (1992), 'The concept of the marketing mix revisited – a case analysis of metaphor in marketing theory and management', paper presented at the Conference on Research Traditions in Marketing, Brussels, European Institute for Advanced Studies in Management, 9–10 January.

Van den Bulte, Christophe (1994a), 'Metaphor at work', in G. Laurent, G. Lilien and B. Bras (eds), *Research Traditions in Marketing*, Norwell, MA: Kluwer Academic Publications, pp. 405–25.

Van den Bulte, Christophe (1994b), 'Can literal truth safeguard models and theories from metaphor?', in G. Laurent, G. Lilien and B. Bras (eds), *Research Traditions in Marketing*, Norwell, MA: Kluwer Academic Publications, pp. 433–4.

van Waterschoot, Walter (1995), 'The marketing mix', in M.J. Baker (ed.), *Companion Encyclopedia of Marketing*, London: Routledge, Chapter 25, pp. 443–8.

van Waterschoot, Walter (1997), 'The marketing mix', in M. Warner (ed.), *The International Encyclopaedia for Business and Management*, London: Thomson Business Press, pp. 3307–14.

van Waterschoot, Walter (1999), 'The marketing mix', in M.J. Baker (ed.), *The IEBM Encyclopedia of Marketing*, London: Thomson, pp. 317–30.

van Waterschoot Walter (2000), 'The marketing mix as a creator of differentiation', in K. Blois (ed.), *The Oxford Textbook of Marketing*, Oxford: Oxford University Press, pp. 183–211.

van Waterschoot, Walter (2007), 'Is the Marketing Discipline Product(ion) Orientated', presentation, EIRASS conference, San Francisco.

van Waterschoot, Walter and Joeri De Haes (2001), 'Entries on the Marketing Mix: Explications and Extensions; Functions; Functional Classification; Influencing Demand; Pragmatic Classifications; Origins of the Metaphor and the Concept; Criticism; Instruments; Multiple Functions of Instruments', in P. Kitchen and T. Proctor (ed.), *The Informed Student Guide to Marketing*, London: Thomson Learning, pp. 175–97.

van Waterschoot, Walter and Els Gijsbrechts (2003), 'Knowledge transfer through marketing textbooks: the Howard and Sheth typology as a case in point', in P. Kitchen (ed.), *The Future of Marketing*, Basingstoke: Palgrave Macmillan, pp. 59–81.

van Waterschoot, Walter and Christophe Van den Bulte (1992), 'The 4P classification of the marketing mix revisited', *Journal of Marketing*, 56(4) (October): 83–93.

van Waterschoot, Walter, Piyush Kumar Sinha, Steve Burt, Joeri De Haes and Annouk Lievens (2004), 'Revisiting the concept and classification of distribution service outputs', working paper, Indian Institute of Management, Ahmedabad, available at www.iimahd.ernet.in/publications/public.

van Waterschoot, Walter, Leen Lagasse and Robert Bilsen (2006), *Marketingbeleid: Theorie en Praktijk*, 11th revised edition, Antwerpen: De Boeck.

# 5

# Market Segmentation as a Metaphor: Whoever Heard of Alexander the Mediocre?

*Malcolm McDonald*

## Introduction

The term 'market segmentation' conjures up images of a whole being divided into smaller parts (segments). Yet, since the dawn of marketing, market segmentation has become a confusing metaphor, badly explained, poorly implemented and, also, one of the last bastions of marketing ignorance. Indeed, a recent *Harvard Business Review* article about 30,000 failed product launches in the US put their failure down principally to inadequate market segmentation (Christensen et al., 2005).

The construction industry is currently booming in many countries in the world. I recently asked one of sixty managing directors at their conference what accounted for his 185 per cent growth in net profits. His reply? 'We had a mild winter'! So I asked him how much of his net profits came from market growth. He didn't know. Then I asked him how much came from market share growth – but obviously, if he couldn't answer the first question, he couldn't answer that. Then I asked him how much came from net price increases. He didn't know. Then I asked him how much came from productivity improvements. He didn't know ... and so on and so on. By now the other 59 managing directors were sitting bolt upright, hoping that this odious little toad of a professor (me!) wouldn't ask any of them such embarrassing questions. There is a grossly mistaken view that in high growth markets, marketing somehow doesn't matter. But even a cursory glance at the fortunes of American and European companies over the past twenty years will reveal that most of them have gone bankrupt since the heady days of growth ended. Of Tom Peters' 43 'excellent' companies (Peters and Waterman, 1982), only six were left only eight years later.

My conclusion? The good thing about not practising professional marketing is that failure comes as a complete surprise and is not preceded by a long period of worry and depression!

The heartbeat of professional marketing has always been market segmentation. The reason no one has heard of Alexander the Mediocre is that, unlike Alexander the Great, he was mediocre. So what makes anyone think that mediocre products are going to reap anything but mediocre results? Going a stage further, what sort of company would make a commodity out of bread, fertilizer, glass, paper, chlorine, potatoes or mobile phones?

Well, just observe consumers buying potatoes in Marks and Spencer in the UK at a premium price. Then ask whether anyone can tell the difference between Castrol GTX, Alfa Laval Steel, SKF bearings, Intel microprocessors and respective competitors. Yet these great companies are able to charge premium prices and have massive global market shares.

Gurus such as Tom Peters, Philip Kotler, the chairman of Unilever, and the like agree that the key elements of world class marketing are:

1. Profound understanding of the market place
2. Proper market segmentation
3. Powerful differentiation, positioning and branding
4. Integrated marketing strategies

The order is significant. Even now, many companies are messing about with their brands without really understanding their market, how it is segmented, or where they are positioned.

Over thirty years of research at Cranfield University School of Management has proved a link between long-term shareholder value creation and excellent strategic marketing, which exhibits the characteristics in the left-hand column of Table 5.1.

*Table 5.1* Key elements of world class marketing

| Excellent strategies | Weak strategies |
|---|---|
| • Target needs-based segments | • Target product categories |
| • Make a specific offer to each segment | • Make similar offers to all segments |
| • Leverage their strengths and minimize their weaknesses | • Have little understanding of their strengths and weaknesses |
| • Anticipate the future | • Plan using historical data |

## Markets we sell to

Companies frequently confuse target markets with products – pensions or mainframe computers for example – this, coupled with a lack of knowledge about the sources of differential advantage against each segment, signals trouble.

Many companies pride themselves on their market segmentation even though these so called 'segments' are in fact *sectors*, which is a common misconception. Everyone with a marketing qualification knows that a segment is a group of customers with the same or similar needs and that there are many different purchase combinations within and across sectors.

But the gravest mistake of all is a priori segmentation. Most books incorrectly state that there are several bases for segmentation, such as socio-economics, demographics, geo-demographics and the like. But this misses the point totally. For example, Boy George and the Archbishop of Canterbury are both (socio-economically) As, but they don't behave the same! Nor do all 18 to 24 year old women behave the same (demographics). Nor does everyone in my street (geo-demographics) behave the same.

All goods and services that are made, distributed and used and the purchase combinations that result make up an actual market, so the task is to understand market structure, how the market works and what these different purchase combinations (segments) are.

First, let us examine the factors that cause markets to break into smaller groups (see Figure 5.1).

When something new is invented, such as television, computers, microwaves, the internet and the like, not everyone adopts them at the same time. Many years ago an American researcher, called Everett

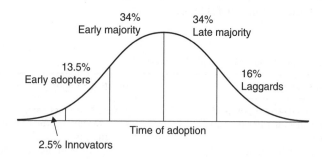

*Figure 5.1*   Non-cumulative diffusion pattern
*Source*: Adapted from Rogers (1976).

Rogers, studied the way in which new products are diffused across markets over time. Imagine that television has just been invented. Let us take any market, Germany will do, and let us imagine that there are only 100 households in Germany. Let us further imagine that there is a law limiting each household in Germany to only one television. Clearly, the potential market for televisions in Germany is 100, but not everyone buys one at the same time. Someone has to be the first to adopt new products. Normally, about 2.5 per cent of any population will be the first to adopt new products. These people are known as 'innovators'. They are very unusual people who enjoy being different.

These people are followed by another group, known as 'opinion leaders'. These people tend to be affluent, well-educated, very privileged, and they are independent thinkers who do not care much what other people think of them. They are, however, crucial in getting any new product or service adopted. We can think of them as the Joneses, in the sense of the expression: 'keeping up with the Joneses'.

This group is followed by a much larger group known as the 'early majority'. These people admire the opinion leaders and can be thought of as the Smiths, in the sense of the expression: 'the Smiths try to keep up with the Joneses'. When these people start to enter a market, there is a rapid growth in sales.

By now, approximately 50 per cent of all those who could adopt the new product, have done so, and it is now that the 'late majority' begin to enter the market. Generally, these people are less privileged, less affluent, and less well-educated, and price often becomes important at this stage in the market.

Finally, the remaining 16 per cent of the population adopt the new technology. Rogers referred to these people as 'laggards'. By now, everyone who could have one has got one. For example, in the United Kingdom, everyone has a calculator, they are very cheap, and the market can now be considered to be a replacement market, in which growth will be dependent on population size, demographics and the like. Clearly, in mature markets, getting growth will be much more difficult.

Although this is not the purpose of this chapter, it is useful to note, before I leave Roger's diffusion of innovation curve, that when launching a new product or service, it is advantageous to know who the opinion leaders are in a market, as these people should be targeted first by the sales force, and by other promotional media, as they will be the most likely to respond. For example, certain doctors will be more open-minded about new drugs, whereas other doctors will not risk prescribing a new drug until it has been on the market for a number of years.

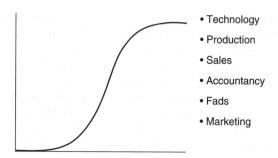

*Figure 5.2*   A market life cycle and different managerial orientations

The diffusion of innovation curve also explains the phenomenon known as the product life cycle, and why, after the 50 per cent point on the diffusion of innovation curve is reached, the market continues to grow, but the rate of growth begins to decline until maturity is reached (see Figure 5.2).

At the beginning of any market, *technology* tends to be the driving business force, largely because new products tend to be at the cutting edge. As the new technology begins to take hold, as explained in the earlier references to the research of Everett Rogers, *production* tends to be very important, because at this stage it is not unusual for demand to be greater than supply. However, as the market grows and new entrants begin to introduce competitive products, *sales* as a function become increasingly important, as the new competition entails a growing consumer choice. A problem frequently occurs at the next stage of the market life cycle, as there is now more supply than demand and frequently organizations attempt to cut costs, so *accountancy* tends to come to the fore. This is often followed by implementing the latest management consultancy *fads*, such as those promulgated by gurus such as Tom Peters in works like *In Search of Excellence*. Finally, however, all organizations come to the same conclusion, which is that they need to understand their consumers and customers better in order to meet their needs, and this of course, is where market segmentation, the subject of this chapter becomes crucial.

All this has been explained in order to introduce the key concept of market segmentation and why it happens. Clearly, in the early days, markets will tend to be homogeneous. But, as demand grows rapidly with the entry of the early majority, it is common for new entrants to offer variations on the early models, as I have just explained, which gives consumers a choice. In order to explain this more clearly, let

*Figure 5.3* The shape of the car market

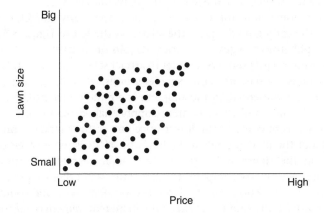

*Figure 5.4* The shape of the lawn mower market

me illustrate the approximate shape of markets (see Figure 5.3). If we were to plot the car market in terms of speed and price, we would see very small, inexpensive cars in the bottom left-hand corner. In the top right, we would see very fast, expensive cars. Most cars, however, would cluster in the middle, what we might call: 'The Mr and Mrs Average market.'

The lawn mower market would look very similar (see Figure 5.4). With lawn size on the vertical axis and price on the horizontal axis, at the bottom left would be small, inexpensive, hand-pushed mowers, with expensive sit-on machines for large estates in the top right-hand corner.

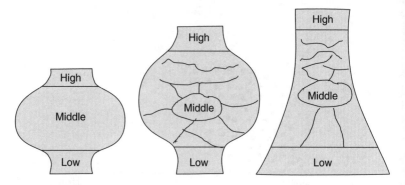

*Figure 5.5*   Early growth, rapid growth and a mature market

That leaves the mass of the market with average size lawns, and average sized lawn mowers, which is where the mass market is.

We can now redraw this to represent the shape of any market, particularly at the early growth stage (the shape on the left in Figure 5.5). But when rapid growth begins, new entrants join the market and offer variations on standard products in order to attract sales, and it is at this stage that markets begin to break into smaller groups, while still growing overall. (This is represented by the shape in the middle.) Eventually, when markets mature, and there is more supply than demand, any market growth tends to come in the lower price end of the market, whilst the top end of the market tends to be immune. (This is represented by the shape on the right.) It is usually the middle market that suffers at this stage, with many competitors vying with each other on price. This, however, is the whole point of market segmentation, for competing only on price is to assume that this is the main requirement of customers, whereas the truth is that this is rarely the case. It is just that a general lack of understanding about market segmentation on the part of suppliers about the real needs of customers in mature markets forces them to trade on price, so encouraging the market to become a commodity market.

The starting point in market segmentation is correct market definition, which is crucial for measuring market size, growth and share, identifying relevant competitors and formulating strategies to deliver differential advantage. Few companies give sufficient attention to correct market definition and few can draw an accurate market map and therefore have little chance of doing anything remotely resembling correct market segmentation at the key influence points or junctions on the map.

At each of these junctions, segmentation is not only possible, but crucial. The methodology for market segmentation is explained fully in McDonald and Dunbar (2005) and this process is summarized in this chapter.

First, however, let us clarify the terminology about customers and consumers.

## The difference between customers and consumers

The term 'consumer' is interpreted by most to mean the final consumer, who is not necessarily the customer. Take the example of a parent who is buying breakfast cereals. The chances are that they are intermediate customers, acting as agents on behalf of the eventual consumers (their family), and, in order to market cereals effectively, it is clearly necessary to understand what the end-consumer wants, as well as what the parents want.

This is only relevant in that it is always necessary to be aware of the needs of eventual consumers down the buying chain.

Consider the case of the industrial purchasing officer buying raw materials such as wool tops for conversion into semi-finished cloths, which are then sold to other companies for incorporation into the final product, say a suit or a dress, for sale in consumer markets. Here, we can see that the requirements of those various intermediaries and the end-user are eventually translated into the specifications of the purchasing officer to the raw materials manufacturer. Consequently, the market needs that this manufacturing company is attempting to satisfy must in the last analysis be defined in terms of the requirements of the ultimate users – the consumer – even though the direct customer is quite clearly the purchasing officer.

Given that we can appreciate the distinction between customers and consumers and the need constantly to be alert to any changes in the ultimate consumption patterns of the products to which our own contributes, the next question to be faced is: who are our customers?

Direct customers are those people or organizations who actually buy from us. They could, therefore, be distributors, retailers and the like. However, as intimated in the previous paragraph, there is a tendency for organizations to confine their interest, hence their marketing, only to those who actually place orders. This can be a major mistake, as can be seen from the following case history.

A fertilizer company that had grown and prospered during the 1970s and 1980s, because of the superior nature of its products, reached its farmer consumers via merchants (wholesalers). However, as other companies copied the technology, the merchants began to stock competitive products and drove prices and margins down. Had the fertilizer company paid more attention to the needs of its different farmer groups and developed products especially for them, based on farmer segmentation, it would have continued to create demand-pull through differentiation.

The segmentation study revealed that there were seven distinct types of farmer, each with a different set of needs. Figure 5.6 shows just three examples of these segments. First, there was a segment we called Arthur (the figure at the top of the slide) after a television character known for his deals. He bought on price alone but represented only 10 per cent of the market, not the 100 per cent put about by everyone in the industry, especially the sales force. Another type of farmer we called Oliver (the figure in the bottom right of the slide). Oliver would drive around his fields on his tractor with an aerial linked to a satellite and an on-board computer. He did this in order to analyse the soil type and would then mix P, N and K, which are the principle ingredients of fertilizer, solely to get the maximum yield out of his farm. In other words, Oliver was a scientific farmer, but the supply industry believed he was buying on price because he bought his own ingredients as cheaply as possible. He did this, however, only because none of the suppliers bothered to

*Figure 5.6*   Personalizing segments

understand his needs. Another type of farmer we called David (the figure in the bottom left of the slide). David was a show-off farmer and liked his crops to look nice and healthy. He also liked his cows to have nice, healthy skins. Clearly, if a sales representative had talked in a technical way to David, he would quickly switch off. Equally, to talk about the appearance of crops and livestock would have switched Oliver off, but this is the whole point. Every single supplier in the industry totally ignored the real needs of these farmers, and the only thing anyone ever talked about was price. The result: a market driven by price discounts, accompanied by substantial losses to the suppliers. ICI however, armed with this new-found information, launched new products and new promotional approaches aimed at these different farmer types, and got immediate results, becoming the most profitable subsidiary of ICI and the only profitable fertilizer company in the country.

Let us now return to market dynamics and what happens to markets at the rapid growth stage. At this stage, new entrants come into the market, attracted by the high sales and high profits enjoyed by the industry. Let us illustrate this with another case history. In the early 1970s, a photocopier company had 80 per cent market share and massive profit margins. This is represented by the big circle in the middle of Figure 5.7. When a Japanese newcomer entered the market with small photocopiers, the giant ignored them. The Japanese product grew in popularity

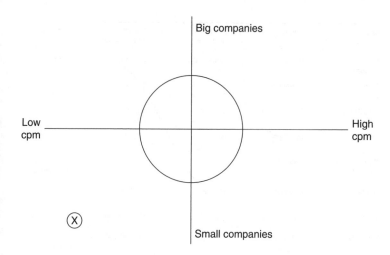

*Figure 5.7* The photocopier market
*Note*: cpm = copies per month.

however, forcing the giant to reduce its prices. Within three years, the giant's share was down to 10 per cent, and the battle was lost. They had failed to recognize that the market was segmented and tried to compete in all segments with their main product, a mistake made by hundreds of erstwhile market leaders. The main point about this case history, is that companies should not attempt to compete in all segments with the same product, but should recognize that different segments or need groups develop as the market grows, and that they should develop appropriate products and services, and position and brand them accordingly.

Let us summarize all of this by showing a product life cycle representation with some generalizations about how marketing strategies change over time (see Figure 5.8). This shows at least four major changes that occur over the life cycle. At the top of the far right-hand column is the word 'commodity', but the point is that this is by no means inevitable, and only occurs in markets where the suppliers do not understand the power of market segmentation, as illustrated in the fertilizer case history. There are other options of course, including the option to get out of mature markets. Another is to move the goal posts as it were, somewhat in the manner of First Direct, Direct Line, Michael Dell, Virgin, Amazon. com, and countless others. The strategy with which this chapter is concerned, however, is market segmentation, which in my view, should be the very first consideration as markets begin to mature.

| Key characteristics | Unique | Product differentiation | Service differentiation | 'Commodity' |
|---|---|---|---|---|
| **Marketing message** | Explain | Competitive | Brand values | Corporate |
| **Sales** | Pioneering | Relative benefits distribution support | Relationship based | Availability based |
| **Distribution** | Direct selling | Exclusive distribution | Mass distribution | 80:20 |
| **Price** | Very high | High | Medium | Low (consumer controlled) |
| **Competitive intensity** | None | Few | Many | Fewer, bigger international |
| **Costs** | Very high | Medium | Medium/Low | Very low |
| **Profit** | Medium/High | High | Medium/High | Medium/Low |
| **Management style** | Visionary | Strategic | Operational | Cost management |

*Figure 5.8*   The product/market life cycle and market characteristics

*Figure 5.9* Fast moving consumer goods value chain

An excellent example of good practice is Procter & Gamble in the US, which supplies Wal-Mart, the giant food retailer. As can be seen from the simple diagram (Figure 5.9), P & G create demand pull (hence high turnover and high margins) by paying detailed attention to the needs of consumers. But they also pay detailed attention to the needs of their direct customer, Wal-Mart. Wal-Mart are able to operate on very low margins because, as the barcode goes across the till, P & G invoice them, produce another item and activate the distribution chain, all of this being done by means of integrated IT processes. This way, they have reduced Wal-Mart's costs by hundreds of millions of dollars.

Closely related to the question of the difference between customers and consumers is the question of what the term 'market share' means.

## Market share

Most business people already understand that there is a direct relationship between relatively high share of any market and high returns on investment, as shown in Figure 5.10.

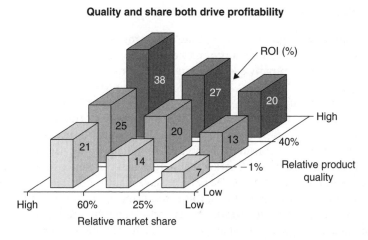

*Figure 5.10* The relationship between market share and return on investment
*Source*: Buzzell and Gale (1987).

Clearly, however, since, for example, BMW are not in the same market as Ford, it is important to be most careful about how 'market' is defined. Correct market definition is crucial for: measuring market share and market growth; the specification of target customers; recognition of relevant competitors; and, most importantly of all, the formulation of marketing strategy, for it is this, above all else, that delivers differential advantage.

The general rule for 'market' definition is that it should be described in terms of a customer need in a way which covers the aggregation of all the products or services which customers regard as being capable of satisfying the same need. For example, we would regard the in-company caterer as only one option when it came to satisfying lunchtime hunger. This particular need could also be satisfied at external restaurants, public houses, fast-food specialists and sandwich bars. The emphasis in the definition, therefore, is clearly on the word 'need'.

To summarize, correct market definition is crucial for the purpose of:

- Share measurement
- Growth measurement
- The specification of target customers
- The recognition of relevant competitors
- The formulation of marketing objectives and strategies

## Market segmentation

We can now begin to concentrate on a methodology for making market segmentation a reality: market segmentation being the means by which any company seeks to gain a differential advantage over its competitors.

Markets usually fall into natural groups, or segments, which contain customers who exhibit a similar level of interest in the same broad requirements. These segments form separate markets in themselves and can often be of considerable size. Taken to its extreme, each individual consumer is a unique market segment, for all people are different in their requirements. While CRM systems have made it possible to engage in one-to-one communications, this is not viable in most organizations unless the appropriate organizational economies of scale have been obtained at a higher level of aggregation, such as at segment level. Consequently, products are made to appeal to groups of customers who share approximately the same needs. It is not surprising, then, to hear that there are certain universally accepted criteria concerning what constitutes a viable market segment:

1. Segments should be of an adequate size to provide the company with the desired return for its effort.
2. Members of each segment should have a high degree of similarity in their requirements, yet be distinct from the rest of the market.
3. Criteria for describing segments must enable the company to communicate effectively with them.

While some of these criteria are obvious when we consider them, in practice market segmentation is one of the most difficult of marketing concepts to turn into a reality. Yet a company must succeed, otherwise they become just another company selling what are called 'me too' products. In other words, what we offer the potential customer is very much the same as what any other company offers and, in such circumstances, it is likely to be the lowest priced article that is bought. This can be ruinous to our profits, unless we happen to have lower costs, hence higher margins, than our competitors.

There are basically three stages to market segmentation, all of which have to be completed.

The first establishes the scope of the project by specifying the geographic area to be covered and defining the 'market' which is to be segmented, followed by taking a detailed look at the way this market operates and identifying where decisions are made about the competing products or services. Successful segmentation is based on a detailed understanding of decision-makers and their requirements. The second is essentially a manifestation of the way customers actually behave in the marketplace and consists of answering the question 'Who is specifying what?'.

The third stage looks at the reasons behind the behaviour of customers in the marketplace and answers the question 'Why?' and then searches for market segments based on this analysis of needs.

The following sections provide an overview of the steps required to complete these three stages and are presented in a format appropriate for conducting a segmentation project using internal resources.

## Stage 1: defining the market

The first step in market segmentation establishes the scope of the segmentation project by specifying the geographic area covered by the project and by clearly understanding from a customer's perspective the 'market' in which the company's products or services are competing with those of its competitors. Where necessary, the scope is modified to take into account the realistic capabilities of the organization.

A clear geographic boundary enables sizing of the market, identification of the localities in which the dynamics of the market have to be understood and, once the segments have been identified, development of the appropriate marketing objectives and strategies for those localities.

Keeping the project within the borders of a single country is a manageable starting point because the stage of market development, the available routes to market and the pattern of marketing activity will probably be the same throughout the country. Even this, however, may be too broad for some companies, simply because their geographic reach is limited by physical and/or economic considerations, or even because their appeal has a strong local sentiment attached to it.

For companies trading in numerous countries around the world, there is clearly an enormous attraction in finding a single global segmentation model that can be applied to every country. However, the experience of 'globalization' has highlighted for many of these companies that they have to 'act local' in order to succeed in their market. This doesn't mean that every country is completely unique in respect of the segments found within it. For the international company, a useful guide to predetermining which countries can be included in a single segmentation project is to ensure that in each of these countries the stage of market development, the available routes to market and the pattern of marketing activity are the same, or at least very similar.

As a reminder, the general rule for 'market' definition is that it should be described in a way which covers the aggregation of all the alternative products or services which *customers* regard as being capable of satisfying that same need. Table 5.2 offers an example from financial services.

### Market mapping

A useful way of identifying where decisions are made about competing products and services and, therefore, those who then proceed to the next stages of segmentation, is to start by drawing a 'market map'.

A market map defines the distribution and value added chain between final users and suppliers of the products or services included within the scope of a segmentation project. This should take into account the various buying mechanisms found in the market, including the part played by 'influencers'. An example of a generic market map is given in Figure 5.11.

*Table 5.2* Some market definitions (personal market)

| Market | Need (on-line) |
|---|---|
| Emergency cash ('Rainy day') | Cash to cover an undesired and unexpected event (often the loss of/damage to property). |
| Future event planning | Schemes to protect and grow money which are for anticipated and unanticipated cash calling events (e.g. car replacement/repairs, education, weddings, funerals, health care) |
| Asset purchase | Cash to buy assets (e.g. car purchase, house purchase, once-in-a-lifetime holiday). |
| Welfare contingency | The ability to maintain a desired standard of living (for self and/or dependants) in times of unplanned cessation of salary. |
| Retirement income | The ability to maintain a desired standard of living (for self and/or dependants) once the salary cheques have ceased. |
| Wealth care and building | The care and growth of assets (with various risk levels and liquidity levels). |
| Day-to-day money management | Ability to store and readily access cash for day-to-day requirements. |
| Personal financial protection and security from motor vehicle incidents | Currently known as car insurance. |

It is useful to start a market map by plotting the various stages that occur along the distribution and value added chain between the final users and all the suppliers of products or services competing with each other in the defined market. At the same time, indicate the particular routes to market through which the products are sourced, as not all of them will necessarily involve all of these stages. (Note at each junction on the market map, if applicable, all the different types of companies/ customers that are found there, as illustrated in Figure 5.12.)

It is useful at this point to split the volume or value quantity dealt with by each junction between the junction types (see Figure 5.13).

The easiest junction at which to start this part of market mapping is at the final users' junction, noting at each junction with leverage the volume/value (or percentage of the total market) that is decided there. Guesstimate these figures if they are not known and note this as a requirement for any follow-up work generated by this first pass at segmenting the market. This is also illustrated in Figure 5.13 in which we see a market in which 30 per cent of annual sales are decided at junctions other than the final user junction.

... including the number of each customer type

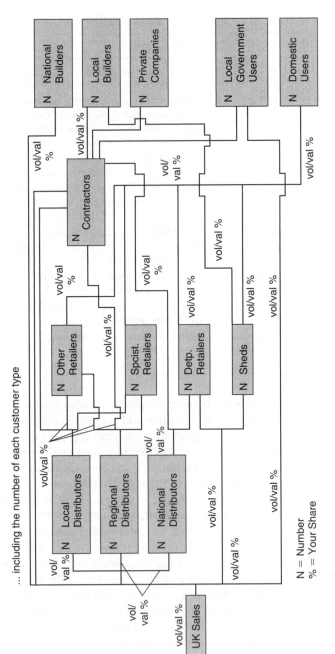

N = Number
% = Your Share

*Figure 5.11*   A generic market map

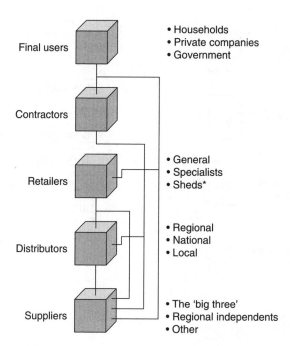

*Figure 5.12*  Market map listing the different junction types
*Note*: * 'Sheds' is the name sometimes used to refer to hardware superstores.

So far, we have built a market map by tracking the distribution and value added chain found between final users and suppliers, and shown the various routes that are taken through the map to link the two together. We then quantified the map. This was followed by expanding the detail to show the different types of companies/customers found at each junction on the map and these were also quantified.

### Stages 2 and 3: who specifies what, where, when, how – and why?

In this step we are developing a representative sample of different decision-makers which identifies the characteristics and properties of a purchase on which decisions are made along with the customer attributes that will be used to describe the decision-makers. Each constituent of this sample is called a 'micro-segment'.

The uniqueness of a micro-segment is that when determining which of the alternative offers is to be bought, the decision-makers it represents demonstrate a similar level of interest in a specific set of features, with the features being the characteristics and properties of 'what' is bought,

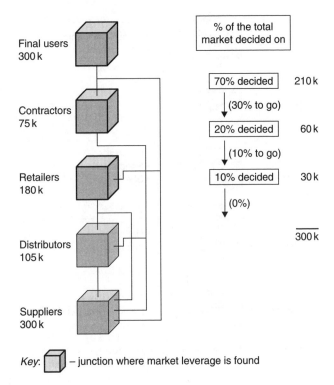

*Figure 5.13*  Market leverage points on a market map

'where' it is bought, 'when' it is bought and 'how' it is bought as appropriate to the micro-segment. To this is added the descriptors which describe who the micro-segment represents along with an estimate of the volume or value they account for in the defined market.

The principle behind this step is that by observing the purchase behaviour of decision-makers and understanding the key constituents of this behaviour, we have a platform for developing a detailed understanding of their motivations. It is, therefore, a critical link with the next step of the segmentation process, which looks at why decision-makers select the particular products and services they specify. This, in turn, becomes the basis on which the segments are formed.

The process chart in Figure 5.14 illustrates a number of steps that will now be described. From this, it is clear that the process begins with market mapping, which corresponds to a deep understanding of the market. This has already been discussed above.

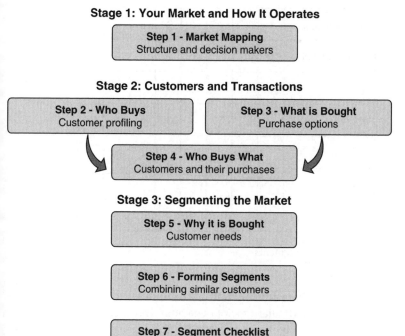

*Figure 5.14*   The market segmentation process

We can now turn to the process again, and move to steps 2, 3, 4 and 5, although it must be reiterated that segmentation can and should be carried out at all major junctions on the market map, not just at the final user junction.

Essentially, these time-consuming steps involve listing all purchase combinations that take place in the market, including different applications for the product or service (see Figure 5.15), principal forms such as size, colour, branded, unbranded and so on, the principle channels used, when – such as once a year, weekly and so on – how – such as cash or credit. Next it's important to describe who behaves in each particular way using relevant descriptors such as demographics. For industrial purchases this might be standard industrial classifications, size of firm and so on, whereas for consumer purchases this might be socio-economic groups such as A, B, C1, C2, D and E or stage in the life cycle, or age, sex, geography, life styles or psychographics. Finally, and most difficult

| Micro-segment | 1 | 2 | 3 | 4 | 5 | 6 | 7 | 8 | 9 | 10 |
|---|---|---|---|---|---|---|---|---|---|---|
| What is bought | | | | | | | | | | |
| Where | | | | | | | | | | |
| When | | | | | | | | | | |
| And how | | | | | | | | | | |
| Who | | | | | | | | | | |
| Why (benefits sought) | | | | | | | | | | |

*Figure 5.15*   Micro-segments

of all, each purchase combination has to have a brief explanation of the reason for this particular type of behaviour. In other words, we need to list the benefits sought, and it is often at this stage that an organization needs to pause and either commission market research or refer to its extant database of previous market research studies. Although there are only 10 micro-segments shown in Figure 5.15, it is normal in most markets for companies to identify between 30 and so micro-segments. Remember, these micro-segments are actual purchase combinations that take place in a market.

To summarize so far, it is clear that no market is totally homogeneous (see Figure 5.16). The reality is that actual markets consist of a large number of different purchase combinations (see Figure 5.17). However, as it is impracticable to deal with more than between 7 or 10 market segments, a process has to be found to bring together or cluster all those micro-segments that share similar or approximately similar needs (see Figure 5.18).

Once the basic work has been done in describing micro-segments, that is, steps 2, 3, 4 and 5, any good statistical computer program can carry out cluster analysis to arrive at a smaller number of segments. The final step consists of checking whether the resulting segments are big enough to justify separate treatment, are indeed sufficiently different from other segments, whether they have been described sufficiently well to enable the customers in them to be reached by means of the organization's

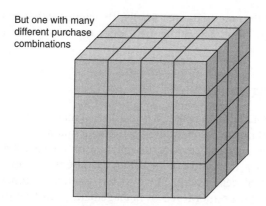

*Figure 5.16*   An undifferentiated market

*Figure 5.17*   Different needs in a market

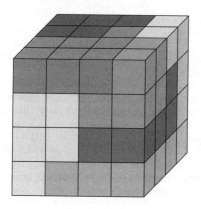

*Figure 5.18*   Segments in a market

communication methods, and finally, the company has to be prepared to make the necessary changes to meet the needs of the identified segments.

## Conclusions

Before summarizing the process of market segmentation, it will by now be clear that market segmentation is fundamental to corporate strategy. It is also clear that, since market segmentation affects every single corporate activity, it should not be just an exercise that takes place within the marketing department, but also has to involve other functions. Finally, the most senior levels of management must lead this initiative if their organization is to be truly market or customer-need-driven.

Table 5.3 summarizes what we have discussed so far. It is obvious that there will be very few markets in the world where all customers have the same needs. Also, once market segmentation has been carried out, positioning products and services to meet the different needs of the different segments is comparatively easy. The difficult bit is segmenting markets. Finally, it is vital to focus on serving the needs of the identified segments, whilst it is dangerous to straddle different segments with the same offer. The photocopier example is only one example of thousands of well-known companies that have suffered from this mistake as markets began to break into segments. The computer industry during the 1980s and 1990s is also replete with examples of this mistake.

Thus, the process of market segmentation consists of five steps: (1) understand how your market works – this involves defining the market and drawing a market map; (2) list what is bought, including where, when,

*Table 5.3*  Understand market segmentation

- Not all customers in a broadly-defined market have the same needs
- Positioning is easy. Market segmentation is difficult. Positioning problems stem from poor segmentation
- Select a segment and serve it. Do not straddle segments and sit between them
  1. Define the market to be segmented and size it (market scope)
  2. Determine how the market works and identify who makes the decisions (market mapping)
  3. Develop a representative sample of decision-makers based on differences they see as key (including what, where, when and how), note who they are (demographics) and size them
  4. Understand their real needs (why they buy, the benefits sought)
  5. Search for groups with similar needs

**Market mapping**

1. Market definition – 'A customer need that can be satisfied by the products or services seen as alternatives'. It is based around what the customers perceive as distinct activities or needs they have which different customers could be satisfying by using alternative products or services.

2. The distribution and value added chain that exists for the defined market.

3. The decision-makers in that market and the amount of product or service they are responsible for in their decision-making.

**Who buys**

1. Recording information about the decision-makers in terms of who they are – Customer Profiling. Demographics, geographics etc.

2. Testing a current segmentation hypothesis to see if it stacks up – Preliminary Segments.

**What is bought**

1. Listing the features customers look for in their purchase – what, where, when and how.

2. Focusing in onto those features customers use to select between the alternative offers available – Key Discriminating Features KDFs.

**Who buys what**

1. Building a customer 'model' of the market – based on either the different combinations of KDFs customers are known to put together, or derived from the random sample in a research project. Can be constructed by Preliminary Segment. Each customer in the model (sample) is called a Micro-segment.

2. Each micro-segment is profiled using information from the data listed in 'Who buys'.

3. Each micro-segment is sized to reflect the value or volume they represent in the market.

**Why**

1. As customers only seek out features regarded as key because of the benefit(s) these features are seen to offer them, the benefits delivered by each KDF should be listed. For some customers it is only by combining certain KDFs that they attain the benefit(s) they seek – benefits should also be looked at from this perspective. These benefits are Critical Purchase Influences CPIs.

2. For thoroughness, benefits can be looked at from the perspective of each Preliminary Segment.

3. Once the CPIs for the market have been developed their relative importance to each micro-segment is addressed (by distributing 100 points between the CPIs).

**Forming segments**

1. By attributing a 'score' to all the CPIs for each micro-segment, the similarity between micro-segments can be determined.

2. Micro-segments with similar requirements are brought together to form clusters

3. Clusters are sized by adding the volumes or values represented by each micro-segment.

**Segment checklist**

1. Is each cluster big enough to justify a distinct marketing strategy?

2. Is the offer required by each cluster sufficiently different?

3. Is it clear which customers appear in each cluster?
If all 'yes', clusters = segments.

4. Will the company change and adopt a segment focus?

*Figure 5.19* Summarizing the market segmentation process

how, and the different applications of the product or service; (3) list who buys, using descriptors such as demographics and psychographics; (4) list why they buy, especially the benefits sought; (5) search for groups with similar needs. These will be the final market segments.

Market structure and market segmentation are the heart and soul of marketing (see Figure 5.19). Unless an organization spends time on this, driven from the board downwards, it is virtually impossible for it to be market-driven, and in any organization that isn't market-driven, the marketing function will be ineffective, or at best, will spend its time trying to promote and sell product or services that are inappropriate for the market. Figure 5.19 describes in more detail each of the important steps in the market segmentation process.

For the details behind each stage see McDonald and Dunbar (2005). Professional market segmentation is hard work and time-consuming. It is worth repeating why market segmentation is so important. Correct market definition is crucial for:

1. Share measurement
2. Growth measurement
3. The specification of target customers
4. The recognition of relevant competitors
5. The formulation of marketing objectives and strategies

And the objectives of market segmentation are:

1. To help determine marketing direction through the analysis and understanding of trends and buyer behaviour.
2. To help determine realistic and obtainable marketing and sales objectives.
3. To help improve decision-making by forcing managers to consider in depth the options ahead.

Without this analytical, in-depth, and critical procedure, market segmentation will remain a metaphor and will continue to be poorly used unless rigorous standards are observed and applied.

## References

Buzzell, R.D. and B.T. Gale (1987), *The PIMS Strategy: Linking Strategy to Performance*, New York: The Free Press.

Christensen, C., S. Cook and T. Hall (2005), 'Marketing malpractice: the cause and the cure', *Harvard Business Review*, December: 74–83.

McDonald, Malcom and Ian Dunbar (2005), *Market Segmentation: How to do it, How to Profit from it*, 2nd edition, Oxford: Butterworth-Heinemann.

Peters, T.J. and R.H. Waterman (1982), *In Search of Excellence*, New York: Warner Books.

Rogers, E.M. (1976), 'New product conception and diffusion', *Journal of Consumer Research*, 2 (March): 220–30.

# 6
# It's a Kinda Magic: Adventures in Alchemy

*Stephen Brown*

## I see a dark stranger

Many years ago, I conjured up a shopper typology. There's nothing unusual about that, I grant you. Classifications of consumers are commonplace in marketing research. It's more than half a century since Gregory Stone (1954) studied the behaviour of 124 female department store shoppers and divided them into four basic types – recreational shoppers, economic shoppers, ethical shoppers, apathetic shoppers – the titles of which are laudably self-explanatory.

In the fifty-something years since Stone's pioneering study, hundreds of shopper typologies have been proposed (Brown and Reid, 1997). Indeed, identifying distinctive consumer types has become something of a postmodern pastime among tabloid journalists, glossy magazine editors and geo-demographic information systems suppliers. Whether it be BMW-owning 'yuppies' or Burberry-bedecked 'chavs', or the free-spending 'dinkies' of legend, or today's designer brand-besotted 'tween-agers', the identification of distinctive consumer categories is meat and drink to today's marketing segmentologists (if there is such a category of professionals).[1]

My own contribution to this admittedly crowded field (Brown, 1998), was notable for two main reasons. First, it contained twelve separate categories, as opposed to the four or six that were standard way back when. I won't bore you with the gory details, but Shopper Type One was aggressive, demanding, impatient, impulsive; Shopper Type Two was slow, steady, deliberate, patient; Shopper Type Three was capricious, flighty, undecided, indecisive; Shopper Type Four was grumpy, fussy, pernickety, stingy. You get the general picture.

The second striking thing about my adventures in classification, was that the twelve-category typology generated a remarkable amount of feedback. As an academic, I'm all too familiar with the eerie silence that follows publication. Ordinarily, my books and articles and learned thoughts, such as they are, disappear into the undiscover'd marketing country, from whose bourn no traveller returns. They are the tumble-weed of thought, rolling across the academic desert, down the side-streets of scholarly Deadwood and, no doubt rightly, come to rest in the intellectual equivalent of Boot Hill.

But my shopper typology was different. Lots of marketing practitioners got in touch, saying that they recognized the shopper types I'd identified. Others wrote to me claiming that they, themselves, belonged to Type Seven or Type Eleven or whatever Type it was. 'That's me, that is!' was the overwhelming reaction. For the first, and sadly only, time in my academic career, I'd written something that unquestionably struck a chord.

There's a twist in the tale, though. My shopper classification wasn't based on a representative sample of consumers or a compendious questionnaire survey, the results of which were squeezed and scrunched and massaged and manipulated with the aid of massive mainframe computers and multivariate statistical methods. Nor was it the outcome of careful qualitative research, based on focus groups, depth interviews, faux-Freudian psychology and the usual projective technique palaver involving inkblots, collages, sentence completion tests or dressing up in romper suits (okay, I made the last one up, but hey).

It was, in fact, a spoof. Yes, a spoof. A spoof based on a book of star signs. I bought a second-hand book about astrology, extracted the supposed characteristics of Capricorns, Leos, Virgos, Sagittarians and so on and imagined how these types of people would react in a supermarket checkout line at peak times or an upmarket designer-label boutique where the sales assistants were indifferent, bordering on antagonistic.

However, the really weird thing about this egregiously spoof exercise is that it resonated ... it connected ... it worked! As I said, the twelve-category consumer classification I'd conjured up, got a reaction 'out there', a reaction that wasn't confined to academics or doctoral students or the unfortunate undergraduates who are forced to work their way through my compendious reading lists (which are heartrendingly heavy in the Brown, S. department)

So, what should we make of such hocus-pocus? Was it fortuitous? Was it a fluke? A bit of fun? An uncanny coincidence? A rogue study that says more about the reprehensible state of postmodern scholarship than the real world of consumer behaviour and marketing practice? A warning of the lunacy that ensues when the narrow path of rigorous marketing science – the supposed route to true knowledge – is abandoned for the multi-lane motorway of pseudo science and New Age nonsense?

Another possibility, of course, is that it's true. Perhaps shoppers *are* affected by the stars. Perhaps consumers have somehow convinced themselves that they're Arians or Pisceans or Scorpios and they act accordingly, be it in an upmarket retail store, a busy supermarket checkout, or anywhere else for that matter. Perhaps my descriptions of shopper types were sufficiently ambiguous to trigger the so-called Barnum Effect (that is, where readers of horoscopes find something to believe about themselves in vaguely-worded predictions for the days and months ahead). As Barnum was arguably the greatest marketer of all time, the latter possibility is certainly appropriate if not necessarily accurate (Brown 2001).

## Pick a card, any card

Regardless of what my act of academic necromancy actually meant, or means, it draws attention to the essentially magical character of marketing. Many commentators have noted marketing's inherent enchantments. Raymond Williams (1993), the great social commentator, termed advertising 'the magic system'. James Twitchell (1996), a professor of English who's written numerous best-selling books about marketing, repeatedly refers to the bewitching blandishments of luxury brands and designer labels. Rachel Bowlby, whose books include *Shopping with Freud* and *Carried Away*, often opines about the hypnotic, mesmeric, spellbinding character of cornucopian supermarket displays. Indeed, it is hard not to walk around, say, a Japanese department store without feeling that one's stumbled into a consumer wonderland, where the products scream 'buy me', 'touch me' or 'try me on for size'.

This is not just a bit of authorial hyperbole, by the way. I have personally interviewed thousands of consumers down the years and, on attending to the expressions my informants employ, it is clear that they interpret the marketscape in magical terms. Again and again, consumers refer to products and brands that possess a kind of otherworldly aura: beautiful Manolo Blahniks that glow numinously in the shop window; exquisite Hermès scarves that physically stop passers-by with a kind of ectoplasmic emanation; gorgeous Fendi handbags that come complete with a corona that dazzles awestruck onlookers and effortlessly outshines adjacent, less lustrous wares.

Further evidence of the sorcerous state of marketing affairs is available from creative artists.[2] In *The Savage Girl*, a novel by Alex Shakar, an employee of a cutting-edge market research agency considers the occult essence of branding. Brand name products, he claims, help consumers construct a wonderfully magical world above the mundane workaday world that they ordinarily occupy. It is a world of enchantment, allure and wish-fulfilment:

> Our world exists only to hold up this other world, this ideal world. It's the world of our dreams, our desires. It's elaborate, it's heavy, and we carry it around with us everywhere. But we don't mind. The more that's up here, the better. Because up here is where we keep all that's best in us. The more that's up here, the richer our imagination becomes ... Products are the material we use to build our world above the world.
>
> (Shakar, 2001: 51)

The world above the world – the world that marketers invoke and are largely responsible for – is a supremely magical world. It is a world of impossibly happy families, impossibly beautiful people, impossibly perfect holidays, impossibly empty roads, impossibly immaculate gardens, impossibly erogenous shampoos, impossibly healthful snacks, impossibly helpful insurers, impossibly open-handed banks, impossibly effective solutions to business problems. It is a world where polar bears quaff Coke, camels chat about cigarettes, green giants are inordinately happy, cars mutate into ice-skating Transformers, frogs squabble over beer ad voiceovers, aliens appear with monotonous regularity and pink, battery-operated bunnies keep on going and going and going. It is a world where price reductions are 'unbelievable', customer service is 'fantastic', sales promotions are 'superhuman', value for money is 'incredible', special offers are 'beyond belief', and the latest product is, inevitably, 'amazing'. It is a world where Walt Disney presides over a mouse-infested Magic Kingdom, where Marks & Spencer, the iconic British retailer, claims to sell Magic & Sparkle, and where consumers of Coco Pops, a sugary breakfast cereal, are urged in a shape-shifting television ad to 'Release the Magic'.[3]

Marketing, in short, is a supernatural sphere of activity where magic is an everyday occurrence. Magic is the rule rather than the exception in Marketopia, Marcadia, Marlysium, or whatever this world above the world is called (Brown and Maclaran, 1996).[4] Indeed, once one's eyes are opened to the inherent magic of marketing, its downright ubiquity becomes ever more apparent. A few examples must suffice:

- A recent TV ad for Tennents lager takes voodoo as its theme. A spurned Haitian virago sticks pins into cans of Tennents and the beer-swilling incumbents of a nearby tavern act as if they had been stabbed, attacked, shaken around and, when she finally hurls a can under a passing car, run over by the proverbial two-ton truck (complete with tyre tracks across the gob-smacked drinker's torso).

- As its name implies, The Witchery hotel in Edinburgh is an upmarket enchantment. The main restaurant is based upon a Tarot card theme and presided over by the Greek god Pan. The lunchtime brasserie is not only called The Secret Garden, after the enchanting children's story by Frances Hodgson Burnett, but it possesses a hidden passageway under the floorboards. The seven residential suites are decorated in a melange of motifs and anachronistic objects d'art that together convey an impression of incredible plenitude, richness, charm. It is marvellous – a place where marvels are found.

- Halloween has been turned into the foremost marketing occasion after Christmas. Once a fairly minor part of the holiday calendar, Halloween is now a multi-million pound marketing opportunity. American style trick-or-treating has transformed a dowdy UK institution – involving bonfires and bangers and a hollowed out turnip or two – into a magical marketing occasion, where sales of scary costumes, toys, party food, fireworks and so forth take off like the proverbial rocket. So popular has Halloween magic become that farmers are plagued by pumpkin rustlers during the run up to the super-spooky occasion.

## Smoke and mirrors

Brandacadabra, admittedly, isn't confined to TV ads or theme restaurants or fright-forward celebrations like Halloween, let alone multi-billion dollar brands like Harry Potter (Brown, 2005a). It is no less evident in the scholarly sphere. The 4Ps, for example, are analogous to the four familiar elements of hermetic legend (earth = place, air = promotion, fire = price, water = product). The contents of many academic articles, especially those in journals like *JMR* or *Marketing Science*, are closer to exercises in necromantic numerology than the mathematical precision of physics (and they're less insightful, if truth be told). The diagrams that pepper our textbooks, with their arrows and circles and pyramids and squiggles, would not be out of place in medieval grimoires (many Lisrel models are indistinguishable from cabbalistic sephiroth). The contents of strategic marketing plans or scenario planning prognostications or Delphi-derived forecasts of future developments/trends/possibilities are contemporary forms of augury (and no more oracular, frankly, than tea-leaf readings).

Consider also the gurus of marketing, or of management generally. Like shamans or witchdoctors or medicine men, they tour the consultancy circuit dispensing occult wisdom to supplicant organizations (Micklethwait and Wooldridge, 1996). Charismatic performers one and all, they claim to possess the seven secrets of success, which they are prepared to reveal provided the appropriate five-figure tribute is paid. These secrets not only sound suspiciously like magic spells or incantations – stick to the knitting, the customer comes first, big hairy audacious goals, there's riches in niches et al. – but they are guaranteed to work provided you truly, truly believe, wish upon a star or sacrifice a goat at midnight under a full moon.[5] Hell, today's retromancers are even capable of raising dead brands, reincarnating passé products and making money from mouldering sales promotions (Brown, 2001).

In this regard, consider Philip Kotler. The much-vaunted father of modern marketing, Kotler is widely regarded as the epitome of mainstream, middle-of-the-road scholarship. His textbooks are required reading for undergraduate students and, as every competing text is a clone of Kotler's original, even those who don't read the master are exposed to his ideas, approach, paradigm. Kotler came to the fore, what is more, when the 'marketing science' revolution was at its height; he unfailingly aligns himself with the rigorous objectives of marketing science; and if anyone deserves to be described as an establishment figure, that person is Philip Kotler.

Yet, when Kotler's works are subject to line-by-line scrutiny, it is clear that his rhetoric is replete with magical metaphors, allusions and conceits. As Brown (2005b, p. 125) observes:

Philip Kotler is equally partial to the paranormal ... He gives space to spectral, bump-in-the night behaviours, as well as 'scarifications', 'presences', 'uncontrollable forces', and 'chills down the spine' of executives. He reports sufficient 'visions', 'spirits', 'miracles', 'icons', 'images', 'signs and wonders', 'Days of Judgment', and 'pacts with the Devil' to put the sainthood to shame. He mentions magic, mysticism, mythology, soothsaying, foretelling, rebirthing, pyramidology, alchemy, time travel, good luck charms and maintains a 'seething cauldron' of magical elixirs, potions and panaceas. He refers to all sorts of otherworldly figures including trolls, leprechauns, giants, ghosts, ogres, aliens and missing links ... He also exhibits a conspiracy culture-immersed interest in brain washing, mind control, subliminal messages and secret societies, which is the twentieth century equivalent of the nineteenth century's fascination with the occult, the esoteric and the unknown.

Although he talks the scientific talk, Kotler walks the magical walk. Bearing in mind that he is as mainstream as marketing academicians get, it's hard to avoid the conclusion that magic is more deeply embedded in marketing than many self-styled 'scientists' imagine. Indeed, science itself is deeply magical. But that's another story (Burton and Grandy, 2004).

## Jiggery-pokery

According to *The Golden Bough*, Sir James Frazer's monumental nineteenth-century study, human societies are characterized by three fundamental worldviews – the scientific worldview, the religious worldview and the magical worldview (Frazer, 1996). These worldviews are sequential, furthermore, insofar as the magical perspective is found in the most underdeveloped regions, the religious is typical of partially developed societies and the scientific is confined to the most advanced nation-states in the west.

No one subscribes to such views today. Apart from their unacceptably chauvinistic imperialism, Frazer's typology ignores the obvious fact that worldviews coexist. The West may be predominantly scientific in outlook, but magical and religious perspectives are apparent in even the most scientific Western societies. If anything, indeed, the hegemony of Big Science is waning now that the unhappy consequences of untrammelled scientific research are becoming increasingly evident. The old ways, the abandoned ways, are back with a vengeance. The rise of both religious fundamentalism and New Age neo-paganism bears witness to this retro-socio-cultural trend (Brown, 1995).

The Frazer typology remains profoundly influential, however, akin to analogous Victorian timelines like Stone Age/Bronze Age/Iron Age and Ancient/Medieval/ Modern. Its influence is especially evident when alchemy is under consideration. Alchemy is ordinarily portrayed as a forerunner of modern chemistry. The medieval alchemists, with their retorts and carboys and tinctures of this, that and the other, were attempting what we now know is impossible: turning lead into gold and distilling the elixir of life. But they nonetheless managed to produce antinomy, oxygen, phosphorous, porcelain and sodium nitrate, as well as forge the laboratory skills that proved invaluable when 'proper' science came to the fore.

Although this narrative is regurgitated in almost every consideration of alchemy (Aveni, 1996; Drury, 2003; Katz, 2005; Martin, 2003), it is a gross misrepresentation of the alchemical ethos. Alchemy wasn't a low-rent antecedent of modern science. It was a worldview, a complete system, in and of itself. Long before it reached sluggardly Western societies, alchemy was practised in China, Egypt, Arabia and Ancient Rome. It obsessed some of the greatest minds of the Scientific Revolution, Newton, Boyle and Ashmole among them. Newton, in fact, devoted more of his time to alchemical experiments than he did to analyses of gravitation, planetary motion or the refraction of light. The cranky scientist's biographers typically treat his alchemical interests as an aberration, or pass over his obsession in silence. Newton didn't see it that way, though. He was an alchemist through and through (White, 1997).

Alchemy, then, shouldn't be regarded as ignorant or wrong-headed, a half-baked attempt to do what modern scientists do with accomplished ease. To the contrary, the alchemical ethic remains alive and well and nowhere is it more apparent than in the managerial sphere. Alchemy is a much better metaphor, I firmly believe, for what actually goes on at the marketing/scholarship/consultancy interface than 'science'. An entire book could be written on the subject, but for the purposes of the present chapter seven key parallels can be briefly identified. The fact than seven is a profoundly magical number is purely coincidental . . .

## Alchemical commerce

The first and most obvious alchemical parallel concerns the philosopher's stone, that special magical ingredient that turns base metal into gold. Every management consultant worth his or her salt – and salt is a key alchemical substance, alongside sulphur and quicksilver – claims to possess the philosopher's stone of management, the supernatural solution that'll turn organizational lead into stakeholder gold. None of them work, as the medieval alchemists themselves found out. But that didn't stop them trying, nor did it dissuade princes, pontiffs and people with more thalers than sense from funding alchemists' quixotic quests. Alchemy was essentially about transmutation, turning one thing into another, and transforming dysfunctional organizations or products or brands or indeed people is what today's alchemists purvey. As educators, similarly, we aim to transform immature undergraduate students – I hesitate to call them dull or leaden – into shiny happy marketing graduates, who are as good as gold and an asset to the organization they serve. That's the theory anyway.

The second alchemical element is equally obvious: *prima materia* or the elixir of life. As Ted Levitt (1991), the marketing alchemist-in-chief, once astutely observed, the purpose of business is to stay in business. Despite economists' assumptions to the contrary, most managers are not motivated by making profits as such – profits are a consequence not a cause of exemplary business activity – but by remaining in the game for as long as possible. Failure, lest we forget, is the norm in business life. Most companies collapse, most start-ups stop, most mergers misfire, most innovations implode, most R&D founders, most CEOs underperform, most advertising is ignored, most mailshots are binned, most pop ups are put down, most new products die young, most sales promotions are here today and gone tomorrow. In such circumstances, anything that promises to put off the fateful day is seized upon by grateful managers, even the less than luminous outpourings of learned journals, which says more about practitioners' desperation than academic acumen. We like to think that we possess the *prima materia* of marketing management, but all the evidence suggests otherwise.

A third, and crucially important, alchemical analogue is the widespread belief among medieval magi – practitioners of the so-called Divine Art – that *they themselves* had to be pure in spirit for transfiguration to take place successfully. If the painstaking process failed, they were personally to blame for not performing the rites properly, or for performing them at the wrong time, or for not being sufficiently pure in spirit to permit the magical change to take place as predicted. The exact same rationalizations are trotted out today when CRM or CSR or re-engineering or six-sigma or corporate storytelling techniques or wire-walking elephant metaphors or whatever it is the witchdoctors are pushing, fail to deliver on their expensive promises. 'You're not doing it properly!' 'Your organization is to blame, not the remedy!' 'You are insufficiently pure in spirit!' which in marketing/branding speak means customer orientation. The basic problem, marketing authorities tell client organizations, with a rueful shake of the head, is that you just don't understand, appreciate, worship, adore – yes, adore – your customers enough. Shame on you!

The fourth alchemical echo is inscribed in an aphorism that encapsulates the Great Work: 'like begets like'. The clustering of shoe retailers in shopping streets; the instant manufacture of me-too imitation products by cut-throat competitors; the regional clusters of complementary organizations in Silicon Valley, Hollywood, Detroit, northern Italy, Mumbai et al.; the bandwagon effect that infects the cultural industries, be it movies or music or computer games; marketers' insatiable appetite for brand extensions and extensions of brand extensions and extensions of extensions of brand extensions; car makers' partiality to model range proliferation, each of which offers innumerable indistinguishable options and specials – and all of which are driving consumers crazy trying to choose from the insane cornucopia of motoring possibilities – are just some among many examples of 'like begets like' in business. As already noted, even the textbooks that inform students of the supposed secrets of marketing success are seen-one-seen-'em-all imitations of Philip Kotler's original. They too exemplify 'like begets like'. Alchemy is everywhere!

A fifth correspondence is contained in yet another snappy alchemical slogan: 'as above, so below'. This aphorism refers to the fact that the macrocosm is in the microcosm and vice versa. As per William Blake's poetic ability 'To see the World in a grain of sand / And a Heaven in a wild flower', the part reflects the whole and the whole is inherent in the part. In fact, if ever an alchemical concept were relevant to marketing it is 'as above, so below'. Every individual manager or organization is expected to absorb and enact the marketing macrocosm – that is, the principles, precepts and basic *weltanschauung* enshrined in our textbooks, degree courses and how-to pronouncements. The part, in other words, is the whole in miniature. The macrocosm, conversely, unfailingly reflects the microcosm and nowhere more so than in the case studies, or best practice exemplars, or benchmarking recommendations, contained in every marketing textbook, degree programme and executive masterclass. It is no exaggeration to state that the alchemical dialectic – as above, so below – underpins much of the strategic and tactical marketing practices of managers, consultants and academics.

The sixth contemporary reverberation is found in the distinction medieval alchemists made between the practical and the philosophical sides of their art. Alchemy wasn't simply a practical proto-laboratory process involving steaming retorts, noisome alembics and bubbling bains-marie. It was a complete philosophical system of psychological self-transformation through a fixed sequence – symbolized by the colours negrido (black), albedo (white) and rubado (red) – with personal enlightenment being the ultimate goal.[6] This practitioner/theorist split is equally evident in twenty-first century marketing, where those who can do and those who can't sit on their well-padded professorial chairs in business schools, thinking great theoretical thoughts that bear no relation whatsoever to everyday marketing reality. In truth, this split is getting ever wider, as practitioners find less and less of relevance in academic journals and academics increasingly target their communication at other academics (Tapp, 2005). The much-vaunted scholarly premises of service dominant logic, I believe, are utterly valueless to those who have to move the merchandise, mind the store, match the forecast and make ends meet (Vargo and Lusch, 2004).

The seventh alchemical resemblance is charlatanry. In their day, alchemists were widely regarded as cheats, chancers, conmen and generally out to rob people blind with their fools' gold and false promises of eternal life. They were often called 'puffers', after the bellows that formed part of their laboratory equipment, but also for their exaggerated claims and hyperbolic statements. Many indeed *were* charlatans and they were often portrayed as such in works of popular culture. Ben Jonson's play, *The Alchemist* and Christopher Marlowe's *Dr Faustus* are perhaps the best-known examples, though countless lesser works tackled the same theme. The parallels with contemporary marketing almost go without saying. From marketers' exaggerated assertions and hyperbolic pronouncements (think ads for beauty products) via their portrayal in popular culture (think *Jerry Maguire* or the novels of Max Barry) to the commonplace perception that they are puffers one and all (as shock-horror exposés from *The Hidden Persuaders* to *No Logo* bear witness), it is clear that marketers occupy a similar position in society to the alchemists of yore. Learned academics, admittedly, stress that 'proper' marketing is customer-oriented, that 'genuine' marketers have customers' best interests at heart, that marketing is 'a good thing' by and large (apart from one or two bad apples). Wider society doesn't see us like that, however (Zuboff and Maxmin, 2003). Let's not pretend otherwise.

## Cross my palm with silver

In addition to the seven foregoing commonalities, several other obvious correspondences are evident. The language of alchemy, for instance, was notoriously convoluted and incomprehensible (the word 'gibberish' is a corruption of Jabir, an important Arabian adept of the eighth century CE). One only has to glance through our leading academic journals to see that contemporary marketing is no different (and as for the circumlocutions and euphemisms of 'management speak' generally, the less said the better). Alchemy, likewise, was driven by detail. Experimental procedures were spelled out very precisely and had to be followed exactly as indicated. The same is true of management, where success in business is often inseparable from taking care of tiny details, making sure things happen when they are supposed to happen, et cetera. Yet another instance is the famous alchemical axiom that was familiar to students of the Divine Art: 'Pray, walk, read, read and reread and you shall

find.' Every single marketing student should recognize this recommendation, though its deeper metaphorical meaning (that constant repetition
is the key to understanding) is equally true of many day-to-day marketing
activities, advertising campaigns among them.

There are, of course, many other forms of magic besides alchemy. Just
as marketing is fragmented into innumerable special interest groups –
Hackley (2007) describes 27 marketing sub-disciplines, everything from
Internal Marketing to International Marketing – so too 'magic' is an
umbrella term than shelters countless modes of supernatural practice.
These include witchcraft, Satanism, paganism, astrology, cabbala, Freemasonry, Rosicrucianism, hermeticism, shamanism, spiritualism, mes-
merism, palmistry, phrenology, theosophy, UFO-ology, homeopathy,
Wicca, wyrd, feng shui, geomancy, gematria, scrying, Tarot, Ouija, stage
magic and many more (Aveni, 1996; Drury, 2003; Katz, 2005).

Most cultural formations are fragmented, admittedly, be it music or
medicine or mathematics or metaphysics or microbiology or macroeco-
nomics or Marxism. But as this chapter has argued, there are striking
similarities between magic and marketing. One only has to consider
celebrity endorsement – the essentially magical idea that lustre is added
to products by mere association with charismatic individuals – to get an
idea of how deeply magical thinking is embedded in marketing practice.
One only has to consider the talismanic magic of luxury brands and how
wearing them helps ward off the evil eye of social disapproval, to get a feel
for the magic that inheres in marketing practice. One only has to remember that the original magi were actually wise men who retailed their amu-
lets, charms and nazaams in the ancient Greek marketplace, to recognize
that selling and sorcery, if not quite one and the same, are as near to each
other as makes no difference. One only has to consider the part played by
mystery in both domains – magicians with their mysterious spells and
hand-waving and alakazaams, marketers with their secret ingredients,
secret recipes and secrets of success – to see than nothing sells like the
numinous, the enigmatic, the intriguing.

In this regard, it is also worth noting the commonplace distinction
between white and black magic. This too is discernible in marketing's
domain, inasmuch as marketing can be used for both good and evil.
White marketing refers to socially responsible activities, as for example
when marketing is used better to inform consumer choice or promote
worthwhile causes such as fair trade, healthy eating, waste recycling,
anti-smoking, breast cancer awareness and so forth. Black marketing
involves the sale of unnecessary or unsafe or exploitative or wasteful
products, or the invention of non-existent ailments or anxieties or

concerns that marketers then relieve for a price: Restless Leg Syndrome, Female Sexual Dysfunction, Social Anxiety Disorder, Sports Utility Vehicles, Voice Activated Central Car Locking, sweatshop T-shirts, size-zero aspirations, Pet Rocks, alcopops ...

## Hey presto!

So what does it all mean? Ah, that would be telling! Suffice it to say that I believe marketers should make more of their impeccably magical credentials. Rather than trying to reinvent ourselves as accountants in marketing mufti (I'm thinking of the metrics movement here) or second-rate information technologists (consumer choice algorithms a-go-go), I believe marketers would be better off selling themselves as suppliers of magic dust, the special secret substance that we (and we alone) sprinkle on mundane brands and me-too products to make them take off and fly on the astral plane of consumer acceptance.

Marketers *can* turn lead into gold. We distil the elixir of modern life. It's time, brothers and sisters, to come out of the magic cabinet. Say it loud and say it proud, I am an alchemist!

## Notes

1. In Ireland, a celebrity economist called David McWilliams has made a television career out of the black art of consumer categorization. His typology includes Botox Betty, Billy Bunker, Patio Man and Miss Pencil Skirt, though 'celebrity economist' is perhaps the strangest category of all.
2. As I argue at length elsewhere, creative artists like novelists and movie makers can provide more meaningful insights into contemporary marketing than bog-standard questionnaire surveys.
3. When the box of Coco Pops is opened, swarms of shape-shifting creatures hurtle around the kitchen, leap over the sink, bounce upon serried ranks of saucepans and cross a countertop chasm with the aid of Marigold rubber gloves, before arranging themselves comfortably in a waiting cereal bowl. Phew!
4. The Garden Centre of Eden, perhaps?
5. This is less outlandish than it seems. Sony executives were recently treated to shock-horror treatment by tabloid newspapers for sacrificing live goats at the launch of the Playstation 3. I kid you not.
6. The same distinction, incidentally, is made in Freemasonry, where brethren distinguish between 'operative' and 'speculative' sides of the craft.

## References

Aveni, A. (1996), *Behind the Crystal Ball: Magic and Science from Antiquity to the New Age*, London: Newleaf.

Bowlby, R. (1993), *Shopping with Freud*, London: Routledge.

Bowlby, R. (2002), *Carried Away: the Invention of Modern Shopping*, New York: Columbia University Press.

Brown, S. (1995), *Postmodern Marketing*, London: Routledge.

Brown, S. (1998), 'Songs of the Humpback Shopper (and Other Bazaar Ballads)', available as free download from www.sfxbrown.com.

Brown, S. (2001), *Marketing: the Retro Revolution*, London: Sage.

Brown, S. (2005a), *Wizard! Harry Potter's Brand Magic*, London: Cyan.

Brown, S. (2005b), *Writing Marketing: Literary Lessons from Academic Authorities*, London: Sage.

Brown, S. and P. Maclaran (1996), 'The future is past: marketing, apocalypse and the retreat from utopia', in S. Brown et al. (eds), *Marketing Apocalypse*, London: Routledge, pp. 260–77.

Brown, S. and R. Reid (1997), 'Shoppers on the verge of a nervous breakdown', in S. Brown and D. Turley (eds), *Consumer Research: Postcards from the Edge*, London: Routledge, pp. 79–149.

Burton, D. and D. Grandy (2004), *Magic, Mystery, and Science: the Occult in Western Civilisation*, Bloomington: Indiana University Press.

Drury, N. (2003), *Magic and Witchcraft*, London: Thames & Hudson.

Frazer, James (1996), *The Golden Bough: a Study in Magic and Religion*, London: Penguin.

Hackley, C. (2007), *Marketing: Culture, Critique and Brand Management*, London: Sage.

Katz, D.S. (2005), *The Occult Tradition: from the Renaissance to the Present Day*, London: Jonathan Cape.

Levitt, T. (1991), *Thinking about Management*, New York: Free Press.

Martin, S. (2003), *Alchemy and Alchemists*, Harpenden: Pocket Essentials.

Micklethwait, J. and A. Wooldridge (1996), *The Witch Doctors: Making Sense of the Management Gurus*, New York: Times Business.

Shakar, A. (2001), *The Savage Girl*, London: Schribner.

Stone, G.P. (1954), 'City shoppers and urban identification: observations on the social psychology of urban life', *American Journal of Sociology*, 60 (1): 36–45.

Tapp, A. (2005), 'Why practitioners don't read our articles and what we should do about it', *Marketing Review*, 5 (1): 3–13.

Twitchell, J.B. (1996), *Adcult USA: the Triumph of Advertising in American Culture*, New York: Columbia University Press.

Vargo, S.L. and R.F. Lusch (2004), 'Evolving to a new dominant logic for marketing', *Journal of Marketing*, 68 (1): 1–17.

White, M. (1997), *Isaac Newton: the Last Sorcerer*, London: Fourth Estate.

Williams, R. (1993), 'Advertising: the magic system', in S. During (ed.), *The Cultural Studies Reader*, London: Routledge, pp. 320–36.

Zuboff, S. and J. Maxmin (2003), *The Support Economy: Why Corporations are Failing Individuals and the Next Episode of Capitalism*, London: Allen Lane.

# 7
# Viral Marketing

*Adam Lindgreen, Angela Dobele, Michael Beverland and Joëlle Vanhamme*

## Introduction

Marketers recognize the importance of encouraging customers and clients to pass along the company's marketing message to family, friends and colleagues. The referral from customers and clients to prospects carries an implied endorsement for the company (and its products and services) – and it's free. Traditional referrals have been verbal, passed from person to person in every-day conversations, but the advent of technology has meant a viral message can travel farther and faster than a traditional referral. We consider here how to achieve this objective through 'viral marketing'.

The phenomenon of viral marketing has both been identified as the stuff of marketing legend and confused with other marketing tools. This may be because definitions of viral marketing have tended not to be focused. As a result, it has been difficult to explain why and how viral marketing works. For example, viral marketing has been linked to standard adoption and diffusion models such as the adoption of Absolut vodka as a gay icon, providing the credibility to diffuse the product into the wider community. We argue that, rather than being a random ground-up phenomenon, largely perceived to be outside the control (or influence) of marketing practitioners, viral marketing is a tool that is within marketers' control and which they can actively use to encourage product adoption and word-of-mouth referral.

While the term viral marketing is most often associated with online referral behaviour (through the internet or communication-based technology), we use the term to explain the exponential spread of a message (a recommendation to use or avoid a product, service, brand, company, or even an idea) from the few to the many in a short space of time.

Viral marketing may involve consumers who know each other (for example, the 'Refer-a-friend' programme of Half.com) and those who do not (for example, Epinions.com and ConsumerReports.org, which both provide a forum for consumers to post objective product reviews for the benefit of others).

This chapter is structured as follows. First, the metaphor of marketing messages as a virus is introduced. Second, a series of vignettes illustrate and exemplify various aspects of viral marketing, as well as bringing in-depth meaning to the metaphor. Third, managerial recommendations are drawn. The chapter finishes with a discussion of viral marketing as a metaphor for managerial usage.

## The metaphor

When customers pass on a company's marketing message to their family, friends and colleagues, and these customers' family, friends and colleagues do the same, a gigantic network evolves rapidly in much the same way as a virus spreads (Dobele et al., 2005, 2007; Lindgreen and Vanhamme, 2005). The network is the total sum of all person-to-person communication about a particular product, service or company at a given time (Rosen, 2001).

Historically, one of the oldest examples of what could be described as a viral marketing campaign are the Gospels and the Christian missionaries preaching the life and teachings of Jesus Christ. Seth Godin's book *Unleashing the Ideavirus*, itself about viral marketing, was originally made available free of charge on http://ideavirus.com, with readers being able to send a full electronic version of the book to their friends. Since then, other famous viral marketing campaigns have been successfully launched, including Anheuser-Busch's Budweiser 'Wassup', Lee's Buddy Lee mascot, Kinetix's free Dancing Baby, Baby Cha Cha launched through the Fox Television show Ally McBeal, Blue Mountain Arts' greeting card service, and Virgin Mobile's Red Academy campaign.

Viral marketing can be used for both promoting and distributing products. For example, the low-budget New Zealand film *Whale Rider* used viral marketing to its full advantage, opening at a few select cinemas and gaining a wider audience via positive word-of-mouth. Viral marketing, of course, fundamentally changes the game, reducing the potential payback window to a few hours and dramatically raising the risk associated with marketing expenditure to ensure widespread product trial or adoption.

Marketers often have only a few days to 'entice audiences before the word, good or bad, leaks out' (Huck, 2003). For example, consumer segments such as Generation X and Generation Y are increasingly becoming media-jaded. A key part of any viral marketing message's success, of course, is the message. For example, Scope mouthwash designed a customized animated kiss that was electronically mailed to its current customers to tie in with the promotional slogan that 'Scope brings people kissably close'. Consumers could forward the e-kiss to family and friends. Other examples include De Beers' website for designing one's own diamond finger rings or Procter & Gamble's Physique shampoo.

Viral marketing strategies can be classified according to the degree of customer activity involved in forwarding the viral marketing message as low or high involvement strategies. Low involvement strategies include 'Send this story to a friend' icons and can be used for web-hosted address books, calendars, list servers, news group readers, and greetings card services. High involvement strategies require the active participation of the customer in reaching new users who may have to download special programs and somehow become involved in the forwarding process. The distinction between intentional viral message dissemination (for example, PayPal or the 'Recommend it' that is known from numerous websites) and unintentional viral message dissemination (for example, Hotmail.com) echoes the low and high integration strategy classification.

High involvement strategies, therefore, require an engaging message if the recipient is to become involved. But what makes a message engaging? First, we have found that consumers voluntarily spread marketing messages if these capture their imagination; are attached to a product that is easy to use or highly visible; are well targeted; are associated with a credible source; and combine technologies.

In addition, it is known that the phenomenon of sharing one's emotions socially with family, friends, and colleagues accounts for a considerable part (about 30 per cent) of the explained variance of referral behaviour. Thus, one key to a successful viral marketing message is to build an emotional connection between a company and its customers. The 'Are You Type 1?' marketing campaign developed for the Levi's brand used creation of curiosity to pique consumers' interest: consumers were asked 'Are You Type 1?' and then encouraged to ask themselves if they could be the person Levi's were looking for. In particular, we have identified the fact that various emotions are at companies' disposal, including the six primary emotions of anger, disgust, fear, joy, sadness and surprise (Table 7.1).

| Emotion | Explanation | Behaviour | Physiological response | Other |
|---------|-------------|-----------|------------------------|-------|
| Surprise | Generated when something (product, service, or attribute) is unexpected or confounds expectation. | • Facial expressions like opened eyes and mouth, and raised eyebrows.<br>• Cessation of ongoing activities.<br>• Sudden and involuntary focusing on the surprising product, service, or attribute.<br>• Heightened consciousness of the surprising product, service, or attribute.<br>• Subsequent curiosity/exploratory behaviour.<br>• Increase in the ability to retain in memory the surprising product, service, or attribute. | • Changes in heart and respiration rates.<br>• Increase in skin conductivity and neural activity.<br>• Different cortical response wave patterns. | • Subjective feeling of surprise.<br>• Spontaneous vocalizations ('Why,' 'Oh,' etc.) |
| Joy | Expressed when a goal has been achieved, or when movement toward such an achievement has occurred. Also, joy is caused by a rational prospect of owning what we love or desire. | • Facial expression of joy is the smile.<br>• Happy people are more helpful and cooperative.<br>• Happy people are more helpful and cooperative.<br>• Often energetic, active, and bouncy.<br>• Prompts the person to aim for higher goals. | • Wanting, hoping, or desiring to have an object when it is not present.<br>• Loving or liking the object when it is already present. | • Smile is used when people are unhappy to mask another emotion. |
| Sadness | Experienced when not in a state of well-being, which is most often derived from the experience of a fearful event. | • No longer wishes for action, but remains motionless and passive, or may occasionally rock to and fro. | • Crying or whimpering. | • Attention can decrease, but when completely focused on the situation at hand it can increase. |

*(Continued)*

*Table 7.1* (Continued)

| Emotion | Explanation | Behaviour | Physiological response | Other |
|---|---|---|---|---|
| | | • Often, focus is turned more toward the self. • Trying to solve the problem in hand. • Seeking refuge from the situation. | | |
| Anger | Response to personal offence (an injustice); this injustice is in that person's power to settle. | • Attacking the cause of the anger through physical contact and verbal abuse. • Anger is extremely out of control (e.g. rage) and freezing of the body can occur. | • Raised blood pressure ('blood boils'). • Face reddening. • Muscle tensioning. | • Culturally dependent. Northern European people show more muscular reactions, southerners show a bigger increase in blood pressure. |
| Fear | Experienced when people expect (anticipate) a specific pain, threat, or danger. | • A system is activated, bringing the body into a 'state of readiness'. • Escape and avoidance. • Facial expression, e.g., 'oblique eyebrows' and resulting 'vertical frown'. | • Internal discomfort (butterflies in the stomach). • Muscle tensioning. • Increasing perspiration and heart rate. • Mouth drying out. | • In the extreme form, making laughing or giggling sounds. |
| Disgust | Feeling of aversion that can be felt either when something happens or when something is perceived to be disgusting. | • Facial expressions like frowning. • Hand gestures, opening of the mouth, spitting, and, in extreme cases, vomiting. • Distancing from the situation, this by an expulsion or removal of an offended stimulus, removal of the self from the situation, or lessening the attention on the subject. | • Decreased heart rate. • Nausea. | • Making sounds like 'ach' and 'ugh'. |

In the following, a series of vignettes illustrate and exemplify the above mentioned aspects of viral marketing, thereby bringing in-depth meaning to the viral marketing metaphor.

## Vignettes

### Vignette one

SMS technology has narrowed the window of time that marketers have to ensure that as many people as possible see their movie during its opening weekend before negative word-of-mouth can spread. Some consumers reportedly text their friends halfway through a movie to tell them whether or not the movie is any good. The word is then transmitted quickly around a wide network of peers and extended to a wider audience via online chat groups. The result is that movies often have dramatic drop-offs between the opening session and the rest of the weekend despite saturation-level marketing. For example, *The Hulk* took in $US62 million in its opening weekend, plummeting by 70 per cent by the end of the week. Moviegoers simply texted their friends during the first showings that the movie was bad and that they should not bother. In contrast, probably one of the most famous viral marketing campaigns is that of *The Blair Witch Project*. The movie's release budget was just $US2.5 million, but it grossed $US245 million in worldwide box office sales. Before the movie was released, Artisan Entertainment, the maker of the movie, created much interest in the movie by giving it the 'air' of a documentary and supporting it with an internet site. People then talked about *The Blair Witch Project* and referred their friends to the site.

### Vignette two

It was a big ad, a very big ad; the juggernaut that was Carlton Draught's Big Ad. The ad was impressive, featuring a large cast of actors (multiplied into thousands by computer graphics) in addition to a 100-voice choir accompanied by the Melbourne Symphony Orchestra in an over-the-top rendition of *Carmina Burana*. The ad was filmed in a remote New Zealand location (think *Lord of the Rings* – rugged mountains and sweeping vistas) with aerial and land photography. In the face of serious ad epics (think British Airways ads circa 1980s) came the epic spoof.

The ad was emailed to Foster's Group employees on Thursday 21 July 2005, two weeks before it was launched nationwide on television. Within 24 hours, the ad had been played by 162,000 people and, by 3 August, this figure had risen to over 1 million people (Table 7.2).

*Table 7.2*  Online viewing of the Big Ad

| Date | Number of views |
| --- | --- |
| 21 July 2005 | Launch to employees |
| 22 July 2005 | 162,000 |
| 3 August 2005 | 1,030,981 |
| 8 September 2005 | 2,001,999 |
| 8 October 2005 | 2,372,853 |
| 8 November 2005 | 2,715,466 |
| 15 December 2005 | 3,005,332 |
| 23 February 2006 | 3,297,065 |

*Source*: Information provided by Felicity Watson at Foster's Group, 24 February 2006.

The ad has been viewed in over 132 countries, from Bangladesh and Jamaica to Germany and the United States of America, and considerable word-of-mouth has been generated through blog (online web logs) discussions. The viral component of this advertising campaign proved so successful that the media budget for television was reduced.

The primary aim of the Big Ad campaign was maximum reach and frequency, and it certainly achieved this aim – 3 million hits are a lot of reach! But as the ad sings, 'it better sell some bloody beer' and it appears that the Big Ad really did so. ACNielsen's Liquor Index suggests that Carlton Draught had the largest growth of any beer brand within Australia for volume and value, thereby giving rival beer brands Vittoria Bitter and Lion Nathan's Toohey's New Real competition, perhaps for the first time. Overall, Carlton Draught packaged beer and draught grew at 13.7 per cent (by value) in the twelve months to January 2008[1] – incredible considering an overall national downturn in beer consumption.

### Vignette three

One may wonder whether by nature there is something innovative in the alcohol market, as our next example is also alcohol: 42 Below, a New Zealand-based vodka (manufactured 42 degrees below the Equator). The company was started by Geoff Ross, of Saatchi & Saatchi and DDB fame. Perhaps all those ideas that were deemed too wacky by his clients finally found a new home? The company's first ad, a tongue-in-cheek explanation of New Zealand and the product, broke seven out of nine New Zealand broadcasting standards and was, temporarily, removed from the website. Not to worry though, for keen viewers had already posted it to YouTube and Ross waited the minimum time before re-posting the ad to the company's website. Thanks to the press coverage of the ad's ban the site was visited by more people than ever.

And he kept the same theme (insulting, swearing, and controversial) for the viral ads which followed and seamlessly managed to insult just about every religion, nationality, and sexuality; practically guaranteeing media coverage and hits. For example, one slogan is '42 Below, drink it straight, or gay'. Further attention was gained through the launch of the 42 Below Cocktail World Cup (possibly to become a paid-network television show and annual event), which manages to combine advertising for the product (42 Below in a range of flavours) and New Zealand (competitors bungee-jumped, white-water rafted, used local produce in their cocktail creations and worked in local pubs in the lead up to the grand final) and the 'Vodka Professor' (Vodka University's Dean of Cocktail Marketing) Dr Jacob Briars who provided helpful hints on all things cocktail (www.vodkauniversity.com).

The overwhelming success of the campaigns has resulted in a much smaller ad budget than the return on investment the ads are realizing, and goes a long way to account for the massive growth in sales of vodka (500 cases in December 2002 to 3500 cases in December 2005). No wonder Bacardi placed a US$91 million dollar price tag on the company in their purchase negotiations. Such successful marketing also provides a great platform for market expansion into South East Asia and for product expansions into gin and bottled water.

### Vignette four

We've saved the best exemplar for last, possibly the most successful viral marketing campaign ever. In terms of buzz creation and hits, Burger King's 'Subservient Chicken' leads the pack. The associated website featured an actor in a chicken suit who would do whatever visitors requested (www.subservientchicken.com) including, for example, clapping, jumping, dancing, and watching television. Suggestions for becoming a vegetarian are met with thumbs down from the chicken.

The site was seeded into several internet chat rooms. Within 23 hours, the site had a million hits; by the end of the first week, hits had jumped to 20 million. In total, the site boasts over 396 million hits and over 14 million unique visitors since April 2004.

The primary target market was 18 to 45-year-old men who spend a lot of time on the internet, playing DVDs and videogames and not watching commercial television as much as they used to. Burger King's campaign goal was for an ad that would 'shock and awe', and in terms of exposure lots of people spent an average of seven minutes on the site.

The website quality is amazingly simple. It's an actor in a chicken suit (definitely not a designer original!) and staged in an every-day lounge. The launch date was timed to coincide with Burger King's launch of a new product (Tender Crisp Chicken Sandwich) and the tagline 'Have it your way'. The website carried a slight variation 'Get chicken just the way you like it', but the link between the company and the subservient chicken is practically non-existent. It took viewers some digging to realize Burger King was behind the website, and they loved that obscurity, as well as the interaction afforded by the site. The subtlety of the marketing message was a hit with cynical viewers perhaps tired of traditional hard-sell marketing messages. And yet, despite the massive number of hits, and the incredible publicity surrounding this particular chicken, *Advertising Age* trashed the campaign for its failure to push the product.

Usually, the success of a viral campaign is judged on two criteria. First, did the message get across? Second, did the message get across to many of the people within the target market? Getting it out to many people is definitely a bonus. However, it is better that your target market is the one who gets the most coverage. Burger King's 'Subservient Chicken' certainly achieved these goals.

## Managerial recommendations

The introduction of electronic media outlets has dramatically facilitated interconnections between companies and their customers. By creating an instantaneous buzz in the promotion and distribution of companies' brands and offerings, viral marketing can hugely lower the cost of promotion, as well as boost the speed of adoption, a critical concern for new product launches. However, viral marketing faces the same clutter-and-noise problems that afflict traditional advertising.

### Fundamentals of viral marketing

In the following we draw out a number of managerial recommendations, grouping these around five fundamentals of viral marketing. The role of emotions is pivotal in viral marketing and will be considered in the following section.

*The target group.*   It is imperative that companies choose carefully which customers should first pass on a viral marketing message, as the creation of the network depends on these customers and the implied credibility they possess. Frankly, you may not want some of your customers talking about you! Motorola increased the success of its viral marketing campaign by using its database containing the email addresses of people who had previously shown an interest in Motorola telephones by registering on the company's website and therefore comprised the perfect target group. Hotmail attached a clickable URL to every outbound message sent by a user: 'GET YOUR PRIVATE, FREE EMAIL AT HTTP:\\WWW.HOTMAIL.COM', which spread to a staggering 11 million users in only 18 months.

*The message.* For viral marketing to work there must be something uniquely powerful about the message, something that encourages would-be advocates to pass on the message. For example, in the case of Viagra the message captures the imagination and highlights a completely new product that lends itself to referrals.

*Capturing the imagination.* The challenge for marketers is to entice consumers with something that provokes their curiosity and encourages them to seek and share information. Steven Spielberg's science fiction movie A.I., for example, did this by including a credit to Jeanine Salla, sentient machine therapist, on the movie's promotional poster. What does a sentient machine therapist do? Curious fans typed Jeanine Salla into Google and the game began, resulting in the creation of a bond between themselves and the movie – even before the movie was released.

*Visible, easy-to-use products.* Brands, products, or services most susceptible to viral marketing are unique (for example, collapsible scooters), highly visible (for example, Gucci baguette bags), naturally susceptible to word-of-mouth discussion (for example, Viagra), early entry (for example, Apple iPod), or simple in the underlying idea (for example, YouTube).

*Credible sources.* The greatest strength of a referral is that it is believable. Each referral carries an implied endorsement from sender to receiver. Thus, marketers can identify opinion leaders in a target segment and provide them with incentives to continue their referring behaviour through their networks and contacts. As long as referrers and referees do not feel used (or bought!) the message is regarded favourably, given the credibility of the source. When launching its T68i mobile telephone with camera, Sony Ericsson used 120 actors who would identify people from desired target segments, approach them, and ask them to take their pictures, with the objective of the campaign being to get the mobile into the hands of potential customers, having them experience its ease of use, and encouraging them to ask questions about it. A clever strategy – but do we need to incorporate a warning? The more companies that 'use' people the more the reputation of the tool is diminished. Further, people don't want to feel as though they were fooled.

*Leveraging combinations of technology.* Many companies combine various technologies to ensure their marketing message spreads to the greatest number of consumers possible. For example, SMS text messaging requires no additional software and is particularly effective in targeting teens who create 'thumb cultures'. Pepsi developed a campaign in which patrons at the Soul Beach Music Festival in Miami had their photographs taken and were then given a DigiCard containing a range of multimedia. The DigiCard was a reminder of the photograph taken, and a vehicle that led participants to the Pepsi site to collect their photographs. As well, the festival sponsorship enabled Pepsi to link its brand directly to an exciting event and the personal experiences of participants who would email their photographs (and the Pepsi brand) to family and friends.

## Emotions

Marketers must achieve fit between emotion(s) and their brand or viral marketing campaign. Some emotions are fleeting and may therefore not serve initiatives involving complex or subtle issues. Surprise is the dominant emotion identified by consumers across a wide range of viral marketing campaigns; surprise is also expressed in combination with at least one of the five other emotions that are covered in the following points.

*Anger* is best suited to single crusades that seek an immediate reaction to injustice, including threats against wilderness preservation, threats from governments, and perceived injustices perpetrated by corporations; or it may be used by companies wishing to mobilize support for their cause (mom-and-pop stores versus Wal-Mart).

*Disgust* is best suited when targeted, intermittently, toward young males, rebel-style brands (for example, Australia's maverick Channel Seven), or cultures that generally find disgusting events humorous (for example, Japan); importantly, disgust-based campaigns must walk a fine line of acceptability and provide a humorous and surprising message at just the right time rather than just being, well, disgusting.

*Fear* is best suited to campaigns combined with either a solution (for example, risky sexual practices and usage of condoms), a punishment (for example, speeding and fines), or links to further information.

*Joy*   is best suited to irreverent or fun brands (for example, Chick-Fil-A); to efforts that seek to encourage interest in a mature category (for example, the Australian Meat Board's Eat Lamb initiative) or to revitalize a brand (for example, Honda); or to target younger consumers (for example, Raging Cow flavoured milk by 7Up/Dr Pepper).

*Sadness*   is best suited to social marketers who seek an immediate response to disasters, particularly acts of God (for example, the Iranian earthquake in 2003); importantly, campaigns should encourage benevolence rather than guilt.

## Summary and final notes

As a metaphor for managerial usage, viral marketing is almost tailor-made. It is also often low cost, although the costs are increasing (for example, we have to develop the message, which could cost a small fortune in terms of graphics and so on). Also, viral marketing is endorsed by the sender – family or a friend or colleague (although it should be noted that not all messages are between friends and family or colleagues, but could be posted on a blog where people do not know each other), meaning that the credibility of the viral message is very high.

Viral marketing has demonstrated its ability to reach a high number of consumers in a short time. It is possible to identify some guidelines for launching a viral marketing campaign, as depicted in Figure 7.1 where for the sake of simplicity the emphasis is on the use of surprise. Obviously, the use of other emotions and the fundamentals of viral marketing (that is, the target group, the message, capturing the imagination, visible, easy-to-use products, credible sources, and leveraging combinations of technology) have to be considered as well.

Companies should understand the target audience (both the customers it wants to forward the message and the group of people it's trying to attract through that message) and consider whether a message fits this audience, as well as the company and the marketing strategy. The company could use contests and promotions; test the intended viral marketing campaign before implementing it fully; integrate the campaign into the company's overall marketing strategy; provide customers with information that enables them to understand the company's value proposition; build in exit barriers so that they stay with the company; and measure the rates of customer advocacy. Companies should avoid spamming and the need to come up with too many incentives in the long run. Some rewards for referral behaviour are acceptable although we do not

114

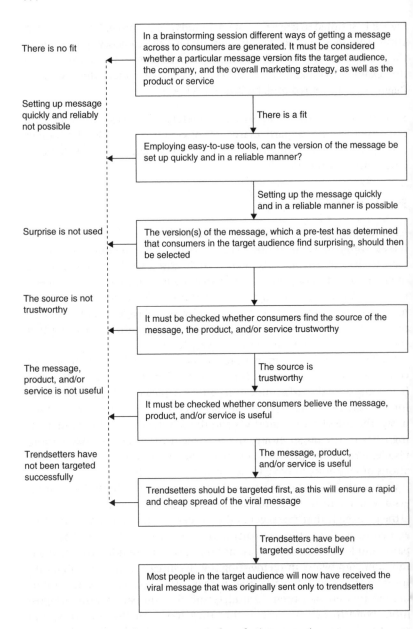

*Figure 7.1* Steps in order to create a viral marketing campaign
*Source*: Lindgreen and Vanhamme (2005: 132).

want to train our recipients to expect them all the time. A reward can be intangible in that it is a recognition with words very favourable for those motivated by, for example, kudos (for example, opinion leaders) and internal rewards (for example, helpful friends). Viral marketers often benefit if they first target trendsetters within their target audience. Such trendsetters are said to account for 8 per cent of internet users, and they each influence about eight other people. Also, the tools that a campaign can employ, including email, chat rooms, bulletin boards, gifts, wish-list registers, or web pages, must be quick, reliable, and easy to use. This means that companies should avoid graphics that take a long time to download ('speed' issue) or forms that take a long time to fill out ('easy to use' issue), as well as programs that are prone to bugs ('reliability' issue). Products or services have to be accepted by the initial consumer and their friends, family and colleagues before being of value (for example, ICQ, which allows people to communicate with each other through the internet only if they use this particular computer program).

We found that people generally engage in viral marketing when they receive freebies (for example, software programs, services); they are given (monetary) incentives including discounts, coupons, tickets and contests; they are concerned about an issue such as the environment or debt relief to poor countries; and they need to create network externalities. Others again are motivated almost entirely by either the need for respect or kudos, or the desire to help others.

We also discovered that a viral marketing campaign's success depends on whether or not the message is funny, humorous, amusing, or cool; quirky, intriguing, or even irritating and controversial – or, in extreme cases, violent or pornographic; or offers important or second-to-none advice that is both specific and relevant to the person.

Products should be services built around the viral message, not the other way around. Obviously, some elements are more suitable for a business-to-consumer setting, while other elements work well in a business-to-business environment. Some industries, including entertainment, music, software, and the internet are especially suited to viral marketing campaigns. This is interesting because e-commerce has been most successful for books, music/CDs, electronics, holidays/travels, and PC hardware and software. Lastly, the use of emotions is important in constructing a campaign that works. Some companies are successful, whilst others fare badly and charge a fee for their products or service. Fees should only be charged if people can identify the benefits offered or a large user base has been established. Also, the fee must be for add-ons to the product or service, not for the basic one.

Studies suggest that viral marketing is effective as a means of drawing high response rates. It is responsible for almost 60 per cent of customer visits to websites. Up to 15 per cent of shoppers who receive a viral message follow the links, with the highest rate in business-to-business markets. The effectiveness of viral marketing is reflected in the value of companies that build their success on viral marketing. For example, ICQ was sold to AOL.com for $287 million in 1998; Microsoft acquired Hotmail.com for $400 million; and Yahoo bought GeoCities! for $4 billion in stock.

Despite the success of companies like ICQ, AOL.com, Hotmail.com and GeoCities!, a few words of caution are in place. First, if consumers believe their right to vet market information is being subverted, the backlash may hurt the company, brand, product, or service.

Second, consumers may also feel they are being exploited by viral marketing campaigns. For example, were the 'fan-generated comments and websites' in *The Blair Witch Project* really from fans or from the movie company? Doubts can have serious implications for marketers attempting to ride the viral wave. When designing a viral marketing campaign, marketers must consider its execution. Are consumers likely to feel cheated or used? And if the worst happens, how will the company deal with negative word-of-mouth before it spreads farther than the original positive message?

Third, the overall ethics of a viral marketing campaign must be considered. Paying actors to extol the virtues of your product or service could be a good idea, but not identifying them as paid employees of a company can have far reaching consequences if you are discovered. For example, in the Sony Ericsson campaign the actors did not identify themselves as paid representatives of the company, thereby prompting consumer group criticism.

## Note

1.   Source AC Nielsen Scan Track 31/01/08 MAT.

## References

Dobele, A., A. Lindgreen, M. Beverland, J. Vanhamme and R. van Wijk (2007), 'Why pass on viral messages? Because they connect emotionally', *Business Horizons*, 50(4): 291–304.

Dobele, A., D. Toleman and M. Beverland (2005), 'Controlled infection! Spreading the brand message through viral marketing', *Business Horizons*, 48(2): 143–9.

Godin, S. (2001), *Unleashing the Ideavirus*, New York: Hyperion.

Huck, P. (2003), 'SMS critique: all publicity isn't necessarily good publicity', *Australian Financial Review Magazine*, 15 (November): 2–3.
Lindgreen, A. and J. Vanhamme (2005), 'Viral marketing: the use of surprise', in I.C. Clarke and T.B. Flaherty (eds), *Advances in Electronic Marketing*, Hershey, PA: Idea Group, pp. 122–38.
Rosen, E. (2001), *The Anatomy of Buzz: Creating Word-of-Mouth Marketing*, London: Harper Collins.

# 8

# Viral Marketing: How to Spread the Word via Mobile Device

*Shintaro Okazaki*

## Introduction

Broadly defined, viral marketing is the process of encouraging honest communication between pre-existing consumer social networks (Phelps et al., 2004). More specifically, it seeks to increase brand awareness exponentially, through processes similar to the spread of a viral epidemic. Thus, the concept of viral marketing fits into the metaphor construct because it highlights information transmission as if it were an infection in living organisms. In a way, this term helps us to comprehend human relationships as a physical bond that can be connected, and therefore also contaminated, by a 'buzz'. Buzz is another metaphor, and describes 'contagious' commentary, about products, services, brands, and ideas, that catches the attention of 'noisy' enthusiasts who spread the word via electronic or face-to-face conversation in social networks. Thus, the buzz helps firms to give people reasons to talk (often in entertaining and/or informative ways) about their products and services, and makes it easier for that conversation to take place. In a sense, this is the major benefit of using this metaphoric term.

The earliest known use of the term 'viral marketing' appeared in *PC User* magazine in 1989 (Carrigan, 1989). In an article about the adoption of Macintosh SEs versus Compaqs, the copycat effect was described:

> At Ernst & Whinney, when Macgregor initially put Macintosh SEs up against a set of Compaqs, the staff almost unanimously voted with their feet as long waiting lists developed for use of the Macintoshes. The Compaqs were all but idle. John Bownes of City Bank confirmed this. 'It's viral marketing. You get one or two in and they spread throughout the company'.

Initially, therefore, the term referred to the phenomenon of catching an idea and imitating it after seeing somebody else adopting it. Ten years later, venture capitalists Steve Jurvetson and Tim Draper became known as the evangelists of the term, when, in 1997, they described Hotmail's email practice (Kirby, 2006). This is probably one of the most cited episodes of viral marketing: Hotmail was appending advertising for themselves to outgoing mail from their users. As the internet rapidly penetrated worldwide (which also gave birth to the term 'electronic word-of-mouth'), consumers began to share their experience through computer-mediated communications, such as email lists, website bulletin boards, Usenet newsgroups, chat, and blogs, among others.

In 1999, *The Blair Witch Project*, a low-budget film, used one of the first viral marketing campaigns to combine entertainment and advertising. The film cost only US$15,000, but the film's website was full of mystery, and attracted 75 million visitors in the first week of the film's release. A tremendous wave of viral chain reactions occurred all over the world.

With the global expansion of such sites as YouTube and MySpace, viral marketing entered a new era. The greater usability of electronic information systems has drastically improved the user interface in consumer 'word-of-mouse'. In Burger King's 'Subservient Chicken' in 2004, a chicken dressed in garters could apparently carry out any command viewers requested. After being seeded into several internet chat rooms, it received 20 million hits in a week. To date, more than 290 million visitors have ordered actions by the chicken through a webcam window.

*I Love Bees* in 2004 was the first promotional ARG (alternate reality game) to create contagious buzz. An ARG is an interactive game that deliberately blurs the line between in-game and out-of-game experiences, often using multiple media, such as websites, blogs, emails, Mp3, real-world puzzles, telephone messages, and cryptic clues to create a fake reality. *I Love Bees* was launched to create an immersive back-story for Microsoft's science fiction videogame *Halo 2*. Enthusiastic fans entered a website and discovered mysterious 'clues', which led to the GPS coordinates of public telephone boxes across the USA. If the participants visited the telephone boxes, they would receive a message and become drawn into an alternate reality, in which they would become players in the creation and distribution of a mysterious plot related to the forthcoming game. Through word-of-mouth, *I Love Bees* attracted over a million visitors before the release of *Halo 2*. The latest viral campaign for *Halo 3*, called Iris, is similar and began in late 2007. In New York City and London, flyers bearing the apparent logo of the campaign are distributed, with the message 'We are not alone' (Marsden, 2006).

## Viral marketing goes wireless

These examples illustrate how viral marketing or 'word-of-mouse' exponentially increased awareness of the promoted object, and also created an enormous online social network. According to an annual study by Ipsos Insight, social networking is quickly becoming the dominant online behaviour globally, with South Korea the world leader, followed by Brazil, China, Mexico and the USA. In addition, the recent growth in use of the mobile device has changed the way in which the social network is expanded. Juniper Research (2007) reports that the number of active users of mobile social networking sites is expected to rise from 14 million in 2007 to nearly 600 million in 2012. Mobile dating and chatroom services currently account for 57 per cent of user-generated revenues, but this proportion will fall to 21 per cent by 2012, as other services increase in popularity. In addition, the volume of downloads from mobile personal content delivery sites, such as SeeMeTV, is expected to increase from less than 200 million in 2007 to more than 9 billion in 2012.

The short message service (SMS) is used frequently as a practical dissemination channel that enables firms to transmit promotional messages directly to their target customers. For example, on the launch of the new S40 model, Volvo used a cross-media campaign in which a message was inserted in print media, inviting consumers to send a text message 'MYSTERY'. In return, the sender received a reply with a link enabling them to download the appropriate video tool to play the teaser trailer directly on their phone. In promoting the movie *Charlie's Angels: Full Throttle*, Sony Pictures offered SMS quizzes and MMS images through a specially designed website, built around a revenue-sharing business model. In McDonald's 'House of Blues' promotion, unique 'Mac' codes were printed on 50 million BigMac boxes in the USA. Consumers typed in the short-code 'RUMAC' to win sweepstakes. Although the exact numbers were not reported, it appears reasonable to assume that these campaigns' success depended largely on the interest and excitement that consumers perceived, and then passed on to their friends and peers. This tendency is probably particularly evident among the young, because the mobile device now plays a predominant role in the life of teenagers.

In 2005–06, according to Childwise's monitor report in the UK, almost 67 per cent of children aged 5–16 had their own mobile phone, as did 90 per cent of those aged 11–16. Up to 95 per cent of teens aged 15–16 also had a mobile phone. In Japan, mobile phones targeting teenagers feature a rounded body coated with gradated colours, which enables girls to customize the phone as an accessory, using chains, key-holders, stickers and so on. Typically, emails are used more frequently than voice call, while GPS-enabled functions allow parents to locate their children. In fact, the mobile phone is becoming the primary form of communication among the young. In Norway, more than 85 per cent of teens and young adults report sending short messages on a daily basis (Ling, 2005). Specifically, girls and boys aged 16–19 send nine and five messages, respectively, per day. Similar numbers have been reported in Japan (Hashimoto, 2003). Teens and young adults also tend to be more responsive to the mobile messages that they receive. One survey suggests that almost 92 per cent view a message as soon as they receive it, compared to 68 per cent of the general population (Ito and Okabe, 2005).

## Why do adolescents spread the word via mobile?

The information provided above shows that mobile-based viral marketing can be very effective, especially for younger consumers. In planning such a campaign, however, firms need to know why young consumers exchange information, and how they do so. For this reason, it appears necessary to identify the various factors determining adolescents' acceptance of a viral marketing campaign.

### Social interaction

There is good reason to believe that young people use the mobile device as a medium of social interaction in which they minimize social structure constraints. In so doing, they learn and exchange the specific values and behaviours necessary to increase their social ties. The goal is to form tightly bounded, densely-knit groups with strong interpersonal connectivity, which can be defined as the 'social benefits derived from establishing and maintaining contact with other people such as social support, friendship, and intimacy' (Dholakia et al., 2004: 244). In an exploration of network- and small-group-based virtual communities, Dholakia et al. (2004) found this construct to be one of the significant determinants of consumers' participation. We believe that this is relevant to mobile-based viral marketing, because stronger ties can be formed through face-to-face contact, but also through electronic networking tools, such as SMS, MMS and emails. Consumers may decide to participate in a mobile-based viral campaign because they are consciously or unconsciously interested in connecting with a potential social network by disseminating, receiving, and responding to a 'buzz', or contagious commentary, about products, services, brands, and ideas, in order to be a part of their peer community.

## Common experience

The earlier examples of *Halo 2's I Love Bees* and McDonald's RUMAC campaigns suggest that it is necessary to create a common experience that can be shared with friends, to provide a 'reason' to talk. Such experience needs to be both entertaining and informative, and neither annoying nor intrusive. One of the most popular experiences may be sharing an incentive or reward upon participation. The creation of effective incentives encourages adolescents quickly to pass on information that is related to the campaign and would benefit their friends. This means an attractive buzz or a good 'reason to talk', because most young consumers tend to seek 'something cool' that enables them to derive social benefits from their network. Such incentives may be monetary or non-monetary. Monetary incentives are instrumental and functional, and would thus stimulate consumers' cognitive processes. Coupons, which are redeemable as a price discount, or music or wallpaper downloads, sweepstakes, product samples and the like are examples of this sort. By contrast, non-monetary incentives are non-instrumental and experiential, and are directly related to consumers' affective process. Playing games, voting in a popular song contest, chatting and so on are examples of this sort. These two forms of incentive are approximately parallel to the hedonic and utilitarian values that have been widely accepted as a useful framework in sales promotion. In practice, firms can combine both types of incentive in one campaign, thus motivating consumers' participation in viral campaigns in a dual manner.

## Agent

Evidence from both academic and trade journals shows that the mobile device can act as an influential agent that delivers the 'seeds' of the buzz in word-of-mouth communications between teenagers, because they tend to identify the mobile device as a very personal item that is an integral part of their everyday life. This feeling is similar to what psychologists define as the perceived psychological attachment. That is, adolescents are likely to feel themselves identified with mobile phones, which express their *raison d'être* or their own inner world. For example, Sato and Kato (2005) point out that children under 16 are now the focus of the huge mobile phone market, especially for short emails, and they note the problems and advantages involved in the desire for this fashion item. Children under 16 often personalize their mobile with their own colour, size, ringtones, chains and accessories, because it is viewed as a personal tool that serves as a bridge of communication. Many people feel that their personality and individualism are reflected in the type and style of their mobile. Largely as a result of this tendency, consumers are likely to expect mobile phones to help them stay connected, informed and entertained. This relationship is essentially isomorphous to what marketing literature terms brand relationship, because teenagers' interactions with the mobile device can be characterized as relational. Here, teenagers use the norms of interpersonal relationships as a guide in their benefits' assessments of everyday communication. Through a sequence of social interactions, benefits are given to others to entertain them, or benefits are given to show concern for others' needs. We believe this self-identification with the mobile device is one of the strong determinants of attitude toward any campaign.

## Content

The content dimension of viral marketing may be influenced by what is most appreciated by peers. Specifically, young consumers tend to share common interests, and follow their opinion leaders in sharing content that has to be both entertaining and informative. Fashion and cosmetics are the most popular product groups to 'talk about'. As a result, young consumers are likely to form special attitudes toward a brand. In the context of adolescent culture, this is illustrated by a strong commitment to fashion and cosmetic brands. For example, a fashion event in Japan, 'Tokyo Girls Collection', attracted 12,600 attendees, and as many as 15 million adolescents watched the live mobile-phone broadcast. This event exemplifies a grass-roots movement that has become so large in Japan that the traditional fashion houses have been rendered anachronistic. In terms of cosmetics, there is now a large market for teens, aided by appealing packaging, suitable products that are safe for children, low prices, child-oriented sales channels, and information sources such as magazines and TV advertisements. Young consumers tend to spread the word on their favourite brands not only via face-to-face conversations, but also via chatrooms, messaging and voice call. All the evidence indicates that the buzz that comments on their favourite brands elicits strong – indeed almost enthusiastic – affection, which in turn motivates their campaign participation.

## A case study in Japan

### Mobile internet penetration in Japan

In Japan, mobile internet penetration, exceeding 90 million, has become mature and saturated. After the introduction of 'i-mode' by NTT

DoCoMo in 1999, the mobile internet expanded rapidly. Unlike the PC internet, i-mode offered low cost, 'always-on' functions, and provided an attractive alternative to the expensive fixed internet connection. Writing emails, playing games, checking interesting news and so on quickly became a national pastime, because Japanese 'salary-men' and students had waited a long time for just such a device to entertain them on their commuter trains (Okazaki, 2004). Of the more than 46 million 3G subscribers (as opposed to 45 million 2G subscribers) in Japan, approximately 48 per cent of the total use i-mode, while the principal competitors, KDDI au and Softbank (formally Vodafone), have 46 per cent and 6 per cent of the market, respectively. All three carriers use a similar system of mobile internet. Every handset leads consumers to a top menu, which includes search and download functions, GPS, news and traffic updates and email. In addition, the mobile internet directory contains links to content-based sites. For example, i-mode had approximately 4200 official and 76,800 non-official sites (as of 2004). 'Official' sites are those that users can access directly by clicking on links in the directory of the menu list, while non-official sites are those to which users have no such access.

Marketers and advertisers rapidly began to adopt the mobile internet for their promotional campaigns. To date, the most extensive use of mobile is in sending advertising and post-campaign information to content-based mobile websites. The most recent and popular trend of this kind is the use of special industrial barcodes called 'QR codes', which are linked to a promotional website or email address that the mobile phone can access. The phone handset can scan the barcode using its camera or other input, decode the information, and then take action based on the type of content. Marketers and advertisers use these QR codes in conjunction with cross-media campaigns, by printing them in magazines and newspapers. In 2004, SONY and NTT DoCoMo developed 'FeliCa', which uses contactless electronic IC chips that can communicate with reading devices when the mobile device is placed near them. FeliCa is used as a multi-functional electronic wallet, which consumers can use for diverse transactions, such as commuter pass, electronic money, membership card and movie tickets, among others, simply by waving their phone in front of enabled sensors. Users must 'charge up' their accounts with credits before making the payment.

Japan is one of the countries in which internet access via mobile devices now exceeds that via PC (Figure 8.1). This enables us to make a stronger case that may have important implications for other countries.

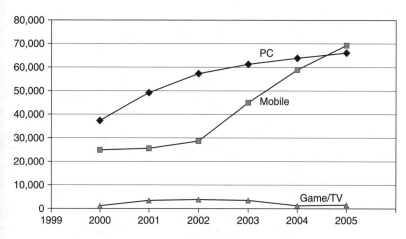

*Figure 8.1* Internet connection terminals in Japan
*Source*: Ministry of Internal Affairs and Communication (2007).

## Viral campaign for a new hair-styling wax

We collaborated with a well-known hair-care brand manufacturer, listed in the first section of the Tokyo Stock Exchange, to plan, design, and execute a viral campaign for a new men's hair-styling wax. This product is an extension of one of its successful brand lines. The viral campaign, called 'kamisuma contest' ('Cool hairstyle contest' in Japanese), was created in collaboration with a mobile advertising agency, D2 Communications.

In this campaign, the promoting company posted the campaign information in a mobile website, called 'GORGON ZORA', and also sent the same information via mobile email newsletter. The 'GORGON ZORA' website targets teenage consumers between 13 and 18, and publishes 'Today's Hot Topics' every day. As of November 2005, its membership had reached 1,130,000, of which 75 per cent were junior and high school students. The gender proportion was slightly skewed towards females, with 41 per cent male and 59 per cent female. This viral campaign targeted only male teenagers, because the promoted product was a new *men's* hair styling wax.

The viral campaign was structured as follows (Figure 8.2):

1. An adolescent mobile user A accessed the 'GORGON ZORA' website or received a mobile advertisement by mobile email newsletter. Both contained the same information.
2. When the user clicked a campaign link, he could jump to the detailed campaign site. He was encouraged to solicit a product sample and use it for his hair styling.

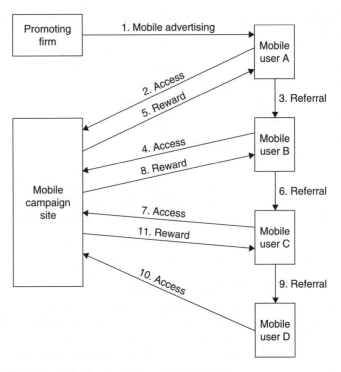

*Figure 8.2*  Structure of the viral campaign

3. Then, he was asked to take pictures of himselves and/or his friends by mobile, and send them to a campaign site via MMS. He became automatically eligible to enter a sweepstake for a gift certificate, and was given a unique reference number. Adolescents who accessed the site could 'vote' for their favourite, or for what they considered hilarious photos.
4. Mobile user A was encouraged to make a referral to his friend, for example, mobile user B, about the campaign. At the time of referral, he passed on his reference number.
5. If mobile user B participated in the campaign and sent his photo with his friend's reference number, then mobile user A was rewarded with electronic coupons for a free music download. This was considered an attractive incentive, because music download is one of the most popular mobile services among teenagers.
6. The viral campaign continued when mobile user B passed the information to his friend, mobile user C, and so on.

*Figure 8.3* Illustrations of photos sent to the viral campaign site
*Source*: Courtesy D2 Communications Inc.

7. Adolescents continued to vote for their favourite photos. At the end of the contest, the 'winners' were announced and rewarded with special gifts.

Examples of the kind of participants' photos posted in the campaign site are shown in Figure 8.3.

### Survey results

After the campaign was completed, 250,000 male adolescents aged 13–18 years were randomly chosen from a mobile advertising agency's opt-in customer database (N = 1,250,000). Structured questionnaires were sent to them directly via mobile messaging service. In total, 9629 adolescents returned the completed questionnaires. The response rate was approximately 4 per cent. Almost 80 per cent of the respondents sent back the questionnaires in the first two days. Almost 60 per cent of the respondents access a mobile website everyday, while approximately 70 per cent of them use PC internet. In the former, 38 per cent check the sites for more than an hour per day.

When they received this survey questionnaire, 33 per cent of the respondents remembered what the 'kamisuma contest' was all about.

With regard to the inward viral effect (that is, how consumers received the campaign information), there were three primary patterns. Approximately 33 per cent learned of the campaign through mobile email newsletters, 30 per cent learned when their friends showed them their mobile screen, and the rest learned from face-to-face contact, mobile website, blogs and so on. With regard to the promoted brand, of those who remembered the campaign, almost 71 per cent recognized its name, and 34 per cent knew the detailed characteristics, primarily because (1) they had used the brand before, or (2) they had seen television commercials.

Approximately 30 per cent of respondents participated in the campaign and/or sent their own photos to the contest site. In terms of the outward viral effect (that is, how consumers spread the campaign information), 12 per cent recommended their friends to participate in the campaign, and 4.3 per cent confirmed that their friends (to whom they had recommended the campaign) had actually sent their photos to the contest site. As many as 22 per cent made referrals through direct or face-to-face contact with their friends. Approximately 12 per cent showed the mobile screen directly, with the campaign notification or the photo contest site. By contrast, 4.7 per cent and 2.8 per cent sent or forwarded mobile emails or advertisements, respectively. With regard to the place of referrals, almost 32 per cent of the participants learned of the campaign from their friends at school, while approximately half learned of it from the notifications in the 'GORGON ZORA' website, or from mobile email newsletters.

Those who actually participated in the campaign, and sent their photos to the contest site, learned of the campaign from their close friends, or school clubs or circles. About 30 per cent of the respondents learned about the campaign at school during break, whereas 20 per cent learned of it at home. With regard to the campaign content, the vast majority perceived it as interesting (47.8 per cent) and enjoyable (26.7 per cent). Almost 43 per cent responded that the campaign had increased their awareness of, or interest in, the promoted brand.

## Lessons learnt: how to plan a successful viral marketing campaign

This case study demonstrates that both beneficial and entertaining experiences can be spread among adolescents, because the mobile device acts as an agent of their social interaction. The experience is a specific benefit to be shared: free music downloads as a utilitarian benefit, and emailing and voting photos as hedonic benefits.

Because the case was studied in Japan, one of the most advanced markets in the use of mobile phones for advertising and marketing, it appears that our implications may be especially useful for practitioners who work in markets that are moving rapidly in the same direction. Some implications can thus be drawn.

First, this case demonstrates that information derived from viral marketing campaigns can be an important source of brand recognition. Adolescent consumers tend to be keen on new personal care products, and the viral campaign served to ignite a chain of talk. Up to 84 per cent of the respondents indicated their intention to purchase the product in the future, while at the time of the survey almost half had already purchased it. Although the direct link between the campaign and purchase intention is far beyond the scope of this chapter, future research may explore this relationship in a scientific manner.

Second, up to 33 per cent of respondents learned of the campaign through mobile messages, such as mobile newsletters, emails from friends, or forwarded campaign notifications (that is, pass-along emails). This leads us to conclude that mobile devices did indeed serve as a powerful agent in the transmission of the campaign information. In addition, although it is not conclusive, this implies that adolescents were able successfully to 'filter' mobile messages, and to distinguish their importance according to their interest. Given the still prevailing SPAM or SPIM problem, this is rather surprising, and may be of special interest to marketers in Europe, where this problem has long been a major obstacle to the adoption of mobile marketing techniques.

On the other hand, the fact that almost 22 per cent of the campaign participants learned the campaign information via face-to-face contact suggests that direct contact is still the preferred way of exchanging information with friends. This may suggest that when planning mobile-based campaigns, marketers and advertisers may want to encourage direct or physical interactions. In the case of this 'kamisuma contest', many photos were taken of a group of two or three friends, which indicates that the participants enjoyed not only sending the photos and voting for them, but also a sense of 'togetherness', or being together. Such social interaction may be indispensable for a successful viral marketing campaign.

## Summary and conclusions

The Japanese case presented in this chapter has important implications. First, mobile-based viral marketing can be a powerful tool for branding. Although the evidence shown in this case is modest, it clearly illustrates that it can be a useful vehicle of campaign information dissemination, in both inward and outward viral effects. Existing consumers' brand awareness was reinforced by giving them a 'reason to talk' in the mobile-based referral campaign. This means that mobile promotion may work better when consumers have a reasonable level of brand familiarity. In this light, mobile-based viral marketing may be especially useful for brand extension.

Furthermore, the case shows that daily social interaction, face-to-face or mobile-based, is extremely important in the transmission of the campaign information. From a practitioner standpoint, firms may find it useful to identify 'opinion leaders' in a strategically segmented group, and then disseminate the information. In this way, firms could achieve two primary goals of viral marketing network members: (1) find a group-to-person 'shortcut' to disseminate the information, and (2) reinforce an instrumental purpose predetermined by their group leader.

The findings of this case appear to provide a structured explanation of viral marketing practices. In this marketing, the firm sought to increase brand awareness exponentially, by creating a stimulating buzz through an entertaining photo contest, which converted into a reason to spread the talk. This study demonstrates that this buzz was transmitted in a structural – rather than accidental – manner. It was spread in relational networks of *social interaction* among friends, via mobile device as a catalyzing *agent*, and created a *common experience* to spread the contagious *content* of a successful trial of the new brand.

In the end, what are the benefits of this metaphor for the analysis of consumer behaviour and viral marketing? Although the complete psychology of this metaphor is far beyond the scope of this chapter, two important conclusions can be drawn. First, marketers and advertisers seem able to develop a notion of 'invisible' physical contact that can be nurtured by entertaining and informative buzz talk. Thus, viral marketing implies that close human relationships can be enhanced through simple nurturing things, such as sending one another a message. Second, this metaphor implies that the buzz becomes stronger, and its strength becomes more stable, as a result of the enduring nature of the friendship. Here, it is important that the 'viral' metaphor promotes the positive interpersonal and emotional nature of those relationships that involve affective connections, links, ties, bonds and so forth. The buzz helps to foster a strong bond that corresponds to a very stable relationship. Probably it is this very benefit that leads firms to use this strategy: as the message spreads among the bonds, the buzz loses its commercial colour, and turns into an enjoyable message from the friendship network.

# Acknowledgement

The author appreciatively acknowledges the generous support provided by D2 Communications Inc. (Tokyo, Japan).

# References

Carrigan, T. (1989), 'New Apples tempt business', *PC User*, 27 September.

Dholakia, U.M., R.P. Bagozzi and L.K. Pearo (2004), 'A social influence model of consumer participation in network- and small-group-based virtual communities', *International Journal of Research in Marketing*, 21: 241–63.

Hashimoto, Y. (2002), 'The spread of cellular phones and their influence on young people in Japan', in S.D. Kim (ed.), *The Social and Cultural Impact/Meaning of Mobile Communication*, Chunchon, Korea: School of Communication, Hallym University, pp. 101–12.

Ito, M. and D. Okabe (2005), 'Technosocial situations: emergent structuring of email use', in M. Ito, D. Okabe and M. Matsuda (eds), *Personal, Portable, Pedestrian: Mobile Phones in Japanese Life*, Cambridge, MA: MIT Press, pp. 257–75.

Juniper Research (2007), 'Report: mobile user-generated content revenues to rise tenfold by 2012', *PRWeb*, 13 August, available at http://www.prweb.com/releases/2007/8/prweb546122.htm (accessed on 23 August 2007).

Kirby, J. (2006), 'Viral marketing', in J. Kirby and P. Marsden (eds), *Connected Marketing: the Viral, Buzz and Word of Mouth Revolution*, London: Elsevier, pp. 87–106.

Ling, R. (2005), 'The socio-linguistics of SMS: an analysis of SMS use by a random sample of Norwegians', in R. Ling and P. Pedersen (eds), *Mobile Communications: Renegotiation of the Social Sphere*, London: Springer, pp. 335–49.

Marsden, P. (2006), 'Introduction and summary', in J. Kirby and P. Marsden (eds), *Connected Marketing: the Viral, Buzz and Word of Mouth Revolution*, London: Elsevier, pp. xv–xxxv.

Ministry of Internal Affairs and Communication (2007), *White Paper: Information and Communications in Japan*, Information & Communication Statistics Database – Year 2005, Tokyo: Government of Japan.

Okazaki, S. (2004), 'How do Japanese consumers perceive wireless ads? A multivariate analysis', *International Journal of Advertising*, 23(4): 429–54.

Phelps, J.E., R. Lewis, L. Mobilio, D. Perry and N. Raman (2004), 'Viral marketing or electronic word-of-mouth advertising: examining consumer responses and motivations to pass along email', *Journal of Advertising Research*, 44(4): 333–48.

Sato, N. and Y. Kato (2005), 'Youth marketing in Japan', *Young Consumers*, 6(4): 56–60.

# 9

# Brand Ambassadors: Strategic Diplomats or Tactical Promoters?

*Claudia Fisher-Buttinger and Christine Vallaster*

## Introduction

The expression 'brand ambassador' appears more and more frequently in both marketing literature and business practice. However, there could not be a broader spectrum of meanings associated with it. While there is agreement that 'brand ambassador' is intended to embrace a wider meaning around the behaviours of a person who acts in support and on behalf of a particular brand, there is disagreement as to the particular mission (strategic, tactical or even self-directed), the nature of the relationship between the ambassador and the represented company (paid for or not, permanent employee or not) and the intended impact (increasing awareness, relationship management, communicating brand values, or negotiating difficult situations). Going back to the roots of the underlying metaphor may help shed some light on which notions of a brand ambassador are more appropriate than others.

In this chapter, we will first look at the original definition of an ambassador, then we will explore and evaluate the various meanings that have emerged in connection with the metaphor of a brand ambassador, and lastly we will discuss the impact for managerial use.

## Origin and meaning of the word 'ambassador'

'AMBASSADOR' (also Embassador, the form sometimes still used in America; from the Fr. *ambassadeur*, with which compare Ital. *ambasciatore* and Span. *embajador*, all variants of the Med. Lat. *ambasciator, ambassiator, ambasator,* &c., derived from Med. Lat. *ambasciare* or *ambactiare*), "to go on a mission, to do or say anything in another's name".[1]

The word 'ambassador' has a humble origin in the Latin word *ambactus*, meaning 'servant'. According to the dictionary, the general meaning of 'ambassador' is 'an informal representative who spreads goodwill'.[2] In more specific terms, an ambassador is:

(a) A diplomatic official of the highest rank, sent by one sovereign or state to another as its resident representative (ambassador extraordinary and plenipotentiary).
(b) A diplomatic official of the highest rank sent by a government to represent it on a mission, as for negotiating a treaty.
(c) A diplomatic official serving as permanent head of a country's mission to the United Nations or some other international organization.
(d) An authorized messenger or representative. Abbreviation: Amb., amb.

Before the development of modern communications, ambassadors were entrusted with extensive powers; they have since been reduced to spokespeople for their foreign offices.[3]

An ambassador's main function, however, is still to advance the interests of a state or institution. These interests usually include promoting trade and security, maintaining access to resources, facilitating cultural ties, and protecting the lives of the state's citizens. Ambassadors are responsible for assessing the political climate in their host country and analysing important events. In former times, ambassadors worked quietly behind the scenes, but the explosion of media outlets around the world has put them in the public eye more frequently.

Ambassador is the most senior diplomatic rank. Diplomacy is the art and practice of negotiation to gain strategic advantage; one set of tools being the phrasing of statements in a non-confrontational or polite manner. Ambassadors, like other foreign envoys, are officially protected from harm by what is known as diplomatic immunity. The host government cannot detain or arrest ambassadors, but has the right to expel them from the country.

## Emerging applications of the metaphor in marketing theory and practice

The term 'ambassador' has been increasingly adopted in the product and branding literature and is widely used in the following contexts:

(a) *Employees* as brand ambassadors (for example, to ensure delivery of the brand promise to the customer, to roll-out a new brand or for brand re-positioning within the organization, or to promote a particular product or service).

(b) *Celebrities* as brand ambassadors (for example, through endorsement).

(c) *Customers* as brand ambassadors (for example, enthusiastic fans).

In the following sections we will explain in more detail the role and responsibilities of the various types of brand ambassadors.

## Employees as brand ambassadors

### General delivery of brand promise

In the most generic meaning of the ambassador metaphor, employees become brand ambassadors when they behave in line with the expectations that are created in the marketplace through the communication of a brand promise.

Any successful brand must align the way it views itself, the way it *wants* to be viewed by others and the way it actually is perceived by others (for example, Kapferer, 2004; Aaker and Joachimsthaler, 2000). Ensuring minimal gaps between these three perspectives is of strategic concern since inconsistency can severely damage a brand, for example by creating expectations that remain unfulfilled. Given that stakeholders experience a brand through every single interaction with a particular company (Davis and Dunn, 2002), it can easily be seen that employees play a crucial role in delivering upon the brand promise (de Chernatony, 2006; de Chernatony and Segal-Horn, 2001). This is particularly true in service-driven industries and in the business-to-business world due to the highly interactive relationship between customer and employee. Take, for example, Honeywell, a US-based technology and manufacturing company providing automotive products, turbochargers, speciality materials, control technologies and products and services for the aerospace industry. On their website they promise the following:

We are building a world that's safer and more secure ...
More comfortable and energy efficient ...
More innovative and productive.
We are Honeywell.
This is the essence of today's Honeywell ... our brand promise.[4]

Furthermore, Dave Cote, Chairman and Chief Executive Officer of Honeywell, has published a letter on the website to his colleagues. In this letter he emphasizes not only the importance of the brand promise, but of the role each individual will play in its delivery, making every single employee a brand ambassador:

> Every Honeywell employee is a brand ambassador. With every customer contact and whenever we represent Honeywell, we have the opportunity either to strengthen the Honeywell brand or to cause it to lose some of its luster and prestige. Generations of Honeywell employees have built our powerful brands with their hard work, spirit of innovation, passion for quality, and commitment to customers. I am counting on every Honeywell employee to continue that legacy as we strive to keep our brand promise and build a better world.

This letter makes it very clear that in this world of engineers, it is not only the technology, infrastructure and quality of underlying products that create the brand, but also every single employee who becomes a loyal spokesperson or messenger for the Honeywell brand. However, in order to advance the interests of the company in line with the brand promise, every employee needs to understand *how* to be a spokesperson for the brand – in other words, they need to know what the brand promise is, how to translate that brand promise into their every-day work context and how to use the brand as a guiding principle when making decisions. Only then will their quest to strengthen the brand and deliver on the brand promise be successful.

This particular application of the brand ambassador metaphor is very broad – it spans the entire organization, thereby drawing more on the idea of an 'authorized representative' than a high-ranking diplomatic officer. While the shared mission of representing the brand may receive sufficient attention and strategic concern, the role of a brand ambassador in this context appears to be less special and a bit inflationary.

### Internal brand roll-out of new or revived brand

Sometimes, brands need to be revived or repositioned in order to regain relevance to both employees and the marketplace. In these situations, behavioural changes, organizational changes and often even cultural changes need to be made. The required change process can often be successfully initiated through a network of influential employees – brand ambassadors – who are strategically selected for this task. For example, when UBS, a global financial services provider, decided to bring all their acquired brands under the aegis of one powerful master brand, they had a big task at their hands – not only did they have to develop a master brand that worked for their various businesses, ranging from a retail bank in Switzerland to a highly prestigious investment bank based in the UK, but it also had to work on a global basis. As their website highlights:

> Clients expect from us the relentless pursuit of their financial success, and they also demand the resources of a global powerhouse. They want proactive advice and a choice of relevant solutions that fit their needs. They want a close relationship with UBS, and for us to understand their individual goals and motivations. If we are to harness the power of our brand so that it is indeed more than just a mere logo but an emotional attachment we have with our clients, it must be truly relevant and credible. We are building a flagship brand to match our position as one of the world's flagship financial services firms.[5]

Once this master brand was focused upon relentless pursuit of financial success with the organization as a global powerhouse, and proactive advice and choice of relevant solutions was designed, it had to be communicated and made accessible to their employees on a worldwide basis. Therefore, UBS developed a strategic network of brand ambassadors that would help communicate the brand content, create excitement about the brand values and help bring the brand to life internally by interpreting it in the day-to-day work context. These brand ambassadors had to be chosen carefully and needed to have good communication and people skills, hold influential positions, and be willing to carry the brand torch. They needed to be equipped with sufficient information and arguments in order to make an impact quickly.

This use of the term 'brand ambassador' appears to be quite consistent with the original ambassador concept. The brand ambassador – a high ranking officer – receives a specific mission to act on behalf of the brand, a mission which requires sophisticated negotiation and communication skills, access to strategic resources and is of the utmost strategic importance.

## Sales promotion

In this context, the brand ambassador represents the product to a public audience. This practice is particularly prevalent in the area of food and drink, hospitality and retailing. For example, companies such as Campari, Pernod Ricard, Rémy Martin, or Moët Hennessy SA – all market leaders for luxury spirits – work with this notion of brand ambassador. It is quite common to use the term brand ambassador in job ads and it is often agencies that search for them on behalf of their clients. For example, the following job ad was posted by Michael Page Australia (excerpt only):

---

**Brand Ambassador/Sales Representative**

- The ideal role for a career focused extrovert
- A company that wants you to have fun while you work

*Job Description*

You will establish and maintain successful relationships with a variety of clients across a given territory, supplying them with product and driving up total sales. Day to day you will be visiting cafés and similar outlets around Brisbane and you will also get to travel at times to important events around the country such as Big Day Out, Mardi Gras, Livid, Falls Festival and other such events.[6]

---

This is simply a sales rep job to which the title 'Brand Ambassador' is applied to make it appear more glamorous and interesting. Even worse, the metaphor is often (ab)used in the context of independent contract work around street promotions. As www.associatedcontent. com aptly describes this particular meaning of the brand ambassador metaphor 'Brand Ambassador: Short-Term Job as a Marketing or Promotions Rep – Fast Money, Fast Pace, and Image-Based Work'. Reading their short summary of what it means to work as a brand ambassador explains where the bad reputation of the term comes from (excerpt only):

- A fast gig as a brand rep is a reasonable way to make quick cash, often in a casual but high-energy environment. Although they do sound like fly-by-night operations, many of these brand ambassador opportunities are legitimate options for college students and others who need to make a little extra money and don't want a long-range commitment.
- Most brand ambassador jobs take place at sporting events, trade shows, conventions, festivals, fairs, bars, and other large public gatherings. Whatever the company chooses to call your job, the real purpose is to market a product or service. The goal is usually something like gaining recognition for a new brand, generating new customers, getting email addresses for a mailing list, etc.

- It is rare that you will be paid by the same company that actually makes the product or provides the service you are promoting. Chances are that the promotions campaign will be run by a separate marketing firm with whom the main company has a contract. Regardless, the company who pays you almost never adds you to their payroll as a regular employee. Instead, you're simply treated as an independent contractor and provided a check in-person or by mail.
- You don't have any say over what you market. Depending on the nature of the promotion, you may be giving out tobacco-themed merchandise, encouraging hapless people to apply for credit, or indirectly encouraging binge drinking.
- There's often a major focus on your appearance. You'll have to deal with having been selected based on a combination of your personality and your looks. If that bothers you, you probably shouldn't pursue a short-term job as a brand ambassador.[7]

Some companies, such as Innocent, the famous British smoothie company, take pride in the training they provide for their promotional staff who distribute smoothies on the street (Hemsley, 2006); nevertheless, the application of the metaphor 'brand ambassador' in this context seems somewhat inappropriate. Organizing and soliciting trials and trainings, handing out free T-shirts and samples and the like hardly seem the tasks you would expect from an ambassador. But where the metaphor really breaks down is the fact that most of these brand ambassadors do not even seem to work for the company who owns the brand – they are hired by a middleman on behalf of the brand owner. This arm's-length relationship makes it very difficult to become a genuine spokesperson. Strictly speaking, this is not a case of using a metaphor with the aim of enhancing communication and getting a point across quickly, but a case of employing a euphemism so that an agreeable or – in this case even glamorous – expression is used (brand ambassador) instead of an offensive term (street marketer) or less pleasant term (sales rep) in order to increase the appeal to the target audience. Thereby these marketing companies seek to make an otherwise undesirable job more respectable, more attractive and more socially acceptable. Not surprisingly, it is this use of the metaphor that is most controversial and even infuriating to those who attempt to keep the definition of the original concept pure:

> Not only do we believe that a brand ambassador is a passionate individual for a particular service or product, but we believe that individual is a loyal and loud advocate that spreads the goodwill in the name

of that company, product or service. It is a dedicated mission that is personal and fulfilling for that person who is NOT there for PR or to push product, but to spread the love, per se.[8]

While this strategy may work in the short term to gain the attention of job seekers, it is to be expected that they will see through this ploy very quickly.

## Using celebrities as brand ambassadors

Companies have long understood the power and impact of associating popular personalities with their brand name and products. Celebrities can come from sports, music, movies and TV, or even politics. Michael Jordan is Nike's 'Air' and Pierce Brosnan is Omega's 'Seamaster', Motorola has engaged David Beckham as a global brand ambassador, Andie McDowell is 'worth it' for L'Oreal and hotel heiress Paris Hilton is the face of sportswear giant Fila.

A successful celebrity brand ambassador can catapult a company into a new era of prosperity by increasing awareness (the target market knows of and is familiar with the brand ambassadors and the endorsed brand benefits from the association), creating elements of trust (the brand ambassador is seen as a credible name/face/voice and – given sufficient brand fit and affinity – is also seen as trustworthy in their projections), and encouraging imitation (they are adored and everyone wants to be like them). However, these connections also bear considerable risk – a brand ambassador can also damage a brand. There is the risk of misbehaviour (What does Paris Hilton going to jail mean for Fila? What did Kate Moss's cocaine scandal mean for Rimmel?), or the danger of a mismatch between the brand's values and those of the brand ambassador's – for example, what might have been the wider impact of the 2007 Luis Vuitton ad campaign using Mikhail Gorbachev as a brand ambassador? Shot by photographer Annie Leibovitz, the ads focus on travel – a 'core value' for the French luxury label – and feature the former Soviet leader in a car, with a Vuitton bag at his side and the Berlin Wall in the background. Examples like this make us wonder about the suitability of the brand ambassador metaphor. While ambassadors according to their dictionary definitions appear to be governed by a long-term dedication to the representation of their principal and a genuine interest in furthering their cause, the authenticity of these celebrity 'brand ambassadors' remains questionable, as their loyalty seems based almost entirely on monetary rewards. Did Eva Longoria not respect the brand ambassador role of her sweetheart Tony Parker when she gave him a custom Piaget watch as a gift while he has pledged loyalty to IWC Schaffhausen? Or was Charlize Theron confused about her allegiance when she wore a watch from the Dior line (with whom she had a perfume contract) although she had pledged exclusivity to Swiss watchmaker Raymond Weil? Credibility wears thin when a particular celebrity is used as a brand ambassador for too many different products (for example, German soccer legend Franz Beckenbauer is highly visible in advertising for a large and very diverse portfolio of brands, including Postbank, Erdinger Beer, mobile provider O2, Adidas, Audi, and media company Premiere) or if they switch competitors in short sequence (for example, Beckenbauer previously endorsed O2's competitor E-Plus). This promiscuity seems at odds with the ambassador concept – it is very difficult to be a loyal and genuine spokesperson for so many brands at the same time or if ambassadors change their stripes so quickly.

## Customers as brand ambassadors

Taking the idea of 'relationship marketing' to the next level, many marketing strategists now believe that they can strengthen a brand by building online communities around them (McWilliam, 2000). Such communities can either be formed by customers or by brand owners. While online communities created and sponsored by brand owners offer more control over the group's evolution and allow for better interaction with key opinion leaders, key buyers and key users, this perceived control sometimes results in a noticeable lack of activity and the absence of the genuine excitement that characterizes many customer-created communities (Fisher-Buttinger, 2002). An interesting attempt to employ customers as brand ambassadors is made by Maker's Mark, the famous Kentucky bourbon. On their website, they introduce their 'embassy' and invite enthusiastic customers to pledge allegiance as an ambassador (excerpt only):

> 'I, as a Maker's Mark Ambassador, do pledge to introduce those who have not yet had the pleasure (poor souls) to the smooth taste of Maker's Mark bourbon. To help friends understand, appreciate and savor what handmade bourbon is all about. To encourage establishments I encounter within my travels to stock Maker's Mark for their thirsty patrons. And to lead by my own example, that every occasion for enjoying bourbon is the perfect occasion for enjoying Maker's Mark.'[9]

In return for their efforts, the ambassadors receive a number of privileges, amongst others their name on a Maker's Mark barrel from which they can buy a bottle. This application of the brand ambassador concept is very similar to that of promotions mentioned above, bar financial remuneration and hence stopping short of making the customer a paid employee.

On the other hand, fans who actively promote a brand for free and out of their own volition are also often called brand ambassadors, citizen marketers or customer evangelists. Unfortunately, they may not always act in the brand's best interest, making it questionable whether leaving the fate of the brand in their hands is the right thing to do (Coyler, 2007). The consequences that fanatical consumers can have on perception of a brand were, for example, illustrated in the much-studied phenomenon of the Hell's Angels who acquired an outlaw-like status and severely endangered the reputation of the Harley Davidson brand (Schouten and McAlexander, 1995). Iconic brands like Apple, various car makes and, more recently, even IKEA (for example, see the 'unofficial IKEA site' that attracts IKEA fans in the spirit of 'positive fanatics' as crafted by IKEA founder Ingvar Kamprad[10] or ikeafans.com who aspire to 'personalising the IKEA experience') seem to attract passionate customers and users, fans who like to spread the word on behalf of their beloved brand. A brand ambassador in this context shows his/her own enthusiastic dedication to a particular brand to others and may or may not attempt to 'convert' them.

While there is a rich pool of research that looks at the questions of why and how such attachment to the preferred object/brand develops (see in the field of attachment or passion, Belk et al., 2003; brand enthusiasm, fetishism, Belk, 2003; brand cult, fandom and devotion, Wallendorf and Arnould, 1988 and Pimentel and Reynolds, 2004), their ability to influence potential consumers to the advantage or disadvantage of the brand needs further research (Pichler and Hemetsberger, 2007). In any case, the ambassador metaphor breaks down in this context due to the lack of authorization and possible sanction in case of misrepresentation. Furthermore, an ambassador is more likely to be understood as a measured personality, not a fanatic. Whether true or not, user-generated content does not always help to spread the good-will of the institution – a role which is definitely ambassadorial.

## Conclusion and managerial recommendations

Metaphors are tools primarily used to facilitate the communication of an abstract concept by relating known information in a new context. They help to infuse concepts with emotions and meanings by evoking associations (Davies and Chun, 2003). By equating one thing to another, a new relationship is highlighted, a new set of characteristics are introduced or new ideas are explored. Metaphors are also used to inspire creativity. For example, the Bible most artfully employs the technique of metaphors. Here, metaphors create powerful images that target the human subconscious and not only get their point across, but often enable the reader to view things in a different light.

Overall, there can be value in using metaphors in the marketing world. By drawing on similarities with known concepts, one can quickly establish a desired notion and meaning within an organization. Furthermore, a certain halo-effect may arise – for example, the term 'brand ambassador' might carry a certain prestige since it refers to a high ranking officer in the diplomatic corps (although it may have suffered from inflation, as explained earlier). If chosen carefully, a metaphor can therefore not only help to explain an abstract concept, but also to position a concept in the organization and to infuse it with positive emotions (Cacciaguidi-Fahy and Cunningham, 2002). Metaphors might even suggest a pattern of associations that can be brought to a situation and may affect competitive strategy (Hunt and Menon, 1995). For example, conceiving of employees as brand ambassadors paints a different picture of an organization than that of 'brand warriors'. While one conjures images of authorized representation and skilful negotiation, the other evokes aggression and warfare, resulting in entirely different processes, structures and required skills.

When employing metaphors, they should be chosen carefully. For example, the term 'brand evangelist' is often used interchangeably with that of brand ambassador although it can be interpreted as carrying a whole host of negative connotations – especially post-9/11 – of religious fanaticism, aggressive mission activities and sermonizing monologies (see Figure 9.1 for a humorous illustration of the brand evangelist).

Metaphors also carry the risks of not being understood or shared. They can only be effective if the intended similarities are clear. For example, the brand ambassador metaphor may not be sufficiently down-to-earth for some employees and hence hinder identification with the role or task.

Another potential danger is metaphor overload. Mixing metaphors or using too many metaphors will reduce their impact and their effectiveness. Evoking competitive strategy as 'warfare', brand enthusiasts as 'brand ambassadors', marketing campaigns as 'viral' and so on may dilute the focus and power of each of these concepts, leaving the audience bored and irritated (Crookston as cited in Henricks, 1997).

Finally, if the metaphor becomes a euphemism, it risks being met with cynicism and rejection. The concept of ambassador implies that

*Figure 9.1*   Brand evangelists

the task at hand is of a certain importance and meaning, requires a certain skill-set and qualifications, a certain personality and probably even standing. There is little connection between these associations and the task of promoting a product in the street – rendering the metaphor unsuitable. In a blog-contribution entitled 'the-bastardization-of-brand-ambassador' a writer pointed out:

> At its core, what they are calling 'brand ambassadors' is street team marketing. This company's employees are unquestioning 'ambassadors' for whatever product or service they are paid to promote – regardless of their experience, knowledge, or passion. Qualifications? They're good looking and brand promiscuous.[11]

Using the term 'brand ambassador' in the context of sales promotion is therefore – from our point of view – the least appropriate application of the metaphor. Also, if every single employee is to become a brand ambassador, the concept is likely to lose its appeal. No country turns every single citizen into a high ranking diplomat, on the contrary, they are chosen carefully and deployed strategically. It is clear that the underlying intention is one of creating advocacy, spreading motivational excitement and contagious enthusiasm, but in our view the use of the phrase 'brand ambassador' in this context is misplaced.

One point that may seem obvious but is important to keep in mind is that metaphors are not true per se (Henricks, 1997). In fact, if examined closely, most of them usually express a logical inconsistency, incongruence or a contradiction (MacCormac, 1985; Morgan, 1980). Employees are not true ambassadors, nor are consumers, even though they may share some of the characteristics of an ambassador in significant ways. They are not high ranking diplomatic officers, they are usually not sent anywhere to represent an organization in a foreign country, but they are representatives in a different way – they are spokespeople for a product or service, they negotiate meaning in a world that inundates the consumer with information and choice.

If metaphors stimulate creativity, offer potentially rich strategic insights, and a way to communicate more powerfully, then management needs to know how to choose compelling and useful metaphors. We suggest looking into the original source and meaning of a word or concept, and evaluating carefully to what extent the metaphor fits the situation in which the term is going to be used. As illustrated by our analysis, there are more and less appropriate applications.

## Notes

1. http://www.1911encyclopedia.org/Ambassador.
2. http://www.dictionaryofdefinitions.com/what-is-the-definition-of-ambassador.html
3. http://www.answers.com/topic/ambassador.
4. www.honeywell.com.
5. www.ubs.com.
6. www.michaelpage.com.au.
7. www.associatedcontent.com.
8. BrainsonFire, Define Ambassador, please, December, 2006, http://www.brainsonfire.com/blog/.
9. www.ambassador.makersmark.com.
10. http://www.positivefanatics.com.
11. http://brainsonfire.com/blog/the-bastardization-of-brand-ambassador/.

## References

Aaker, D.A. and E. Joachimsthaler (2000), *Brand Leadership*, New York: The Free Press.
Belk, R. (2003), 'Shoes and self', *Advances in Consumer Research*, 30: 27–33.

Belk, R., G. Ger and S. Askegaard (2003), 'The fire of desire: a multisited inquiry into consumer passion', *Journal of Consumer Research*, 30 (December): 326–51.

Caddiaguidi-Fahy, S. and J. Cunningham (2002), 'The use of strategic metaphors in intercultural business communication', *Managing Global Transitions*, 5 (2): 133–55.

Coyler, E. (2007), 'The fanatic: a brand's best friend?', brandchannel.com, June 18, http://www.brandchannel.com/start1.asp?fa_id=372.

Davies, G. and R. Chun (2003), 'The use of metaphor in the exploration of the brand concept', *Journal of Marketing Management*, 19: 45–71.

Davis, S.M. and M. Dunn (2002), *Building the Brand-Driven Business: Operationalize Your Brand to Drive Profitable Growth*, San Francisco: John Wiley & Sons.

de Chernatony, L. (2006), *From Brand Vision to Brand Evaluation: Strategically Building and Sustaining Brands*, Oxford: Butterworth Heinemann.

de Chernatony, L. and S. Segal-Horn (2001), 'Building on services' characteristics to develop successful services brands', *Journal of Marketing Management*, 17 (7/8): 645–69.

Fisher-Buttinger, C. (2002), 'New media branding with online communities', unpublished doctoral thesis, University of Innsbruck, Austria.

Hemsley, S. (2006), 'Inspiring the ambassadors', *Marketing Week*, February, 37.

Henricks, M. (1997), 'In other words – metaphor use in business', Entrepreneur, available at http://findarticles.com/p/articles/mi_m0DTI/is_n1_v25/ai_19128554/pg_2 (accessed 30 September 2007).

Hunt, S. and A. Menon (1995), 'Metaphors and competitive advantage: evaluating the use of metaphors in theories of competitive strategy', *Journal of Business Research*, 33 (2): 81–90.

Kapferer, J.-N. (2004), *The New Strategic Brand Management: Creating and Sustaining Brand Equity Long Term*, London: Kogan Page.

MacCormac, E. R. (1985), *A Cognitive Theory of Metaphor*, Cambridge, MA: MIT Press.

Morgan, G. (1980), 'Paradigms, metaphors, and puzzle solving in organization theory', *Administrative Science Quarterly*, 25 (4): 605–22.

McWilliam, G., (2000), 'Building strong brands through online communities', *Sloan Management Review*, 41 (3) (spring): 43–54.

Pichler, L. and A. Hemetsberger (2007), ' "Hopelessly devoted to you" – towards an extended conceptualization of consumer devotion', *Advances in Consumer Research*, 34: 194–9.

Pimentel, R.W. and K.E. Reynolds (2004), 'A model for consumer devotion: affective commitment with proactive sustaining behaviors', *Academy of Marketing Science Review*, (5): 1–45.

Schouten, J.W. and J.H. McAlexander (1995), 'Subcultures of consumption: an ethnography of the new bikers', *Journal of Consumer Research*, 22 (June): 43–61

Wallendorf, M. and E.J. Arnould (1988), ' "My favorite things": a cross-cultural inquiry into object attachment, possessiveness, and social linkage', *Journal of Consumer Research*, 14 (March): 531–47.

# 10
# Negative Comparative Advertising: When Marketers Attack

*Fred Beard*

Advertisements that directly or indirectly compare or associate a marketer's products with those of an identifiable competitor on the basis of some relatively specific point of difference are called, appropriately enough, comparative ads. Gaining widespread acceptance in the early 1970s, their use had previously been rare among mainstream marketers. However, by the mid-1980s, it was obvious, in the US at least, that comparative advertising had become one of mainstream marketing's most frequently used advertising strategies.

For more than a decade there have been signs of a metamorphosis of comparative advertising into an increasingly confrontational and aggressive format, as some marketers attempt not only to differentiate their products and brands from competitors by claiming superiority, but also to disparage them. Industry observers have identified a likely basis for this aggressive strategy: 'Madison Avenue is taking cues from the hard-hitting tactics of political advertising: go negative on your opponent early and often' (McCarthy, 2007: 6B).

Called 'political attack advertising', the metaphorical slinging of mud at political opponents has also increased since the 1980s. Perhaps for some of the same reasons – for example, it often seems to be devastatingly effective – major brand leaders, many of whom previously avoided a marketing tactic associated with desperate second-raters, are employing an aggressive format of advertising that can be conveniently and metaphorically referred to as 'commercial attack advertising'.

Exemplified early on by the 'Cola Wars' and 'Burger Wars' of the 1980s – and more recently by the attacks of Miller Brewing and Apple Computers on competitors Anheuser-Busch and 'PC' – attack advertising is clearly linked to one of marketing's most widely recognized metaphors: marketing as 'warfare'. Applying this metaphor and its associated military terminology, attack 'campaigns' equate to 'tactics' in broader 'offensives' against marketing 'enemies'.

In this chapter, the managerial implications stemming from a marketer's decision to 'go negative' and employ advertising as a tactical weapon to strategically 'attack' one or more competitors are explored. Perhaps because its truly widespread use has evolved so recently, published research on negative comparative advertising is nearly nonexistent. However, advertising theory and relevant findings from research on comparative advertising and political attack advertising provide a solid foundation for this chapter's conclusions about the utility of the attack advertising metaphor and when, who, what and how advertisers should attack.

## Background

In the 1970s, the US Federal Trade Commission began encouraging advertisers to use comparative advertising because the agency believed it would provide consumers with more useful information. Although its widespread adoption took a little longer in the European Community (EC), Directive 97/55/EC (European Parliament and Council of the European Union) established that comparative advertising should be permitted as long as, among other requirements, it wasn't anti-competitive, unfair or misleading.

Researchers Karen James and Paul Hensel (1991) offer some helpful suggestions as to when and how a comparative ad, in which a competitor is identified merely for the purposes of claiming superiority, becomes an attack. The two are best differentiated based on (1) the degree to which the targeted brand is identified, (2) whether the direction of the comparison is differentiative as opposed to associative (that is, products are presented as different rather than similar), and (3) the extent to which consumers perceive the advertising to be particularly malicious or unfair. As with other advertising strategies, the implications of employing attack advertising should be assessed in terms of its likely effects on the three categories of message effects that provide the foundation for advertising's 'hierarchy-of-effects' models and the setting of advertising objectives. These include: (1) cognitive (attention, awareness, knowledge), (2) affective (liking and brand preference), and (3) conative (purchase intention) advertising process outcomes.

Early hierarchy-of-effects models, such as Lavidge and Steiner's (1961), proposed that advertising works by making consumers aware of a product (cognition), then by persuading them to like the product (affect), and finally by encouraging a purchase (conation). Later models, namely the

FCB Grid (Vaughn, 1980) and the Rossiter-Percy Grid (Rossiter et al., 1991) propose that consumers don't always seek or process information in the sequence predicted by the classic LEARN-FEEL-DO hierarchy. They may vary, for instance, depending on the level of involvement in making a product choice (high versus low involvement) or whether the motivation to purchase is mainly rational versus emotional – 'thinking' versus 'feeling' product decisions in the FCB Grid and 'informational' versus 'transformational' decisions in the Rossiter-Percy Grid.

Regardless of the decision-making sequence consumers follow, both marketing planners and advertising researchers continue to use the three categories of message effects to establish objectives and predict advertising's situational effects.

## Cognitive process outcomes

Once people pay attention to an ad, it's generally hoped they will process some information and consequently learn something. In both the study and practice of advertising, among these hoped-for cognitive outcomes are attention and awareness. Attack advertising's effects on attention and awareness should also be evident in its effects on other important and related variables, such as credibility, believability and perceived informativeness.

### Attention and awareness

Dhruv Grewal et al. (1997) conducted a comprehensive meta-analysis of 22 years of empirical research directly comparing the effects of comparative advertising with non-comparative advertising. Their findings confirmed the conclusions of many empirical studies and literature reviews: comparative ads, on the average, generate more attention, increase message awareness, increase brand name awareness, and encourage greater message processing than non-comparative ads.

Although a widely cited meta-analysis of negative political advertising conducted by Richard Lau and his colleagues (1999) found no statistically significant difference between negative and positive political ads and their effects on memory, most studies of political attack advertising suggest it elicits more attention, is more easily recalled and considered more involving, useful and informative.

*Theoretical explanations.* There are also theoretical explanations for why negative information and, consequently, attack advertising, enhances cognitive message effects. Referred to as 'negativity bias', some research in advertising, marketing, communication and political science has shown that negative information is more memorable and influential than positive information. This may be because it is more unexpected and novel, less ambiguous, more credible, appeals to emotion rather than logic, and because people assign greater weight to negative information when making evaluations in social settings and about individuals. James and Hensel (1991) provide a thorough review of the available research on this topic.

*Effects on attention and awareness by brand positions.* Experience and practice in the marketplace have long suggested that new brands and smaller competitors, rather than brand leaders, have more to gain from the use of comparative advertising, and, consequently, attack advertising. An observation by Bernd Michael, deputy chairman of advertising agency Grey Europe, directly links this prevalent belief to attention: 'the argument for using comparative advertising is at its most compelling for small advertisers wishing to take on major, established brands. Here it provides a tool for gaining attention on a limited budget' (cited in Shannon, 1999: 32).

Research on comparative advertising generally supports the idea that effects on attention are greater for new brands and low-share competitors. However, Grewal et al. (1997) concluded that the message awareness for a comparative ad is greater than a non-comparative ad when the sponsored brand's relative market position is equal to or greater than the comparison brand's. And although comparative ads were not more informative overall than non-comparative ads, they did find that comparative ads are perceived as more informative when the sponsored brand is an established one rather than a new brand or a market leader.

### Believability

One might expect that source believability would be less for comparative ads than non-comparative ads, and that's what the research generally confirms. However, and like the effects of comparative advertising on attention and awareness, Grewal et al. (1997) found that the effects on message believability vary based on market positions. In this case, the advantage goes to smaller brands and advertisers. They also concluded that when an advertiser's market position is equal to or greater than the comparison brand, comparison ads are less believable than when market positions are less than the comparison brand's.

Only one study is available to suggest how the effects of comparative advertising on believability are likely affected by its elevation to an attack. Comparing high- and low-negativity comparative ads with a positive comparative ad, Sorescu and Gelb (2000) found that the low-negativity ad scored significantly higher not only on measures of believability, but also on fairness of its content, approval of its content, informativeness and overall ad evaluation. It also significantly outperformed a positive comparative ad on measures of believability, informativeness and overall evaluation. Sorescu and Gelb propose that low-negativity attack ads might be more believable because they are perceived as more credible and less unfair.

### Affective process outcomes

Affective outcomes and objectives address the ways in which advertising encourages favourable feelings toward an ad and brand. Attitude-toward-the-ad ($A_{ad}$) has been especially important since some groundbreaking studies – conducted by Haley and Baldinger (1991) and Mitchell and Olsen (1981) – revealed it is one of the strongest predictors of an ad's sales success and that it has a significant effect on attitude-toward-the-brand ($A_{br}$). $A_{br}$ is typically measured in terms of how good or bad or likeable or unlikeable people say a brand is.

Studies of commercial comparative and political attack advertising suggest that people don't like either of them very much (Brabbs, 2001; Johnson-Cartee and Copeland, 1989). In general, women are more opposed to negative commercial ads than men, and older and more highly educated individuals are more opposed to both negative commercial and political attack ads (Garramone, 1984).

Although Grewal et al.'s (1997) research confirms that comparative ads generate more negative $A_{ad}$ than non-comparative ads, they also found that they tend to generate more favourable $A_{br}$. Richard Petty and John Cacciopo's (1981) Elaboration Likelihood Model (ELM), according to James and Hensel (1991), offers a useful framework for explaining the effectiveness of negative comparative ads in light of their negative effects on $A_{ad}$.

Negativity bias predicts that attack ads activate the ELM's central route to persuasion, that some consumers will form supportive arguments, and, consequently, be persuaded by the attack. However, since comparative advertising tends to encourage more counter-argument and source derogations (Swinyard, 1981), especially if the source lacks credibility or the ad is not believable, some consumers will not be persuaded. In the case of neutral responses, or when consumers are unmotivated or unable to process the message, peripheral cues, such as humour, music or positive $A_{ad}$ will become relevant and whatever attitude change occurs will be weak and temporary.

Observing that some research has shown that $A_{ad}$ is not a significant predictor of brand choice in the case of comparative advertising, James and Hensel (1991) argue: (1) that negative comparative advertising is mainly processed cognitively via the ELM's central route as opposed to affectively, (2) that brand cognitions dominate $A_{ad}$, and (3) that it will be more effective for consumers who are highly involved.

These conclusions are consistent with the experiences and practices of some advertisers. Mark Goldston, CEO of United Online (owner of the NetZero internet service) acknowledged *USA Today* Ad Track data showing consumers didn't like the ads in which NetZero attacked competitor AOL. However, he also pointed out that he was unconcerned about the ads' negative affect: 'They're designed to make AOL customers "kick themselves" and question why they're paying more for AOL. "These ads are not going to create joy and happiness in people. We want them to say, I feel silly. Maybe I'll switch"' (cited in McCarthy, 2007: 6B).

### Negative attitudes and the potential for backlash

Experience and research on both negative comparative advertising and political attack advertising strongly suggest that one of the principle risks associated with an attack is the potential for backlash, that is, negative attitudes toward the advertiser resulting from the perception that the attack was unfair or excessively malicious. The likelihood of backlash, and how it might vary by brand positions or the nature of an attack, is especially important to account for because even though comparative advertising doesn't encourage positive $A_{ad}$, it does, on the average, encourage $A_{br}$.

*Effects on negative attitudes and backlash by brand positions.* Again, research on comparative advertising suggests the impact of an attack on both $A_{br}$ and the potential for backlash depends on the market positions of the attacker and victim. Grewal et al. (1997) found comparative advertising is more effective in enhancing attitudes toward the sponsored brand when (1) the comparison brand is established in the product category but is not the market leader, (2) when the sponsored brand's market share is less than that of the comparison brand, and (3) when the sponsored brand is new to the category. Others, such as James and Hensel (1991), similarly predict that favourable outcomes, including positive $A_{br}$, are most likely to occur for new brands and that negative comparative advertising by market leaders will generally result in backlash because 'picking on the little guy' is almost always perceived as a violation of fair play standards.

*Evaluative versus factual attacks.*   Grewal et al. (1997) concluded that the effects of comparative advertising on favourable attitudes are greater when the ad contains evaluative messages (that is, information that is subjective in nature) rather than factual ones (information that is more objective in nature). They suggest this occurs because, in some cases, comparative ads may encourage affective responses. Sorescu and Gelb (2000) also argue that some attack ads appeal to emotion, rather than logic, and that people accord more weight to negative information when evaluating social situations and forming evaluations about people. The print ad for Miller Brewing brands Miller Lite and Miller Genuine Draft in Figure 10.1 offers both evaluative (more taste) and factual (half the carbs) attacks. On the other hand, the Diet Pepsi spot in Figure 10.2, which explicitly identifies competitor Diet Coke, offers only an evaluative attack (more cola taste) to differentiate the brand.

*Product versus image attacks.*   If a comparative ad is raised to the level of an attack, it is likely that attacking a competitor's product is less risky than attacking the company itself. Sorescu and Gelb (2000) compared a negative image ad attacking Toyota's competitors for exporting US jobs with a negative product feature ad and a positive comparative ad. The negative image ad generated lower ratings on all their measures – approval of the message, fairness, believability, informativeness and an overall rating – among the total set of respondents, including those who drove a Toyota. Some research on political attack advertising also supports the conclusion that attacks on political issues generally encourage more favourable attitudes toward the sponsoring candidate and the ad than do attacks on images.

Theoretically, as well, there are reasons to attack products rather than reputations. James and Hensel (1991) argue that people are more influenced by information they obtain from someone else about a third entity if that information pertains to the entity's factual performance or actions.

*Direct versus implied attacks.*   Direct attacks (the identification of specific negatives about a comparison brand) create the greatest likelihood of backlash, partly because they violate fair play standards and partly because they directly criticize the consumers of the denigrated brand. One pair of researchers, Karen Johnson-Cartee and Gary Copeland (1987), propose that implied attacks in political ads are more effective because they prompt people to generate their own arguments. A near-perfect example of an implied attack ad is one from a campaign for Juniper Networks, a marketer of high-performance network infrastructure (see Figure 10.3).

153

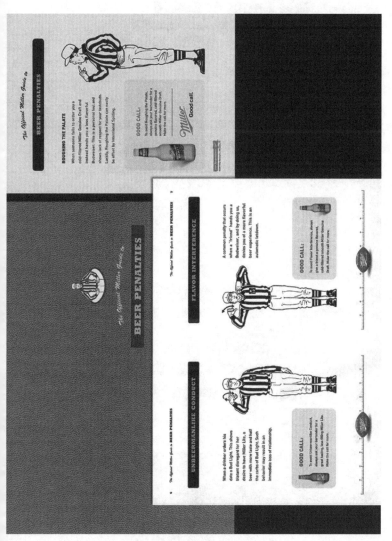

*Figure 10.1*  Miller Brewing launches both evaluative and factual attacks on Anheuser-Busch

*Figure 10.2*   Diet Pepsi's evaluative attack on Diet Coke

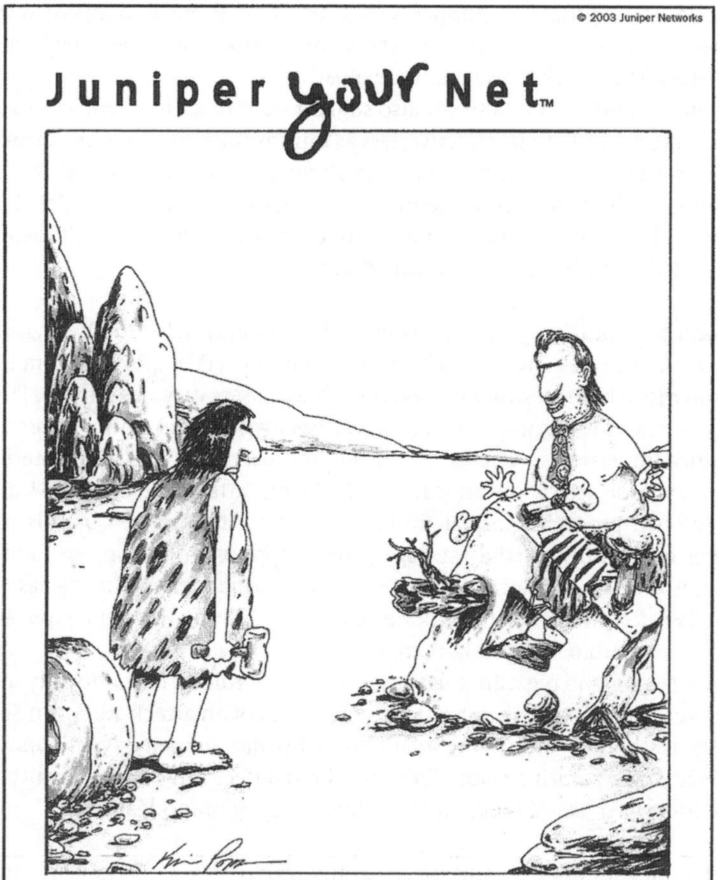


*Figure 10.3* Juniper Networks and an implied attack on Cisco

The ad implies that had Juniper Networks' competitor Cisco invented the wheel, it would have had an excessive number of useless bells and whistles. The attack is also mainly evaluative.

Sorescu and Gelb (2000: 36) also suggest that 'negative elements in an ad can contribute to its effectiveness as long as they are either believable, or offset by some positive elements about the sponsor, so that the ad would still be perceived as neutral on a negative-to-positive scale'. This may help explain why so many attack ads are satirical and clearly intended to be humorous (Beard, 2007).

*Effects on attitudes by user segments.*   Sorescu and Gelb (2000) extended research on attack advertising by exploring how users of sponsored brands, comparison brands, switchers and third-brand users vary in response. They began with the assumption that advertisers who attack competitors are mainly interested in effects on third-brand users and switchers. Studies of a Tylenol attack on aspirin and a Toyota attack on Ford, GM and Mitsubishi produced similar findings. Users of the targeted brands had lower evaluations of the messages, lower approval of them, and lower ratings of their fairness, believability and informativeness. In the case of the Tylenol attack ad, third-brand users and brand switchers expressed more favourable responses on approval and believability.

A related issue regarding usage groups is the role of brand loyalty and its likely impact on the potential effectiveness of an attack ad. Arjun Sen, a US restaurant industry consultant, who has helped several brands develop comparative claims, recently linked declining brand loyalty to the increased use of comparative advertising by brand leaders:

> For all the talk of brand loyalty, only 8% to 10% of people are stubbornly brand loyal ... There is a huge group of people who can be swayed. Now that the market is saturated, it's a new move for big guys to say 'I'm going to take you out today.'
>
> (cited in MacArthur, 2007)

Tactically, James and Hensel (1991) propose that an attack might be more effective for users of the comparison brand if it is endorsed by an independent third-party source.

## Conative process outcomes

Conative process outcomes and advertising objectives capture how advertising encourages desire among consumers for a product or brand and the ultimate decision to purchase it. Observers note that both comparative commercial advertising and political attack advertising are frequently used because they are believed to have powerful and direct effects on behaviour. The findings of Grewal et al.'s (1997) study confirm that comparative ads, on the average, increase both $P_i$ (purchase intention) and purchase behaviour more than non-comparative ads.

However, the effects vary by market positions, with the advantages again going to new brands and smaller competitors. Grewal et al. (1997) found that comparative ads, versus non-comparative ads, result in greater intention to purchase when (1) the comparison brand is the market leader and (2) the sponsored brand's market share is less than the comparison brand's.

Effects on $P_i$ also vary with the inclusion of credibility enhancers and factual versus evaluative information. Grewal et al. (1997) conclude that comparative ads with enhanced credibility significantly increase $P_i$, compared to non-comparative ads. Credibility enhancers discussed in the literature include the use of credible sources, two-sided messages, and the supporting of claims with factual information. Grewal et al. (1997) also conclude that comparative ads containing factual information, rather than evaluative information, account for higher $P_i$ than non-comparative ads. Thus, although evaluative information appears to have more positive effects on $A_{br}$, factual information is more effective in enhancing $P_i$.

## Implications and conclusions

Linguists note the difference between 'dead' metaphors, which have become part of a literal vocabulary, and 'live' ones, which continue to require some interpretation. William Grey (2007) proposes a third category he calls the 'dormant' metaphor': expressions 'used unselfconsciously as part of our literal vocabulary, although when we take note of them it is evident at once that they cannot be straightforwardly literal'.

Attack advertising, as a contribution to marketing thought and managerial use, is arguably a dormant metaphor, since it has considerable literal meaning with many users likely unaware of its metaphorical character rooted in a military lexicon. Yet it remains figuratively useful. An attack ad is something very different from a merely comparative ad. The attack advertising metaphor, at the very least, captures an advertiser's intent not only to establish the superiority of a brand, but also simultaneously to inflict damage on an opponent.

Perhaps the most obvious proof of the utility of the attack advertising metaphor, however, is how well it provides a context for exploring the managerial implications of employing a frequent, but potentially risky, advertising message strategy. Although caution is necessary when drawing inferences from the literature to specific industry applications, many of the implications that follow are well supported by theory, empirical research findings and the practice of successful mainstream marketers.

## When to attack

Research on comparative advertising and political attack advertising, as well as negativity bias and relationships based on the ELM and the situational grid models of Rossiter et al. (1991) and Vaughn (1980) strongly imply that if message objectives are cognitive in nature, then that's when attack advertising should be most effective. Moreover, since comparative advertising enhances $P_i$ and purchase behaviour, attack advertising should also be effective in situations where advertising objectives include encouraging purchase behaviour. These and other implications regarding when to use attack advertising include the following:

- Attack ads will be very effective for high-involvement product decisions (for example, home appliances, insurance, new products), where (1) perceived risk in making a poor choice is high and (2) consumers seek and process functional information to facilitate rational decision-making.
- Attack ads should also be effective for low-involvement product decisions (for example, food, household items) where (1) consumers enter the hierarchy-of-effects sequence with a mainly convenience-driven purchase, (2) brand loyalty is typically low and repeat purchases mainly a function of habit, (3) advertisers often attempt to exploit any meaningful difference, (4) advertising functions primarily as a reminder, and (5) $A_{ad}$ isn't very important.
- Attack ads will be less, but still somewhat, effective for influencing low-involvement 'feeling' or 'transformational' product decisions (for example, beer, soft drinks, candy), where (1) decisions are motivated mainly by personal taste and the desire for social status, (2) advertising succeeds mainly by getting attention (Vaughn, 1980), and (3) $A_{ad}$ is important.
- Attack ads will be least effective for high-involvement 'feeling' or 'transformational' product decisions (for example, jewellery, fashion apparel), where purchase decisions are driven mainly by feelings, attitudes, and self-esteem and the main goal of advertising is to encourage positive affect.

- Across all product categories, attack ads will be most effective when target audiences are younger and less educated consumers rather than older, more highly educated consumers.
- Men, especially younger ones, will respond most favourably to an aggressive attack ad.
- Attack ads will be least effective for users of the targeted brand; however, if users are targeted, the advertising will be more effective if (1) brand loyalty in the product category is low, (2) independent third-party sources are used, or (3) positive peripheral cues or an implied attack are used to distract consumers from counter-argumentation and source derogation.

## Who to attack

For the most part, if marketers are offering new products or have larger competitors, attack advertising will be effective. However, there are a few situations where larger advertisers are justified in using attack advertising, which helps explain recent industry trends. The implications for whom to attack are the following:

- Marketers of new brands and those with larger competitors will benefit most from attack advertising, across all advertising effects outcomes and product categories.
- Larger, established advertisers can safely attack competitors, gaining both message awareness and favourable brand attitudes, if the attacker is relatively the same size and not perceived as a brand leader.
- Larger marketers and brand leaders should never attack smaller competitors.

## What and how to attack

Research on political attack advertising and negative comparative advertising suggests implications regarding how negative an attack can safely be, the potential for backlash, evaluative versus factual attacks, and how attacks might be fine-tuned using other advertising tactics.

- Attacking product attributes and benefits will encourage less backlash and be more effective than attacking a competitor's image or reputation.
- High-negativity attack ads will generate greater attention and awareness, but will also generate greater backlash and be perceived as less credible, believable, and fair; consequently, they should never be used for high-involvement products (where such advertising effects are important in the decision-making process) and rarely, if ever, for other product types or advertising situations.

- An especially negative attack will be more effective if its believability is enhanced via credibility enhancers or offset by a positive element, such as humour. This effect should hold across all advertising situations.
- A marketer's use of attack advertising will grow less effective over time as the advertising becomes less novel and distinct and as the advertiser builds up a reputation for unfairness.
- An evaluative attack will be more effective for low-involvement products because it enhances $A_{br}$ and $P_i$; conversely, a factual attack will be more effective for high-involvement products by discouraging counter-arguing and source derogation.

## Other issues and caveats

Politicians have a big advantage over commercial advertisers when they use attack advertising: they don't have to tell the truth. Thus, any marketer considering an attack ad or campaign must take into account the possibility that the competitor will take legal action. Launching an attack increases the likelihood that the marketer of the targeted brand will take legal action. Indeed, one advertiser contacted for permission to reproduce an ad in this chapter courteously declined because the company is involved in litigation regarding the ad in question and another declined on the recommendation of attorneys.

It is also important to note that some states in the US, such as New York, have anti-dilution statutes that prohibit implying the inferiority of competitors' products. Attorneys Ethan Horwitz and Jessica Parise (2005) offer an excellent overview of the legal issues involved in the decision to launch a comparative advertising campaign, negative or not.

A second issue addresses what marketers should do if they are the victims of an attack. Should they respond? Although research on political attack advertising suggests that counterattacks do enhance somewhat the backlash against the sponsor they fail to enhance favourable attitudes toward the victim. Yet, the prevalence of cola wars, burger wars and pizza wars strongly suggests that advertisers do frequently allow themselves to be drawn into responding to an attack ad or campaign. As a final caveat, anyone considering the escalation of overt hostilities would be wise to consider the regrets of one such casualty of a 'spaghetti sauce war':

> At a certain point, [Unilever] realized, 'Hey, the category has declined every year for several years,' said one marketing services executive, 'and between [Unilever and Campbell], we're spending $60 million a year to convince consumers that our spaghetti sauce is really crappy'.
>
> (cited in Sorescu and Gelb, 2000: 26)

# References

Brabbs, C. (2001), 'Two-thirds find comparative ads "unacceptable"', *Marketing*, 20 September: 4.

European Parliament (1997), 'Directive 97/55/EC of European Parliament and of the council of 6 October 1997 amending Directive 84/450/EEC concerning misleading advertising so as to include comparative advertising', http://www.legaltext.ee/text/en/T70690.htm.

Garramone, G.M. (1984), 'Voter responses to negative political ads', *Journalism Quarterly*, 61: 250–9.

Grewal, D., S. Kavanoor, E.F. Fern, C. Costley and J. Barnes (1997), 'Comparative versus non-comparative advertising: a meta-analysis', *Journal of Marketing*, 61(4): 1–15.

Grey, W 2000, 'Metaphor and meaning', *Minerva*, 4, http://www.ul.ie/~philos/vol4/metaphor.html, accessed 18 July 2007.

Haley, R.I. and A.L. Baldinger (1991), 'The ARF copy research validity project', *Journal of Advertising Research*, 31 (April/May): 11–31.

Horwitz, E. and J.S. Parise (2005), 'Top 10 things to know before you launch a comparative advertising campaign', *Metropolitan Corporate Counsel*, June: 29.

James, K.E. and P.J. Hensel (1991), 'Negative advertising: the malicious strain of comparative advertising', *Journal of Advertising*, 20(2): 53–69.

Johnson-Cartee, K. and G. Copeland (1987), 'Setting the parameters of good taste: negative political advertising and the 1986 election', paper presented at the International Communication Association Convention, Montreal.

Johnson-Cartee, K. and G. Copeland (1989), 'Southern voters' reaction to negative political ads in the 1986 election', *Journalism Quarterly*, 66(4): 888–93, 986.

Lavidge, R.C. and G.A. Steiner (1961), 'A model for predictive measurements of advertising effectiveness', *Journal of Marketing*, 25 (October): 59–62.

Lau, R.R., L. Sigelman, C. Heldman and P. Babbitt (1999), 'The effects of negative political advertisements: a meta-analytic assessment', *American Political Science Review*, 93(4): 851–75.

MacArthur, K. (2007), 'Why big brands are getting into the ring', Adage.com, accessed 10 June 2007.

McCarthy, M. (2007), 'NetZero ads get in competitor AOL's face', *USA Today*, 28 March: 6B.

Mitchell, A.A. and J.C. Olsen (1981), 'Are product attribute beliefs the only mediator of advertising effects on brand attitude?', *Journal of Consumer Research*, 18 (August): 318–32.

Petty, R.E. and J.T. Cacioppo (1986), *The Elaboration Likelihood Model of Persuasion*, New York: Springer Verlag.

Rossiter, J., L. Percy and R. Donovan (1991), 'A better advertising grid', *Journal of Advertising Research*, 31 (October/November): 11–22.

Shannon, J. (1999), 'Comparative ads call for prudence', *Marketing Week*, 6 May: 32.

Sorescu, A.B. and B.D. Gelb (2000), 'Negative comparative advertising: evidence favoring fine-tuning', *Journal of Advertising*, 29(4): 25–40.

Swinyard, W.R. (1981), 'The interaction between comparative advertising and copy claim variation', *Journal of Marketing Research*, 18 (May): 175–86.

Vaughn, R. (1980), 'How advertising works: a planning model', *Journal of Advertising Research*, 20 (October): 27–33.

# 11
## Why Do They Lag and Why Should We Care?

*Jacob Goldenberg and Shaul Oreg*

### Introduction

A vast amount of attention has been paid to 'Innovators' and 'Early Adopters'. Firms need them, marketers love them, and they are typically respected and even envied. You can see people gather around the person who brought to work the newest generation mp4 player, who bought the latest GPS navigator, or who was first to install Windows Vista. People draw close with admiration, as if they were witnessing the invention of fire. Without them, firms would probably have difficult times in surviving, because if they do not adopt first, the mass market will likely not either. Some argue that Innovators are not very smart consumers: they buy a very expensive version of a new product, the product they buy still has many problems and bugs, and they will probably have to purchase a different version once a dominant design is introduced. Nevertheless, it is clear that they are prime in the social process of innovation adoption.

Far less attention has been paid to those who are typically last to purchase. These individuals' choices are at best ignored and at worst ridiculed. They are called 'Laggards', and they are assumed to be the last to adopt, when prices are already very low, and therefore it is considered pointless to invest any energy in persuading them to adopt earlier. Firms expect little of them, having virtually no faith in gaining profits from them.

In this chapter we challenge this point of view and suggest that it may be premature, and somewhat hasty, to brush away further consideration of this late adopting sector. We suggest that while Laggards are late to switch their products, once they *do* they often surpass the rest of us with their new purchase. Through what we call the *consumer leapfrogging effect* we describe how a typical Laggard may come to play the role of an Innovator.

We liken the Laggard to the bullfrog, which won't rush to find new foods, but once it leaps, bounds an incredible distance. After describing the leapfrogging effect we move on to talk about its theoretical and practical implications. As we will show, expediting Laggards' leaps may prove to be quite lucrative.

## Why should we be interested in resistance to innovation

Innovators and other early adopters are believed to be the leaders of new trends, and when they adopt they spread the word and spark the entire adoption process (Rogers, 2003). They are like the busy bee, cruising from flower to flower, fertilizing each as it passes by. Some may say that without them, we would all be sentenced to a life with perhaps new, yet boring, products that lack innovativeness, creativity or imagination.

Perhaps if this were the whole picture there would be no point in trying to understand individuals' resistance to innovation. But, in fact, this is only part of the story. Let us consider, for example, a famous Innovator: Cosmo Kramer, from the TV programme *Seinfeld*. Seriously, the man has invented a sea-scented deodorant, a brassière for men, a coffee-table book about coffee tables (which is a coffee table as well), and was the first to adopt super jet showers.

Yes, society looks much more intersting when such individuals are around. But the real questions is, does anyone take their advice seriously? Probably not. Would you take Kramer's advice about a new ipod? A new generation cell phone? Would you buy the sea-scented deodorant if Kramer recommended it?

Now perhaps Kramer is not the typical Innovator in every sense of the term, and indeed, with his many quirks, he is certainly one of a kind. Yet in several respects he possesses many of the primary characteristics of the typical Innovator. He is open-minded, creative, and willing to take risks. However, some of these characteristics are precisely what make many of us sceptical and hesitant about his proposals.

Creators of new ideas love Innovators because they are open-minded and because their only resistance is perhaps to resistance itself. Most people, however, are at least somewhat hesitant before adopting new products or ideas. Resistance, for most, is a central part of the decision-making process.

Theoretically, one could argue that resistance is merely the opposite of innovativeness and that Laggards constitute the mirror image of

Innovators. We argue that a true understanding of innovativeness can only be achieved by understanding resistance. More specifically, most consumers are *not* Innovators, and rather than defining them through the innovativeness that they lack, it is much more meaningful to define them through the resistance that they possess.

Contrary to the common view, that resistance, as a primary source of lagging, is a boring and dull phenomenon, we argue quite the contrary. Resistance involves rich and fascinating phenomena. It leads to surprising behaviours and sometimes, perhaps counterintuitively, may be a source of substantial benefit to firms.

A few years ago, Wagner Kamakura (Duke University Professor of Marketing), mentioned to one of the authors that 'Innovators are actually suckers: they purchase an expensive product that performs poorly and is full of bugs, and are happy with it.' In other words, we argue that resistance is not necessarily a negative attribute. It is human, it generally involves a rational basis, and it often provides the main thrust behind successful innovations. Although we cannot see resistance, resistance is the story that underlies and governs the dynamics typically seen in penetration curves and sales charts. Understanding this invisible force and uncovering its consequences aims not only at minimizing negative effects, but also at improving our effectiveness and efficiency in innovation management. Let us, therefore, consider the lagging phenomenon.

## Laggards

Laggards constitute one of the five segments identified by Rogers (2003) and have been defined as those who are last to adopt an innovation (following 'Innovators', 'Early Adopters', the 'Early Majority' and the 'Late Majority'). Although some understanding of the Laggard phenomenon can be gained through studies on resistance to change, academic research that has focused directly on Laggards is quite scant. In Figure 11.1 we present a famous classification of the adoption of an innovation over time.

First let us distinguish between lagging and resistance. Consider a recent case, involving the introduction of the new official NBA (the US national basketball association) basketball in June 2006, to replace its predecessor of 35 years. The new ball was said to include a new design and a new material that together offer a better grip, feel and consistency than the previous leather ball. Players' resistance emerged immediately. Shaquille O'Neal, Miami Heat centre, commented: 'I think the new ball is terrible ... It's the worst decision some expert, whoever did it,

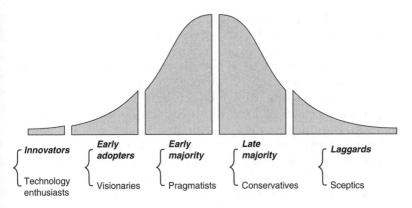

*Figure 11.1* Rogers's (2003) 'Adopting Segments'.

made ... The NBA's been around how long? A hundred years? Fifty years? So to change it now, whoever that person is needs his college degree revoked ... Whoever did that needs to be fired. It was terrible, a terrible decision. Awful. I might get fined for saying that, but so what?' (ESPN.com, 2006). Similarly, Miami Heat guard, Dwyane Wade commented that '[this] will require another adjustment period. Now I've got to make another adjustment with a ball that I haven't shot with at all and it's going to be a challenge ... That means it's going to take a lot of late nights for me' (ESPN.com, 2006).

Neither Shaquille nor Dwyane Wade wanted to invest efforts in switching. In fact, resistance to the ball was so strong that the NBA commissioner decided to switch back to the previous ball. If it was up to Shaquille, Dwyane or their friends, as long as they play there is no need to innovate, especially not with the ball they are used to.

Are they Laggards?

## What do we know about Laggards?

Because research on late adopters has been so scant, we do not know much about the size of this group. The classification of the five consumer segments in Figure 11.1 is based on deviations in a normal distribution. Accordingly, Laggards constitute 16 per cent of the market. Other classifications based on different rules are generally consistent with this definition (for example, Mahajan et al., 1990).

Demographically, Laggards have been characterized by low incomes, low levels of education, low social status, and low social mobility

(Rogers, 2003). Such characterizations suggest that lagging constitutes a stable characteristic, which therefore does not warrant any further investigation or investment since, presumably, there's not much that can be done to change Laggards. Let us note that there is some kind of circularity here: because Laggards are assumed to comprise a less attractive segment, there is sparse research on this behaviour. But because there is not too much research on this, marketers do not know how to approach these 16 per cent of the consumer population.

We consider here why we *should* be interested in highly resistant consumers and will argue that, due to the consumer leapfrogging effect, their economic impact is considerably underestimated. In the following section we demonstrate how infrequent, yet substantial leaps, create the atypical situation of a typical Laggard who becomes an Innovator.

## The consumer leapfrogging effect

Consider John, who enjoys listening to music as he jogs every morning. John uses his 1985 Walkman and is used to cassettes. His entire music collection is recorded on cassettes and he has always preferred the Walkman to switching to a portable CD player or any other contraption. That his friends all make fun of him for sticking with his old cassette-playing companion, while they have all upgraded their devices, makes little difference to him. John certainly knows what he likes.

Now, what kind of consumer is John? By definition, Innovators are first to adopt a new product, and Laggards are last. However, accompanying these definitions the terms 'Innovator' and 'Laggard' bear with them several connotations concerning the character of the adopter. Based on the description above, is John likely to be a Laggard? His preference for an antiquated product and his unwillingness, and even resistance, to upgrade would appear to characterize him as one. Indeed, Laggards are often described as localites and traditionalist. However, do such behavioural inclinations to resist necessarily correspond with late adoption?

We argue that John is not necessary a Laggard and moreover, that in some cases John may fall under the definition of an Innovator. We propose that dispositional resisters may also be predisposed to skip product generations, that is, to *leapfrog*. In other words, contrary to what their behavioural tendencies seem to imply, dispositional resisters may often show up as Innovators on product adoption curves, rather than Laggards.

Diffusion models generally look at each product as distinct from and as independent of other products, and assume that, over time, all members of that potential market will either adopt or decide not to adopt and will no longer constitute part of the market. However, this is often not the case. In many cases, products evolve in the form of successive product generations that satisfy the same need but through an entirely different technology, each of which can be considered a new product in itself. Music players that came out after the Walkman are a good example: although completely different from the Walkman in how they are used, in their technology, and in their quality, CD players and mp3 players address the same fundamental need of listening to music 'on the move' (walking, jogging or travelling). In these cases, adoption curves are often incomplete, and encompass much less than the entire market.

Imagine now that John has finally realized that the sound generated by his Walkman is indeed much poorer than that produced by all of his friends' players, and that he has come to recognize that the equipment is much bulkier and heavier than the newer products. After all these years, even John acknowledges that it is time to buy something new. In fact, we could even consider the possibility that John's Walkman simply broke down. At any rate, the question is: what kind of player will he purchase? Will he buy a portable CD player? Or, maybe a Mini-Disc? If John decides to skip a generation or two, perhaps he will go all the way and choose the mp4 player? In this case, would it be a surprise if John simply bought the most recent version of the iPod?

Assume that after discussing the issue with his friends, John decides to buy the most technologically-advanced player. An examination of John's time of purchase, as it appears on the mp4's adoption curve, would identify John as a classic Innovator, among the first to purchase the new product. Generation-skipping may make John an Innovator, based on his position on the product's life cycle curve, despite his dispositional tendency to resist innovations.

Like John, almost all resisters come to a point where they ultimately upgrade their products. What makes them resisters is not that they never upgrade, but that they upgrade *less frequently* than others. One question is how far will they upgrade? Although the newest products may often be more expensive than mid-range ones, the more substantial switching costs for John are likely to involve the adaptation to the new technology. For John, upgrading would mean abandoning the hundreds of cassettes he has accumulated over the years and purchasing new CDs or the rights to download music to his mp4 player. In this respect, it should make little difference to him whether he switches to a portable CD player or to the mp4.

Thus, even though resisters take much longer to upgrade than other consumers, once they upgrade they may very well upgrade to the latest technology available. Contrary to other consumers, however, resisters have held on to their old products long enough for several new generations of products to join the market. Thus, when resisters upgrade they will often need to skip several generations in order to reach the most recent technologies. This is the phenomenon that we call the consumer leapfrogging effect.

When products do not involve generations, resisters are always among the last to adopt, which by definition, makes them Laggards. For these products, then, the terms Laggard and resister may be used interchangeably. However, when an industry's products involve several generations (for example, Walkmans, portable CD players, Mini-Discs), the behavioural and dispositional sources of lagging do not necessarily correspond with the formal definition. Contrary to the accepted definition of Laggards – as those who are last to purchase the product – it may be more appropriate to define them, in these contexts, as those who hold on to their products longest and who are the last to switch.

The tendency to lag, therefore, is not synonymous with being a Laggard. Research on the concept of resistance to change has uncovered individual differences in people's inherent inclination to resist changes and new ideas and products (Oreg, 2003). Some people are more likely than others to resist or avoid trying out new things. Such inclinations fall in line with the overall profile of the typical Laggard. When a new product is introduced, dispositional resistance manifests itself in late adoption. Indeed, resistance to change has been found to correlate with time of adoption across a variety of products such as cordless phones, VCRs and software packages (Oreg et al., 2005). However, when multigeneration products are involved, the ultimate kind of lagging can be exhibited in a certain generation being skipped altogether. As in John's case, skipping generations can coincide with the early adoption of other generations. Thus, whereas the underlying tendency to resist remains the same, the nature of the product involved (that is, single versus multiple generations) determines how resistance will be manifested: in lagging, or in leapfrogging, which creates the potential for early adoption.

## Why should we care?

Now that we've reached a deeper understanding of the lagging and leapfrogging dynamics, and understand that even typical resisters may become leaders of the adoption curve, we can no longer ignore the economic value of Laggards. Let's return to John, who decided to adopt the mp4. The direct effect of his purchase on company sales derives from the simple fact that one more person has purchased the product. The size of this effect is obviously negligible. However, there is another effect that John is responsible for – the *indirect effect*, more commonly known as the word-of-mouth that John spreads. John shows his new 'toy' to his friends; people see him jogging with his cool new player; and may even ask him about it. It has been shown in many studies that the indirect effect is much larger than the direct effect, because it initiates something similar to a snowball. The more people adopt the innovation the more powerful the effect (for example, Hogan et al., 2003).

When John used his Walkman, his word-of-mouth about the product was insignificant, because the people around him already possessed portable players, most of them probably better and more advanced than his own. On the other hand, when John shows up with his new mp4 player, his word-of-mouth will now count as that of an Innovator. This effect is, in fact, larger than that of a more typical Innovator because John is not Kramer; he is a solid, responsible Laggard. John never gives in to pressures to adopt, and when he does, it is typically a risk-free purchase. This means that John's adoption signals that anyone (even a resister such as himself) can purchase and easily use the new product. John becomes a symbol of safe adoption of a completely new product. Without noticing it, John becomes a leader.

If people like John, still holding on to their Walkmans, decided to leapfrog today, the mp4 would be a likely candidate for their new purchase. However, were they to hold on to their Walkmans a little longer, they might well skip even the mp4 and end up purchasing a newer-generation product, maybe one that does not yet exist. For each product, a resistant population exists that will potentially skip, and thus never purchase, that product. This population constitutes a challenge for firms who want to speed up the adoption process.

The potential gain in addressing these resisters comes from firms' potential to convince them to leapfrog earlier than they would have done. In other words, if Apple were somehow to convince John, and his like, to abandon their Walkmans today, instead of waiting for the next product, they would benefit from both the direct and indirect effects on iPod sales. Otherwise, they would be certain to miss out on these benefits at this point in time, and likely miss out on them entirely in the case that these consumers end up adopting a next-generation product, manufactured by another firm.

The analysis and calculations of the real economic value of the leap-frogging effect are beyond the scope of this chapter. The reader can find technical details in Bass (1969). Let us summarize the main conclusions of that research.

Quantifying the indirect effect created by resisters' leapfrogging in order to assess the value of pursuing the resister population is not difficult. As noted earlier, when a resister leapfrogs, the firm's profits increase for two distinct reasons. The direct profit comes from the fact that an additional purchase takes place, which leads to an increase in the firm's net present value (NPV). This, however, is a small effect. On the other hand, the impact of the indirect effect of an early-adopting resister is substantial (assuming, of course, that the resister is satisfied with the product). As mentioned above, late adopters have very few potential adopters around them, so their word-of-mouth effect is negligible. However, when resisters leapfrog, they become surrounded by potential adopters, subject to their influence. The visibility of the new product thus increases. In such a case, leapfrogging may prove to accelerate the adoption process.

By constructing a firm's diffusion and NPV equations it is possible to calculate what happens to the product's adoption curve once a small subgroup of resisters leapfrog and become among the first to adopt the new product at hand. For example, let's assume that a firm can convince 1 per cent of resisters such as John (that is, 0.16 per cent of the entire market, based on the estimated proportion of Laggards in the population) to make their leap today, rather than wait for their 'natural', leap. This would result in an average profit increase of 14 per cent. If 10 per cent of resisters were persuaded to pre-empt their leap, the average profits would increase by 89 per cent, on average.

These findings demonstrate that leapfrogging may have an important impact on firms' revenues. Even if a small portion of such Laggards can be persuaded to leapfrog earlier than they would have done, firms' profits should be expected to increase substantially because of the acceleration in the entire adoption process.

Therefore, whereas the management and marketing literatures generally suggest disregarding the resistant segment of the consumer population, the findings above suggest otherwise, in particular when product categories involve an intrinsic process in which new generations supersede old ones. For such products, the Laggard concept needs to be considered more carefully and not confused with the related, yet distinct concept of resister.

## Note

This chapter is based on Goldenberg and Oreg (2007).

## References

Bass, Frank (1969), 'A new product growth for model consumer durables', *Management Science*, 15(5): 215.

ESPN.com (October 3 2006), 'Shaq: "Whoever [changed ball] needs to be fired"', available at http://sports.espn.go.com/nba/news/story?id=2610976, Associated Press (accessed 15 June 2007).

Goldenberg, Jacob and Shaul Oreg (2007), 'Laggards in disguise: resistance to adopt and the leapfrogging effect', *Technological Forecasting and Social Change*, 74: 1272–81.

Hogan, John E., Katherine N. Lemon and Barak Libai (2003), 'What is the true value of a lost customer?' *Journal of Service Research*, 5(3): 196–208.

Mahajan, V., E. Muller and R.K. Srivastava (1990), 'Determination of adopter categories by using innovation diffusion models,' *Journal of Marketing Research*, 27(2): 37–50.

Oreg, Shaul (2003), 'Resistance to change: developing an individual differences measure', *Journal of Applied Psychology*, 88(4): 680–93.

Oreg, Shaul, Jacob Goldenberg and Rachel Frankel (2005), 'Dispositional resistance to the adoption of innovations', paper presented at the annual meeting of the European Association of Work and Organizational Psychology, Istanbul, Turkey.

Rogers, Everett M. (2003), *Diffusion of Innovations*, 5th edition, New York: Free Press.

# 12
# Relationship Marketing as a Marriage

*Adam Lindgreen, Roger Palmer and Michael Beverland*

## Introduction

Until marketing emerged as a distinct business function between World War I and World War II, few economists had shown any interest in the behaviour of customers or the role of intermediaries. Throughout the 1950s and 1960s, however, the marketer came be to seen as a mixer of the 4Ps: product, price, place and promotion. The 4Ps framework – also known as transaction marketing – was to dominate marketing for the next many years (Lindgreen et al., 2004). Transaction marketing focuses on attracting new customers in a broad market or specific segment against a background of unfulfilled demand, and satisfies growing demand through the use of marketing techniques, portfolio analysis and the means of production.

Changes have since then significantly affected marketing practice, however. For example, the decline of manufacturing industries saw the concomitant rise in service industries: an increased emphasis is placed on the development of services and the way in which they can be incorporated into goods, such that marketing and quality align as a coherent value-creation chain (Lindgreen, 2004). In the mature market context of the twenty-first century, few or no new customers exist; mergers and acquisitions reduce the number of current customers; and the commercial significance of remaining customers increases (Brookes and Palmer, 2004). Transaction marketing, therefore, is likely to be less effective because its focus is largely on attracting new customers. Relationship marketing, in contrast, emphasizes the value of maintaining customers to grow profits and sales. Relationship marketing, most often, is defined as 'attracting, maintaining and … enhancing customer relationships' (Berry, 1983: 25). Increasingly, therefore, marketers are looking toward relationship marketing as a promising marketing approach.

Transaction marketing manages the 4Ps. Relationship marketing, in contrast, encompasses database tools to target and maintain customers; to establish dialogues or relationships between a company and its individual customers; and to assure the development of personal interactions between employees and individual customers and the positioning of the company within a wider marketing network (Palmer et al., 2005). In short, in relationship marketing the customer is treated as a client rather than a face in the crowd.

Empirical observations testify that relationship marketing is in vogue, with companies investing considerable amounts of money in relational marketing programmes. In fact, a relational marketing approach is now often the price of entry, not a competitive differentiator. So the time has come to ask critical questions of relationship marketing. We consider the 'relationship marketing as a marriage' metaphor that has become common currency among marketing practitioners.

This chapter is structured as follows. First, the metaphor of relationship marketing as a marriage is introduced. Second, a series of vignettes illustrate and exemplify various aspects of relationship marketing, as well as bringing in-depth meaning to the metaphor. Third, managerial recommendations are drawn. The chapter finishes with a discussion on relationship marketing as a metaphor for managerial usage.

## The metaphor

The influential author Levitt (1983) understood the sale (that is, 'attracting') as a courtship. Once the sale was completed, the marriage (that is, 'maintaining' and 'enhancing') between the company and the customer commenced. Transaction marketing is largely concerned with attracting customers and completing the sale. The transactional perspective gives little guidance or even credibility to the concept of sustaining and managing the customer once the transaction has been completed. Relationship marketing, however, overtly addresses this issue by putting in place a framework that enables managers to understand how sustaining and managing customers can be achieved. Perhaps also from the managerial perspective this framework has a further benefit; it legitimizes the continued investment of resources into current customers. The traditional badge of achievement, particularly from a sales perspective, is the winning of new business, but now managing and maintaining the business already gained is regarded as not only commercially worthwhile, but even respectable.

There is some support in the literature for the view that buyer-seller relationships develop through distinct stages. In England, Tynan (1997, 1999; see also O'Malley and Tynan, 1999), examines buyer-seller relationships in terms of five stages: to meet, to go out, to go steady or to court, to marry and to divorce. In the US, Dwyer et al. (1987) also use five stages to describe buyer-seller relationships: awareness, exploration, expansion, commitment and dissolution. The latter authors characterize the first four stages as follows (ibid.: 21):

- Awareness: Unilateral considerations of potential exchange partners.
- Exploration: Dyadic interaction occurs. A gradual increase in interdependence reflects bilateral testing and probing. Termination of the fragile association is simple.
- Expansion: A successful power source exercise marks the beginning of expansion. Mutual satisfaction with customized role performance supports deepening interdependence. Additional gratifications are sought from the current exchange partner, rather than from an alternative partner.
- Commitment: Contractual mechanisms and/or shared value systems ensure sustained interdependence. Mutual inputs are significant and consistent. Partners resolve conflict and adapt.

The four vignettes below illustrate and exemplify some of these aspects of relationship marketing, thereby bringing in-depth meaning to the marriage metaphor.

## Vignettes

### Vignette one

The Fine Wine Delivery Company in New Zealand takes a strategic view of its relationships with wineries, ensuring that its previous tactical, emergent strategies are formalized (Beverland and Lindgreen, 2004; Lindgreen et al., 2003). For example, members of the whole supply chain are brought together, and relationships are deepened. The Fine Wine Delivery Company will invest in relationships that are successful or promising, thereby furthering its differentiation and defence position. On the other hand, the company will end relationships that are neither successful nor promising, thereby divesting important resources for other purposes.

Further, through the industry body, the Wine Institute of New Zealand, both wineries (compulsory membership) and other parties (voluntary membership) have been working together over the past decades to promote overseas the New Zealand wine industry and its products.

The Fine Wine Delivery Company enhances its customer relationships through, for example, special offers made to high-margin, loyal customers on its mailing list. Customers are also invited to high-profile or exclusive tasting events.

However, there are some wine brands to which The Fine Wine Delivery Company is tied, as customers have come to take these for granted. In these cases, the company continues to be supplied with such brands, but the suppliers have the upper hand in determining the nature of these business relationships.

The Fine Wine Delivery Company may be seeking to strengthen its relationships with some suppliers, but at the same time it continues to look for new opportunities, including purchasing from new suppliers to provide one-off products to its preferred customers, to target new niches, or to try out new product styles and ranges.

### Vignette two

The UK-based Meat and Livestock Commission was established in 1967 to improve the efficiency of livestock production, marketing and distribution. With the devolution of governmental power to the Scottish Parliament and Welsh Assembly, the Meat and Livestock Commission itself evolved into a series of bodies that more adequately represented the political reality. In 2002, the English Beef and Lamb Executive was established in order to improve the marketing of these meat products (Palmer et al., 2006). The Meat and Livestock Commission, the English Beef and Lamb Executive, and similar bodies – both in the meat and other industries – represent supra-industry bodies. Their role is to address the environment within which the industry operates. In the meat industry in particular there have been plenty of challenges in recent years, with problems such as mad cow disease and foot-and-mouth outbreaks, but such bodies also concern themselves with ongoing activities, such as education and responding to trends in diet and eating habits. In addition, they provide support throughout the supply chain in order to ensure market responsiveness, efficiency, and integration of activities including the development of new techniques.

Bodies such as these do not direct the industry in the sense that they facilitate structural change, and they are careful not to favour one company or group of companies within the supply chain over others. Rather, their role is to facilitate relationships and to ensure that communication within the supply chain enables appropriate responses to technological and market developments.

### Vignette three

The telephone and online banking service Firstdirect was once described by George Day of the Wharton Business School as the best telephone banking service in the world. The traditional high-street retail bank offers a physical presence and local service for its customers, but there are limits to the service that it can provide, in particular opening hours, especially at weekends. In addition, a large number of simple transactions can now be conducted asynchronously, by post or by the use of automated teller machines. By contrast to conventional banks, Firstdirect has invested resources not in a network of retail branches but in a series of call centres. Staff are chosen not for their knowledge of banking procedures and systems, but for their ability to work in teams and interact with customers. Culture and attitude are even more important than technical capabilities.

By developing strong and positive relationships with customers and providing an excellent level of service, Firstdirect has developed an enviable reputation, as well as winning a string of awards and recognitions for its work (Clark and Baker, 2004). In fact, in an environment where many bank customers are at best apathetic about the service they receive in return for the charges that they pay, Firstdirect is one of the few banks whose customers will actively recommend its service to others. Firstdirect customers are enthusiastic, committed and loyal to the extent that they have become in some cases an unpaid sales force, promulgating positive word-of-mouth and demonstrating a very high quality relationship.

### Vignette four

The supermarket chain Tesco was originally known for its 'pile it high, sell it cheap' philosophy, a price-led and evidently transactional approach to doing business. Yet since 1995, Tesco has doubled its market share and assumed market leadership in its domestic UK market, become the largest internet retailer in Europe, the third-largest retailer in the world after Wal-Mart and Carrefour, and now earns the majority of its revenue outside its UK base. Tesco has become a global player, with ambitions to develop further, particularly in the non-food sector.

One of the catalysts for Tesco's dramatic growth has been the Tesco Clubcard, an early generation loyalty card of the type pioneered by the airlines. The Clubcard enables customers to gain points – in effect a modest discount on the purchase price – each time they shop (Humby et al.,

2006). The Clubcard is swiped at the checkout and this enables Tesco to link the customer's purchases and demographic data. The most important item of data is the postcode, and this and other details are obtained when the customer completes the Clubcard application form. Detailed analysis of this large volume of data – 17 million customers a week now visit Tesco stores – enables Tesco to obtain insight into customers' buying behaviour and to manage its product range accordingly, and also to offer promotions and incentives to segments that the data indicates will find them attractive. Customers regularly shop at Tesco stores in order to receive the benefit of the deferred discount. Further promoting the relationship has been fundamental to the extraordinary retail phenomenon of Tesco.

## Discussion of vignettes

As is evident from the four vignettes above, there is some merit to the metaphor of relationship marketing as a marriage. Companies become aware that they have a need and that the other is a feasible partner (meeting). They then explore business opportunities (going out); the other should be able to add value through resources such as cash, contacts, manufacturing capacity, technical knowledge or distribution capabilities. If they can assist each other in the achievement of common goals they may expand their business dealings, thereby becoming increasingly interdependent partners (going steady). Common goals include expanding a product line, gaining access to a domestic or international market, cutting costs, warding off competitors and sharing information. Following that, the companies commit themselves to one another, pledging to continue the business relationship (marriage). Eventually, once their objectives have been reached the companies may end their relationship with the other (divorce).

However, the companies described in the vignettes also identify the fact that buyer-seller relationships are a bit more complicated than first meets the eye. When a company-customer relationship is looked upon as a marriage this implies that the relationship is contractual, exclusive and long term. We consider these and other aspects below.

## Contractual relationship

Many business-to-business relationships and agreements are underpinned by a formal contract. However, contractual commitments have not just a legal basis, but also are symbolically important as they demonstrate commitment, often through a formal process of signing. In a marriage ceremony, the bride and groom will formally sign the marriage certificate, almost invariably in the presence of witnesses, signifying the contractual nature of a much wider relationship. If the contract is seen not just as a legal document, but as a defined framework within which the relationship operates, it can be seen that industry bodies such as the Wine Institute of New Zealand and the English Beef and Lamb Executive have clearly defined boundaries to their operations. Considering the consumer examples, customers of Tesco have to make a formal application for a Clubcard and in the process surrender their personal details in return for the discount and other benefits offered by the Clubcard. The relationship is voluntarily entered into by both parties.

### Exclusive relationship

Two partners in a marriage may be nominally monogamous, but still they may pursue extramarital sex, and sometimes they even divorce each other. Once there is marriage, the possibility of 'the pursuit of a mixed reproductive strategy' arises, meaning that a customer may be in a relationship with a certain company, while simultaneously seeking 'extramarital sex', that is, relationships with other companies (Diamond, 1992). Consumers are sometimes referred to as 'promiscuous buyers'. Particularly with no-involvement products, consumers may purchase from a portfolio of similar products while often expressing a preference for one particular brand (Knox and Walker, 2001). However, this preference does not constitute an exclusive relationship with the brand – such exclusivity is more associated with high-involvement products.

A discussion of relationship marketing as a marriage should therefore also include a discussion of adultery and the eventual breakdown – divorce – of a company-customer relationship. In fact, dissolution of a company-customer relationship could be understood as the final stage of a marriage, with the company and customer having to meet in court and arrange for a settlement.

### Long-term relationship

There are several reasons why a company would not necessarily want a long-term relationship with its suppliers or customers. For example, the company could be under pressure to create business relationships quickly, thus making maintaining and enhancing a relationship difficult. A company could also seek out one-off business deals, including deliveries of low-priced materials for its production.

Alternatively, there are mutual benefits in closer cooperation or in the development of closer ties. The concept of the network helps to explain this. The automotive industry, exemplified by Toyota and its production system, shows how suppliers are linked in close relationships referred to as tiers. First-tier suppliers provide not just components, but complete sub-assemblies of vehicles, such as engines and transmissions, braking and electrical systems. This requires close integration and longer-term commitment in order to achieve the necessary economies of scale. Other examples include such things as collaborative design and development and sharing of information systems to match supply against demand. Suppliers may even locate their production plants adjacent to their customers, representing a very high level of commitment by both parties, in order that integration and cost saving can be optimized.

It is evident within supply chains that there has been a significant trend toward reducing the number of suppliers – even to single sourcing – and concurrently for suppliers to accept more responsibility for value creation and management of behalf of their customers. Hence, such suppliers gain greater long-term assurance of business from their customer due to the high level of commitment, but in return must achieve consistently high standards and undertake more responsibility on behalf of their customers. A packaging supplier to the food industry, for example, now not only supplies containers for microwave meals, but must also accept responsibility for recipe and range development and package design.

## Managerial recommendations

Before celebrating the death of transaction marketing, caution must be exercised. Often companies are more anxious than a virgin on prom night in pressing ahead to implement fancy – and expensive – relationship marketing programmes despite the fact that not all customers want to have such a close relationship to the company (Lindgreen and Pels, 2002). A portfolio of customers requires a range of marketing solutions. What in fact results is a hybrid: a coexistence of transactional and relational relationships rather than the sole application of one or the other. Buyer-seller relationships can be considered as spanning a continuum from transactional to relational with companies occupying a position along that continuum. Companies should recognize and interpret the interaction style of their customers and adapt their own behaviour accordingly; expecting the client to change behaviour and style of business simply because the supplier would like to do so is generally an unreasonable assumption. Different types of companies have different types of practices, and some companies adopt multiple styles of relationships with their customers. Also, and as described in vignette one, there is a relationship between changes in market dynamism and the form and intensity of buyer-seller relationships. Companies routinely form, build upon, and exit relationships in response to a changing environment and changing strategic needs. The debate should therefore not be about whether to emphasize or de-emphasize relationships under certain conditions, but should rather focus on which buyer-seller relationships to invest in further or divest oneself of, and which relationships to maintain on a transactional level.

Often, companies do not give thought to such considerations. It is therefore not surprising that despite assiduous attempts to cuddle up many companies remain singles. To maintain and enhance relationships with its customers there are a number of paths that a company should follow (Hunt, 1994).

### Choosing customers selectively

It is important to consider the customer's motivation for purchase. Is there an attitudinal commitment, as exemplified by the Firstdirect vignette, or could this be mistaken for behavioural loyalty, which would need to be approached differently?

### Structuring customer relationships carefully

It is axiomatic that companies should only offer things for which the customer is prepared to pay. If the supplier enhances the offering in order to promote the quality of the relationship this may not be reciprocated by the customer who will nonetheless be happy to accept the largesse of the supplier.

### Devoting time to maintaining and enhancing customer relationships

Relational techniques such as key account management and customer relationship management provide tools that enable relationships to be effectively managed. In the worst cases these can simply become large and unwieldy repositories of data. However, as exemplified by the Tesco vignette, effective data management guides and informs the management of customer relationships as well as providing measures of performance.

### Keeping lines of communication open

In many organizations, market research has evolved into customer insight and market sensing. This entails not just passively gathering data, but interacting with, interpreting, and responding to customer and market feedback. Close customer contact is essential to maintaining the relationship. At Firstdirect, staff's interaction with customers is essential to the bank's marketing strategy; and in the case of The Fine Wine Delivery Company, customers are invited to exclusive tasting events and what they tell staff about their preferences for wines provides valuable information to the company.

## Be trustworthy

There are a number of well-defined models of business and consumer buyer behaviour. Many of these suggest what can be done to customers through a series of steps or processes, but overlook the importance of the emotional and attitudinal perceptions of the customer. When was the last time you bought something from somebody you didn't like? Trust and its reciprocal commitment are at the basis of relationships.

## Summary and final notes

This chapter has considered what is meant by the 'relationship marketing as a marriage' metaphor. The more important aspects that make the use of the marriage metaphor difficult at times were also discussed. However, other aspects were left out, including the following. Most marriages are between two partners. Typically, however, in business-to-consumer marketing a company has relationships with many customers, and in business-to-business marketing a relationship may be varied depending on whether a single individual is involved in a business transaction or several individuals are consulted before a transaction can go ahead.

Overall, if you are in business and intend to survive and to reap the benefits of your marketing investment we advocate that you give serious thought to how you can analyse, create and deliver value to your customers (Lindgreen and Wynstra, 2005). If the best way is through transaction marketing then so be it; the customers are happy, and you save from not investing in a marketing programme that would not deliver on its promises.

## References

Berry, L. L. (1983), 'Relationship marketing', in L.L. Berry, G.L. Shostack and G.D. Upah (eds), *Emerging Perspectives on Services Marketing*, Chicago: American Marketing Association, pp. 25–8.

Beverland, M. and A. Lindgreen (2004), 'Relationship use and market dynamism: a model of relationship evolution', *Journal of Marketing Management*, 20(7-8): 825–58.

Brookes, R. and R.A. Palmer (2004), *The New Global Marketing Reality*, Basingstoke: Palgrave.

Clark, M. and S. Baker (2004), *Business Success through Service Excellence*, Oxford: Elsevier.

Diamond, J. (1992), *The Rise and Fall of the Third Chimpanzee*, London: Vintage.

Dwyer, R. F., P.H. Schurr and S. Oh (1987), 'Developing buyer and seller relationships', *Journal of Marketing*, 51(2): 11–27.

Humby, C., T. Hunt and T. Phillips (2006), *Scoring Points: How Tesco is Winning Customer Loyalty*, London: Kogan Page.

Hunt, S. H. (1994), 'Seven questions for relationship marketing', *Proceedings of the Marketing Education Group Conference*, University of Ulster, July 4–6.

Knox, S. and D. Walker (2001), 'Measuring and managing brand loyalty', *Journal of Strategic Marketing*, 9(2): 111–28.

Levitt, T. (1983), 'After the sale is over', *Harvard Business Review*, 61(5): 87–93.

Lindgreen, A. (2004), 'The design, implementation, and monitoring of a CRM programme: a case study', *Marketing Intelligence & Planning*, 22(2): 160–86.

Lindgreen, A. and J. Pels (2002), 'Buyer-seller exchange situations: four empirical cases', *Journal of Relationship Marketing*, 1(3/4): 60–93.

Lindgreen, A. and F. Wynstra (2005), 'Value in business markets: what do we know? Where are we going?' *Industrial Marketing Management*, 34(7): 732–48.

Lindgreen, A., M. Antioco and M. Beverland (2003), 'Contemporary marketing practice: a research agenda and preliminary findings', *International Journal of Customer Relationship Management*, 6(1): 51–72.

Lindgreen, A., R. Palmer and J. Vanhamme (2004), 'Contemporary marketing practice: theoretical propositions and practical implications', *Marketing Intelligence & Planning*, 22(6): 673–92.

O'Malley, L. and C. Tynan (1999), 'The utility of the relationship metaphor in consumer markets: a critical evaluation', *Journal of Marketing Management*, 15(7): 587–602.

Palmer, R., D. Croston, A. Garvey and S. Mead (2006), 'Marketing of beef and lamb in England: the role of EBLEX', *British Food Journal*, 108(10): 808–23.

Palmer, R., A. Lindgreen and J. Vanhamme (2005), 'Relationship marketing: schools of thought and future research directions', *Marketing Intelligence & Planning*, 23(3): 313–30.

Tynan, C. (1997), 'A review of the marriage analogy in relationship marketing', *Journal of Marketing Management*, 13(7): 695–703.

Tynan, C. (1999), 'On metaphors, marketing and marriage', *Irish Marketing Review*, 12(1): 17–26.

## Further reading

Beverland, M. (2003), 'Organizational evolution in the Australian and New Zealand wine industry', unpublished PhD thesis, University of South Australia.

Lindgreen, A. (2000), 'The emergence and rise of relationship marketing', published PhD thesis, Cranfield University.

Palmer, R. (2001), 'A theoretical model of relationship marketing in market maturity', unpublished PhD thesis, Cranfield University.

# 13
# Products and the Life Cycle

*Roger Palmer and Adam Lindgreen*

## Introduction

It was between the First and Second World Wars that the concept of marketing first started to emerge as a business practice. This was largely with consumer goods companies such as Procter & Gamble and Lever Brothers, although the early contribution of General Motors under the guidance of Alfred Sloan also demonstrated early good marketing practice. Within these organizations, tools and techniques such as branding and product management were emerging and developing as routine business activities. Consistent with this, disposable income amongst consumers was increasing, and perhaps for the first time large numbers of people were able to buy not just what they needed, but what they wanted as well.

The classic role of the product manager was to understand current and emerging customer needs and to manage the product range in order to meet those needs and optimize profitability. This means that product managers need to initiate new product development in response to new needs, or in anticipation of creating demand for new products, and then to manage those products over the product life cycle before finally withdrawing the product. In order to manage cash flow the conventional advice is to have a number of different products at different stages of the product life cycle, and a product manager has to balance these factors using acquired skill, judgement and experience.

Over the last 20 years or so, with the emergence of relationship marketing, it has increasingly been realized that introducing more products does not necessarily result in increased sales although there are still tangible increases in cost. As competition has increased, more attention is being paid to managing not just products, but also markets and customers. As products become more similar, differentiation is achieved by other means, such as through service. Also, profitability becomes dependent on managing both product and customer profitability, using techniques such as segmentation.

The product life cycle was the focus of considerable attention and research particularly during the 1960s and 1970s. Despite the development of new perspectives of marketing such as relationship marketing and the service-dominant logic, the product life cycle remains a persistent and dominant concept in the minds of marketers.

This chapter starts by discussing the metaphor of the product life cycle and then presents two illustrative vignettes. Some of the key features illustrated by these are then discussed, and the relevance to managers is addressed. The chapter concludes with some final notes and a brief list of references and further reading.

## The metaphor

Within the management disciplines two classes of metaphors dominate the debate – military and biological. The military metaphor is used almost unconsciously, as we discuss how to 'attack competitors' and 'aggressively win market share'. Biological metaphors, however, also have a rich tradition in the areas of both business strategy and marketing. Penrose (1952) is largely credited with opening the debate when she discussed evolution with respect to the firm; this is captured in the terms 'competition' – which we regularly use as firms compete in a Darwinian sense for market space – and their '(ecological) niche' (Beverland and Lindgreen, 2004). The debate continues to this day, with the life cycle metaphor being extended to explain concepts such as recycling (Ayres, 2004).

A favourite experiment for schoolchildren in a biology class is to grow plants from seeds to flowering and senescence. At intervals, the plants are harvested and dried, and the resulting dry matter is then weighed. If the dry weight of the plants at various stages of growth is then plotted over time the result is a life cycle. Virtually all biological organisms can be described in this way, from bacteria living just an hour or two to a Redwood Sequoia surviving for several thousand years. With the only certainties in life being taxes and death, as they say, we too conform to this phenomenon.

The product life cycle is perhaps one of the most widely used metaphors in marketing. It is discussed in virtually every textbook, and it serves as a model or framework by which managers can understand how products progress in the market place. Very few products actually

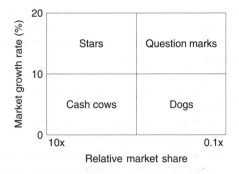

*Figure 13.1* The Boston matrix

conform to the smooth S-curved shape used in diagrams, but it is a powerful aid to assist managers in understanding the complexities of products and markets.

The concept of the product life cycle is also incorporated into other tools, most notably the share-growth or Boston matrix (Figure 13.1), and it is also fundamental to the concept of economies of scale. This suggests that as the total number of units produced increases, there is the opportunity to reduce the cost of each unit by spreading fixed costs more widely, buying more effectively, and improving the economics of production. This could perhaps be achieved by moving from batch production to mass production, and finding savings in other areas such as logistics. Hence the Boston matrix uses relative market share on the horizontal axis, and the rate of market growth on the vertical axis, resulting in the four well-known boxes on the matrix: question marks or problem children, stars, cash cows and dogs. These boxes relate to the four stages of the product life cycle respectively: introduction, growth, maturity and decline. The Boston matrix is often used to suggest strategies, such as milking cash cows or eliminating dogs, but this has hazards for the unwary, which are discussed later.

In the following, two vignettes illustrate and exemplify the above mentioned aspects of the product life cycle, thereby bringing in-depth meaning to the metaphor.

## Vignettes

### Vignette one

In 1979, Sony introduced the first of the groundbreaking Walkman range of products, thus opening up what might be termed the mobile music category. First utilizing cassette tapes and later CDs, which were introduced in the early 1990s, some models also incorporated radios to provide a wider range of benefits. The emergence of digital technology and the accelerating pace of change, however, generated new opportunities in this market space. Sony surrendered its dominance of this category to Apple at the start of the new millennium when the latter introduced the iPod.

Before the advent of the iPod, downloading music from the internet and preparing CDs required a degree of technical expertise, as well as being legally questionable. Spotting this trend and recognizing the problem that its popular desktop computer of the time did not have a CD capability, Apple developed the iPod together with the iTunes website. This made it easy and simple for consumers not only to download, store and play their music, but to do so legally and at a modest price. In October 2001, Apple introduced the 5-GByte iPod to the US market at a price of $US399. The stylish design and ease and simplicity of use quickly turned the product into a must-have fashion accessory. Six months later, the 10-GByte version came to the market at a price of $US499, and the price of the original music player dropped to $299. Every few months after this saw the introduction of either a slightly larger machine or a different version, perhaps one suited to displaying photographs as well as playing music, or a very small and much lower-cost version, such as the iPod Shuffle. With the introduction of each new product, the price of the previous version was usually revised downwards.

The pace of innovation and development has continued, with the much anticipated introduction of the iPhone in the US on 29 June 2007. The iPhone not only plays music, but as its name implies has much extended capability. Such is the success of the product that a million units were sold within a couple of months of launch. Originally priced at $US599, within two months the price came down to $US399, coinciding with the launch of another Apple product, the iPod Touch. So annoyed were the original purchasers of the iPhone that Steve Jobs, the Apple CEO, quickly apologized to customers and arranged for a $US100 credit for the disgruntled purchasers, which could be spent at Apple stores. Apple is now beginning to offer video and TV content as part of its product offering, and it remains to be seen how this will be accepted and developed in the market place.

### Vignette two

The name of Christopher Sholes is perhaps not one that is immediately recognized by many, but his contribution to business life was groundbreaking. His invention – the typewriter – was marketed by Remington, originally armament and sewing-machine manufacturers, in 1873. Later developments included the typewriter ribbon, a thin strip of material impregnated with ink; this was struck by a moving arm, the tip of which had the impression of a letter on it. The typewriter keyboard activated the many arms necessary in order to reproduce the alphabet and punctuation marks, from 1878 in both upper and lower case. Operators soon became efficient at the use of the typewriter, causing the arms to collide and jam the mechanism. This was resolved by the introduction of the now familiar QWERTY keyboard, which was originally intended to slow down the speed at which the typist could enter data and thus avoid the jamming problem. By the 1880s, two competitors had entered the market – Calligraph and Hammond. By the 1890s, they were joined by Smith Premiers, Denmores and Yosts as the market continued to expand. Technical developments continued to improve performance and ease of use, and in the 1920s the market consolidated to four major manufacturers: the original Remington company, together with Underwood, Royal and Smith-Corona, each having about an equal market share.

The original typewriters were very substantially built, with a cast-iron frame and the paper wound round a carriage. As the key was depressed, the carriage moved to the left the equivalent of one letter width in order to produce the appropriate spacing. The next major technical development was by IBM (originally International Business Machines) who introduced the 'golfball' typewriter in the early 1960s. The letters were contained around a small sphere and rather than the carriage moving the sphere or golfball moved instead. The IBM Selectric was also electrically powered, making it much easier to use.

The first word processors for office use were introduced in the early 1980s, and the first word-processing program, WordStar, appeared in 1979. From that point, typewriters rapidly disappeared from offices and are now museum pieces. By the mid-1980s, WordStar was the dominant word-processing software despite its awkward screen commands; instructions to alter the nature of the text had to be entered as commands in text format on the screen. The program was superseded by WordPerfect and then Microsoft Word, which allow the now ubiquitous WYSIWYG facility ('What You See Is What You Get'). With the coming of age of open source software, it is now possible to download fully functional word processing, indeed suites of commonly used office software, effectively free of charge. The Openoffice software suite contains the usual range of office applications and is based on the StarOffice suite of software owned by Sun Microsystems. In June 2000, the software was made 'open source', enabling enthusiasts and independent software writers to enhance the program, which is now provided free of charge (see www.openoffice.org).

## Discussion of vignettes

### Product life cycles and technology life cycles

The two vignettes illustrate a number of interesting characteristics concerning the product life cycle. Perhaps one of the most striking of these is the role of technology. As can be seen from both the example of the iPod and the typewriter, technological developments make product innovation possible. However, technologies are not of themselves new products. It is the application of the technology to features of the product that makes the upgraded product valuable to customers. Hence the technology life cycle mirrors and leads the product life cycle. The typewriter enjoyed a remarkably long life cycle, but rapidly disappeared as the application of computer technology to word processing replaced it. By contrast, Apple innovates rapidly and almost makes its own products obsolete. In fact, Steve Jobs has been quoted as saying that he would rather compete with himself than with others in the market. The furore that accompanied the reduction in price of the iPhone suggests that it is possible to innovate too quickly with respect to the needs of the market. This illustrates something that managers intuitively understand, that is, that life cycles are getting shorter as technology enables more and different products. The original typewriter had a life cycle measured in decades; the iPhone lasted only two months before the price element of the marketing mix was changed.

### Level playing field

Products do not operate in markets in isolation and whilst the product life cycle might be used with respect to a product, managers should be aware that there are wider issues that impact on product success. A factor that is increasingly important, due to the influence of technology, is the adoption of standards that create a 'level playing field'. If we continue the biological metaphor the term 'environment' could apply. When originally introduced, the typewriter went through a period of early market development, as the problem of efficient operators causing the actuating arms to jam became apparent. This resulted in the development of the QWERTY keyboard now standard in many markets despite the fact that it was deliberately designed to be awkward to use. In the 1930s, the Dvorak keyboard was developed on the basis of efficiency studies, but despite its potential benefits it has failed to usurp the original keyboard.

## Protocols and standards

The development of standards is an interesting example of how companies cooperate in order to compete: once protocols are established, customers feel confident to commit to purchase, which can presage rapid growth in sales. Sony has lost out in the marketplace to Apple and is criticized for its commitment to technological innovation rather than responding to and driving market growth. The current battle in high density video format, with Sony strongly promoting its Blu Ray technology, has led to uncertainty on behalf of consumers reluctant to commit to one or other of the competing technologies, which may subsequently be rendered obsolete; at this time, Sony seems to have won the day. Previous technologies such as the CP/M operating system, the eight track cartridge, Betamax video, and the digital audio tape (DAT) have all been superseded. As the PC market demonstrates, the adoption of the IBM standard for PCs, together with the Microsoft operating system, led to rapid market growth.

## Price skimming and penetration pricing

As the market develops and expands, it becomes more attractive to other potential competitors. A growth market is often characterized by new market entrants. The typewriter example shows how an attractive market drew in new players. As volume builds, there is also the opportunity for economies of scale. As the cost of production decreases, there is the opportunity to reduce price, which in turn generates higher volumes, as the product becomes more attractive. As the example of the iPhone demonstrates, the price reduction may be early and rapid, leading to dramatic market growth. Apple sold one million iPhones in the two months following its launch, and is planning on sales of 10 million in the first year. The opportunity to manage price can be a critical competitive factor. Keeping the price high – what is known as price skimming – gives high margins and a much earlier return on the investment in new products. By contrast, dramatic and early price reductions – what is known as penetration pricing – gives early and rapid gains in both volume and market share and can lead to a low-cost position in the market. If costs are sufficiently low this can give a high level of competitive advantage, as it means that competitors simply cannot compete or even contemplate entering the market – would, for example, anybody like to compete on price with Ryanair?

## Disappearing products

Inevitably, market growth will slow, as the market becomes mature. It can be difficult to determine this point due to the interaction between price and volume, but with maturity there comes a rationalization of competitors. The typewriter market in the 1930s, for example, shrank to four major competitors with roughly equal market shares. Finally, as the market declines, volume and profitability reduce significantly and the industry is left with perhaps one or two competitors who provide maintenance or replacement volumes of product, or indeed can disappear completely. Mechanical typewriters, together with thermionic radio valves, shoe-trees, steam trains and black-and-white televisions are just some of the products that have been superseded.

## Product classes and subclasses

The concept of the product life cycle helps to explain and make sense of these sometimes complex and dramatic market developments. With this in mind there have been many attempts to develop the concept into a practical management tool. However, this has posed a number of sometimes quite intractable problems. As has already been mentioned, there are four stages usually associated with a life cycle, but there is no clear and distinct cut-off between the stages, and it is only really with hindsight that these can be ascertained. It is also necessary to be clear as to what is known as the unit of analysis. The second vignette discusses typewriters, but within that class of products there are numerous subclasses. The very earliest machines wrote only in capital letters, and it was some time before 'overstrike' machines superseded 'understrike' typewriters. This refers to the way in which the actuating arm strikes the paper. With understrike machines the operator could not see what was being typed without lifting the carriage, a problem overcome by the introduction of overstrike products. So when considering life cycles what exactly are we talking about? With regard to the class of products called typewriters there might be particular types of typewriters, but, of course, we should not confuse these types with brands. A brand can have a continuing life, whilst products sold under the brand can be constantly changed, repositioned and reinvented. The Sony Walkman brand was applied to many different types of products. Coca-Cola may be a global brand, but hundreds of product and flavour variants are sold under that brand name.

## Marketing as a science

There was a view prevalent, particularly in the 1960s, that marketing could be treated as a science. In other words, that marketing expenditure could be directly related to sales results, and that it would be possible to predict how the amount and nature of marketing spend would result in financial benefits to the firm. Prodigious effort was made by researchers trying to analyse the product life cycle in order that marketing expenditure could be tracked through to financial results. This resulted in all sorts of classification schemes for product life cycles, as well as much mathematical modelling in an attempt to take the abstract concept of the product life cycle and turn it into a managerial tool that could predict the outcome of various expenditures.

It should, however, be borne in mind that the product life cycle has only two variables – time on the horizontal axis and some form of measure of sales or growth on the vertical axis. We live in a world that is sufficiently complicated that it is very difficult to reduce it to two simplistic measures. One article on the subject noted that 'the 23 variables … are not intended to be exhaustive [but] the starting point for further [work']' (Rink and Swan, 1979). This rather begs the question of how many variables will be 'exhaustive' in an attempt to mathematically model the ultimately random nature of markets.

## Managerial recommendations

From the previous discussion we can understand that managers can use the concept of the product life cycle as a way of understanding in general how products might perform in markets. In other words, it is a descriptive tool, but it should not be regarded as a predictive tool. It cannot help us to understand what will happen in the future, and it should be used not as a basis for decision-making but as an aid to analysis. Deciding to stop advertising because we think that sales will decline in the future could just cause that to happen!

With the Boston matrix, derived from the product life cycle, it is quite common to see strategies ascribed to each box of the matrix. It is now almost part of management folklore that 'dog' products should be eliminated from the range, yet products can be revived and reinvigorated by insightful marketing, and with proper evaluation dog products could be much more useful than the simple prescriptive strategy of the Boston matrix implies. It seems implausible that all the permutations and possibilities for marketing with a multitude of product and market combinations can be reduced to a series of simple 2 × 2 matrices and one-line strategies.

The four stages of the product life cycle – introduction, growth, maturity and decline – would suggest that at each stage different decisions need to be made consistent with the overall strategic objectives. The role of price has already been discussed, but the other elements of the marketing mix (product, place and promotion, or more) can also be managed. The example of Apple shows how products (that is, product) are successively introduced in order to maintain sales, optimize margins and to stay ahead of competitors. Similarly, as markets mature, products tend to become more similar, referred to as product parity. The power of the brand (promotion) or dominance of distribution channels (place) provide us with the means by which we can differentiate our product on something other than price.

When considering the product life cycle the following particular points should be taken into account.

### Prescription and prediction

Each firm and product is different, and managers should use the product life cycle to assist in their understanding and then develop their own, unique solution, thereby avoiding the blanket application of a generic strategy.

### Current status

It is only apparent with the benefit of hindsight where the product is on the life cycle and at which stage. The transition between stages is also difficult to determine.

### New products

The product life cycle, together with its derivative the Boston matrix, tends to overemphasize the importance of new product introductions against the importance of managing volume against price in order to optimize margins and product life. Over the life cycle, products have to recover the cost of development and introduction and to create the revenue to offset the costs of marketing; also, it is often only in the later stages of marketing that the product is cash positive, generating free cash flow for investment. Hence maintaining products and increasing their life can be disproportionately profitable.

### Definitions

There are interesting discussions to be had as to what is meant by the product in terms of the unit of analysis. Also, there needs to be consideration as to the nature of the market. To take a product focus could lead us to think that we are in, for example, the mobile phone market which might mean that the threat from the iPod is ignored. This is a form of myopia that is encouraged by a narrow interpretation bounded within our thinking of what constitutes the product life cycle. The product life cycle, although ubiquitous in management thinking, is just one way of understanding the interaction between products and markets.

## Final notes

The difficulty of the managerial application of the product life cycle is illustrated by two famous articles by leading marketing authors. In 1965, Levitt published in *Harvard Business Review* an article entitled 'Exploit the product life cycle'. In 1976, in the same highly respected management journal Dhalla and Yuspeh published their article 'Forget the product life cycle concept!' Of course, knowledge progresses and nobody can make an absolute claim to the truth, but interestingly both articles referred to the same company and the same product – DuPont and its product nylon – to justify their arguments. Levitt presents a detailed analysis of how the life cycle can be used as a tool to formulate and drive business strategy, together with an extensive analysis of sales of nylon to support his argument. By contrast, Dhalla and Yuspeh in their article say that 'there are several cases of companies that have ignored the PLC concept and achieved great success through imaginative marketing strategies. The classic example of the 1940s and 50s is DuPont nylon.'

Managers should be wary of the literal and simplistic acceptance of the product life cycle. It is hoped that this review of products and the life cycle and the discussion of some of the associated issues of which managers need to be aware have helped toward a clearer understanding of what we know of this very famous metaphor in marketing.

## References

Ayres, R. U. (2004), 'On the life cycle metaphor: where ecology and economics diverge', *Ecological Economics*, 48(4): 425–38.

Beverland, M. and A. Lindgreen (2004), 'Relationship use and market dynamism: a model of relationship evolution', *Journal of Marketing Management*, 20(7–8): 825–58.

Dhalla, N. K. and S. Yuspeh (1976), 'Forget the product life cycle concept', *Harvard Business Review*, 54, January–February: 102–12.

Levitt, T. (1965), 'Exploit the product life cycle', *Harvard Business Review*, 43, November–December: 81–94.

Penrose, E. T. (1952), 'Biological analogies in the theory of the firm', *American Economic Review*, 42: 804–19.

Rink, D. R. and J. E. Swan (1979), 'Product life cycle research: a literature review', *Journal of Business Research*, 7(3): 219–42.

## Further reading

Avlonitis, G. J. (1985), 'Product elimination decision making: does formality matter?' *Journal of Marketing*, 49(1): 41–52.

Berenson, C. and I. Mohr-Jackson (1994), 'Product rejuvenation: a less risky alternative to product innovation', *Business Horizons*, 37(6): 51–7.

Berkowitz, K. and H. Rudelius (1986), 'Managing the product, times', *Marketing*, Mosly College Publishing: 253–81.

Lambkin, M. and G. Day (1984), 'Evolutionary processes in competitive markets: beyond the product life cycle', *Journal of Marketing*, 53, July: 4–20.

Shipley, D. (1998), 'Marketing strategies for growth, maturity and decline', in C. Egan and M.J. Thomas (eds), *The CIM Handbook of Strategic Marketing: a Practical Guide for Designing and Implementing Effective Marketing Strategies*, Oxford: Butterworth-Heinemann, pp. 48–60.

Wind, Y. and J. Claycamp (1976), 'Planning product line strategy: a matrix approach', *Journal of Marketing*, 40(1): 2–9.

Wood, L. (1990), 'The end of the product life cycle? Education says goodbye to an old friend', *Journal of Marketing Management*, 6(2): 145–55.

# 14
# Don't Blame it on the Metaphor: Marketing, Metaphors and Metamorphosis in the Internal Market

*Ian Buckingham*

> 'We've reached a critical point of inflection in the war for talent and it's now time for a paradigm shift if we're to dominate the moral high ground.'
>
> (OD Director, UK Financial Services)

I met the person who came out with this sentence a couple of years ago – to spare his blushes, let's call him Babel. He proudly wore the label 'Head of Organization Development' and worked for a web-based financial services firm which had a reputation for funky marketing. He represented a truly maverick brand, much heralded for its iconoclastic, irreverent approach but which, unfortunately, also had an alternative financial performance record. I would show you a copy of their 'strategy on a single page' if I could, but suffice to say, looking at it for the first time was rather like being a Victorian explorer faced with a hieroglyphic carving on a stone tablet. This A4 tablet was packed with symbols and acronyms which might as well have been runes and had so many mixed metaphors that it looked as though it had been chiselled by an army of schizophrenic stonemasons.

He talked proudly of their collaborations with a series of specialist management gurus – although for collaboration read abdication. The 'tablet' said everything and nothing. The metaphors and figures of speech weren't wrong, the problem was that they were overcrowded and horribly out of context. His team had absorbed key thinking indiscriminately and were feverishly attempting to align their passionate but rather confused employees behind their chaotic OD strategy. In the meantime, they were wrestling with their senior leaders, puzzled by the absence of early adopters in the top team.

Sadly, Babel-speak, as it came to be known, became so infamous that the employees invented a game which they came to call BS Bingo. An enterprising cultural guerilla had created a spreadsheet populated by the most infamous and prevalent metaphors being perpetuated by Mr Babel and his team. On the increasingly popular internal communication black market, he offered a financial incentive for his contemporaries to seek out, cite and mark off those metaphors appearing in officially sanctioned communication within a given period of time. The first to spot and report back a 'full house' of BS metaphors within that period was awarded the BS Bingo prize. Needless to say, you were at a distinct advantage if you were a middle manager and attended the Babel-sanctioned conferences and engagement events.

Two years on and Babel left to start up his own consultancy. This has since folded, unfortunately. The funky financial services company has just been sold by its parents after years of underperformance and the OD and communication team was severely 'right-sized' a year ago. It didn't have to be that way as they had some very good ideas. Passionate as they were, they were seduced by compulsive creativity; they took for granted or obfuscated the obvious and forgot to deliver the basics consistently well. They lost their audience in a mist of purple prose. It will come as little surprise that external customer satisfaction statistics suffered during Babel's tenure. I've seen few more compelling arguments for the power of language as an influence on the brand and the bottom line.

As we all know, a metaphor is a linguistic tool, a figure of speech that uses one thing to mean another and makes a comparison between the two. At their best metaphors add a powerful dimension to communication by conjuring up imagery which, in turn, evokes emotions that help with understanding, empathy and impact. Used properly, they help to transform our understanding by evoking a sensory dimension that brings words to life. But in my experience as someone who has consulted on internal communication and change management across industries, more often than not, metaphors are more abused than well used in the internal communication market, not because they're ignored in favour of a dull relay of facts (although that does happen as well), but because communications largely either become tied up in organizational politics or the user simply fails to differentiate between internal and external markets.

The organization in question employed metaphor extensively. It was at the very heart of their brand. But obsessed with being different in a fairly undifferentiated market, they lost touch with their core internal culture. They forgot that, despite their rebellious brand proposition, their people needed clarity and to be properly engaged with the goals and culture of the business if they were to deliver. In pursuit of the more maverick qualities associated with innovation they also lost touch with one of the defining features of an organization, namely that effective communication demands a clear structure, a form of discipline that helps it to become customer- rather than initiator-centric.

Without an explicit understanding of the need for a consistent language to support a balanced set of values, being different became more important than being effective. Rather than involve employees in the creation of their communication, they 'cherry-picked' it from the far flung fields of prevailing, pan-industry management lore. In the process, they became confused about the core tenets of their brand (as it manifested itself internally and externally) and the internal communication which resulted made their standard discourse very confusing.

Obviously metaphors aren't the only linguistic tools at the disposal of the internal communication market. To enhance the quality of writing, effective communicators call upon the more explicit simile, also called an open comparison and prefaced with 'like' or 'as' within the phrase, or the analogy, which shows similarity between things that might initially seem different. Analogy in particular is often used to help provide insight by comparing an unknown subject to one that is more familiar (useful in complex business environments or in unnerving change management scenarios). It can also show a relationship between pairs of things and is useful for illustrating points and adding interest to otherwise dry subjects. The most effective use of these communication tools is within the creative and engaging disciplines of storytelling where we expect to suspend disbelief as our innate understanding of the rules and rhythms elicits a learned response – so long as the story is correctly signposted of course. Abused, however, these communication tools and devices only serve to make the communication problem worse.

To get some idea of typical use and abuse, Figure 14.1 shows a sample, collected over six months, of some of the stand-out headlines from the mainstream internal communication stemming from the newsrooms of around ten organizations from six different business sectors. The sample includes verbal and written communication aimed at a variety of internal stakeholders. I've arranged the most commonly recurring outputs into four simple categories.

Have a look at them, think about your own company and indulge yourself in your own version of BS bingo for a moment.

Interestingly, what I've termed emotional references were the rarest. This does seem to support the point that communicators adopt macho,

| **Macho/Militaristic:** get in the game, play the game, lead the game; take the moral high ground; align the troops; customer champion; war for talent; cutting/bleeding/ leading edge; focus campaign; burning platform; tanks on our lawn; rearguard action to fight off the acquisition; vulnerable to predation; search for the hero campaign; dog eat dog | **Emotional:** bleeding heart; change and the stages of grief; capturing hearts and minds; love the customer |
|---|---|
| **Elemental:** seismic shift; critical point of inflection; the change process downstream; in rhythms with seasonal trading patterns; upstream ideas; sands of change; milestone on the change journey; natural point of inflection; magic dust of innovation; firestarter; paradigm shift | **Biological:** the project life cycle; turning hierarchy on its head; staff are the eyes and ears of the business; project planning season; appraisal season; stomach for change; appetite for change; have a heart campaign |

*Figure 14.1* 'BS Bingo' matrix

clichéd, de-personalized metaphors and motifs more readily. In *Brand Engagement* (Buckingham, 2007), in the context of the drive for authenticity as a way of engaging with employees, I make the point that 'emotions are unpredictable, can be difficult to control and therefore are potentially threatening to a leadership trying to maximise performance'. In light of the modest piece of research detailed above, I believe that sensitive, nurturing emotional metaphors are in the minority because communicators feel that there is:

1. A form of macho management parlance that, irrespective of industry, is a perceived mark of belonging to the management cadre (the political perspective), and
2. That emotional references are either seen as inappropriate or too exposing (they reveal too much about what the communicator really feels).

I don't believe that this is necessarily a sexist observation (nearly 70 per cent of the communicators in this mini survey are female), but I do strongly believe that these factors are key inhibitors of employee engagement and act as a barrier to authentic communication, which is, conversely, one of the cornerstones of effective internal communication.

These two factors aside, the metaphor suite adds colour, interest and vibrancy and undoubtedly helps to nudge communication up the employee engagement continuum, if used appropriately. Overused, clumsily applied or worse still, used cynically or in the wrong context, the metaphor suite becomes synonymous with laziness, deviousness, incompetence and patronizing management speak. This type of abuse manifests itself within the internal market as communication that is 'too clever by half'. It is characterized by insincerity and spin.

Regardless of industry or sector, in my experience, employee surveys very frequently highlight the proliferation of what is generalized as 'management speak', including the abuse of metaphors, figures of speech and acronyms. They tell of how they find this irritating and distracting at the very least and potentially hugely disruptive. It slowly poisons brands from within by misrepresenting and adversely affecting the true internal culture and, far from helping bring them closer together, acts as a barrier to relationships between employees and leaders. But other than providing the equivalent of internal dictionaries to de-code the most commonly used examples (yes, a number of organizations I've worked with, despite protestations to the contrary, have actually invested significant funds this way), skills-development activity geared towards the understanding, creation and application of a common and appropriate internal language is extremely rare. Culture development initiatives are probably the closest most professionals come to broaching this issue as part of a wider investigation into traits, norms, mores, common values and behavioural drivers of performance. The reality is that understanding and reflecting the prevailing linguistic norms is an implied right of passage into the managerial suite in most businesses and is therefore something of an ordeal.

For many years, internal communication was seen as an off-shoot of marketing and largely reported to the marketing head. Recent evidence suggests that corporate communication and, rightly or wrongly, HR are starting to assume increasing responsibility for employee engagement (see the Melcrum study in Buckingham, 2007). This subtle power struggle is a sign that internal communication is gradually gaining increased status, as the importance of employees as deliverers of the promises made by brands via marketing receives increasing recognition. It may also be a signal that the marketing function lacks the appetite and aptitude to influence the internal market appropriately.

Whilst there are clear similarities between the internal and external communication markets, especially in industries where the distinction between customers and staff is blurred, the internal market differs from the customer-facing market in a significant number of ways. This means that a blanket approach to communication based upon the use of marketing methodology is essentially a flawed model. Employees are more savvy, more informed and more innately cynical than customers. They literally know the product inside out and, more importantly, understand and control the means of production. They also have a feel for the core values and motives of the business owners and managers. They demand greater authenticity in internal communication which has implications for the use of metaphor.

Employees have to be engaged with the aims, objectives, values and methodologies of the business if they're to be truly effective and, in turn, they need to be convinced and entertained if they're to be truly engaged. It's a very old-fashioned view to believe that, in today's society, liberated by freedom of expression and access to powerful sources of information, employees can be won over by PR, coerced, cajoled or conscripted. They can't be adequately engaged through repetition of marketing campaigns for customers re-run for internal audiences. Employees increasingly demand that they be consulted and involved. Yet employee focus groups in general have yet to attain the same status or level of sophistication as those developed for customers.

There's nothing innately wrong with the list of colourful language, peppered with metaphor, simile and analogy, gathered during our brief period of research. Clearly some of it works as it is fit for purpose within the culture in which it is prevalent. But in my view the most common mistakes organizations make when adopting the metaphor suite as a hopeful route to metamorphosis are:

1. Failure to fully understand the prevailing culture.
2. Adopting a 'one size fits all strategy' to both internal and external communication and for different parts of the business.
3. Focusing on push rather than pull communication as a result of lack of employee involvement.
4. Not recognizing that excessive differentiation and over-elaboration is most likely to be a signal of lack of confidence rather than an absence of competence.

I'll illustrate these points with reference to another client, a major UK retailer. The company in question is a multi-site international retail firm. Their business strategy is reliant upon just-in-time supply chain management and the provision of a 'no frills' customer service experience in return for low retail prices, their key differentiator in the market. They have traditionally viewed their staff as relatively poorly skilled manual workers; corporate assets operating clearly defined processes. Communication was traditionally of the push variety and followed the same patterns, metaphors and motifs as customer communication (for example, campaigns to be 'first choice', 'unbeaten on price'), centrally-designed campaigns with clear benefits for the company itself, based around product and process awareness and complete with foolproof instructions prescribed by central dictat. There was very little two-way communication, no iteration of a central story or journey, little effort invested in engagement skills training for managers, extremely little communicated about the importance of employees to the business, and supervisor and all real employee consultation was undertaken formally through trade union representatives.

The communication system was clearly entrenched in a hierarchical, bureaucratic, tell and sell model punctuated by quirky campaigns at the expense of engagement based upon intimacy, legacy and relationships. And for a long time it worked relatively well. But in more recent years the leadership began to notice a rise in absenteeism, higher employee turnover and an absence of innovation and new ideas. Not only were they missing out on creative opportunities (why should staff volunteer new ways when they were treated like faceless numbers?), but employee feedback was dammed behind walls of due process. Before they could address the problem the communication dam burst and at the worst possible time – the lead-up to the festive season.

Partly driven by changes to legislation, partly by an internal drive for change, the organization was forced to renegotiate the staff terms and conditions of employment. Owing to the inflexibility of the existing system, they elected to take a campaign approach, reiterating the benefits of the changes via a poster and presentation promotional campaign, rather in the way that they would sell new lines or seasonal furniture. In the background they attempted to thrash out a deal with the unions.

Relationships quickly locked into a power struggle between managers, staff and unions. Supervisors were powerless to translate what was happening for staff as they had neither the true context, mandate, confidence or competence, nor the breadth of vision, and the organization fast approached a retailing meltdown at their most important trading time. There were a number of factors, but the root cause was an outmoded approach to communication. The poster campaign was highlighted as the catalyst, the classic step too far. It was clearly employing customer sales techniques which the staff were very familiar with, including clumsy metaphors to sell the benefits to staff. Almost too well trained in the basic tenets of marketing, staff understood that they were being manipulated and were suspicious of the motives of the management, were insulted by the underlying conceit and were understandably more concerned about what they saw as a threat to their fundamental rights and privileges than the cleverness of the internal campaign.

The approach taken to resolve this deadlock, was to enlist the help of independent, professional third parties, quickly to gather information about the root cause of the issue and then to shift instantly out of spoon-fed solution mode and enter into genuine consultation with their employees rather than their formal representative bodies. Backed by these findings, the leadership team sanctioned a complete overhaul of the communication infrastructure from the overarching strategy through to what they actually called point of sale, tactical communication materials:

- A consultation forum was established which included a full cross-section of employees.
- A full-time, professional and specialist internal communication manager was appointed.
- Work was undertaken with the top team to develop an inspirational vision (in consultation with the employee forum) and a route map which paid homage to past achievements and looked to the future.
- The vision was built around the core brand values of the business which became the cornerstone metaphors for the communication strategy.
- Look, feel and tone of voice was carefully influenced to focus on nurturing and to stress appreciative insights rather than criticism.
- Although the centre maintained a coordinating and strategic role, regional and site-specific communication functions were established to add local colour and flavour to communication.
- Tactical in-store communication was changed to predominantly face to face and an emphasis placed on two-way communication.
- Supervisors received engagement skills development training.
- New measurement systems were introduced to obtain employee feedback on a more consistent and regular basis.

Only when this proposed programme of fundamental changes was developed and the commitment of the senior leadership obtained were the employees ready to listen to the rationale behind and details of the amendments to their terms and conditions. The ultimate irony is that the changes were genuinely beneficial to both parties.

This case illustrates a great many things but of most relevance to the core thesis of this book is the power of metaphor and the need for communicators to differentiate between internal and external markets when applying classic marketing techniques.

## The importance of the story

Moyers: Do you see some new metaphors emerging in a modern medium for the old universal truths?
Campbell: I see the possibility of new metaphors, but I don't see that they have become mythological yet.

(Campbell, 1988)

A great deal of internal communication, rather like a lot of marketing, is obsessed with tactical, campaign-think. As a result, the cracks show in the joins between creative campaigns and the proliferation of mixed metaphors becomes a signal of an absence of a coordinating overview. Campaigns and tools are interesting because they're new, they're gimmicky, they're bite-size and give the impression of deliverables, of activity. The same can be said for funkily-named projects (Phoenix, D-day, Iron Mask and Zenda are a few of my current favourites). Stand-out terminology and phraseology is fine but unless the project team is complementing rather than competing with their peers on the overall critical path, is their unique form of expression really of any pragmatic use? In my experience, a lot more time should be spent on making the communication grounded, connected and engaging, there should be more focus on quality and a lot less on diversity and quantity.

The ancient communication art of storytelling has ironically emerged in recent years as a way of fulfilling the demanding internal communication brief. Pre-dating writing, as it does, storytelling comes with a set of rules we're all instinctively familiar with, including the creative use of the metaphor and myth.

The extensive body of work by mythologist and master storyteller Joseph Campbell, for example, teaches important lessons about the universality of storytelling patterns. One of his defining achievements is his work concerning the monomyth, in which he represents a storytelling blueprint as the journey of the hero, representing Everyman, and which occurs in three distinct phases:

- departure
- initiation, and
- return

Campbell has provided compelling cross-cultural evidence that we are all attuned to these essential storytelling patterns and conceits through our innate understanding of and need for mythology and that we have an innate craving for these patterns in our most important communication. In contemporary times, this certainly includes communication in the workplace. A basic understanding of these patterns is important to the properly contextualized use of metaphor in internal communication as it can be a powerful way of developing, relaying and sharing:

- the **Outer Story** (the corporate vision, mission, values, direction, plan and strategy)
- the **Inner Story** (fit with individual goals, ambitions, values, hopes and fears)
- the **Connected Story** (how employees embrace and are delivering the promises made by the brand)

It requires genuine engagement to make this happen and avoid the confused and disjointed story; the clichéd story or the power play. That's what Campbell alludes to when he says 'I see the possibility of new metaphors, but I don't see that they have become mythological yet?'

For some time now I've been making the point that the key communicators in any business aren't the heroic figureheads (see Buckingham and Kitchen, 2005), but the line managers and supervisors, what I call 'chief engagement officers' (ceos). It is this community who are the workaday custodians of the internal manifestation of the brand; it is they who are responsible for customer service, employee engagement and delivery of bottom line results. They also tend to be the population who are most objective and open to skills development, feedback and support.

Along with my colleagues at the Bring Yourself 2 Work Fellowship, I've broken down the key components of the ceo engagement skills profile (see Figure 14.2). Within a storytelling and experiential learning framework we've developed a number of bespoke skills development programmes for organizations including BP, Shell and Ernst and Young, which include an exploration of the power of figures of speech and, indeed, metaphor in pursuit of enhanced business performance. The programmes have been received with a great deal of humour, genuine engagement and not a small amount of relief.

I wouldn't quite describe it as an epidemic but the sublimation of engaging communication into intimidating and confusing corporate-speak is certainly an illness to which we're all susceptible. But the

*Figure 14.2*   Profile of a 'chief engagement officer'

proliferation of purple prose, whether in written or spoken form, should be recognized for what it is – the indefatigable creative spirit bursting free from the corporate straitjacket. Creativity should be encouraged as a driver of expression, involvement, innovation and engagement but it shouldn't be at the expense of understanding or business performance. In an increasingly competitive and confusing corporate environment where the management of the brand from within becomes an imperative, engagement skills are increasingly important within businesses and can be greatly enhanced with a little gentle guidance in the right areas. As I said at the beginning, the metaphors themselves aren't to blame.

## References

Buckingham, Ian (2007), *Brand Engagement: How Employees Make or Break Brands*, Basingstoke: Palgrave Macmillan.
Buckingham, Ian and Philip Kitchen (2005), 'Who is responsible for corporate communications?' *Admap*, July/August, www.by2w.co.uk.
Campbell, Joseph (1988), *The Power of Myth*, New York: Doubleday.

# 15
# Marketing, Metaphors and Metamorphosis: Marketing Management as a Caring Profession

*Michael Thomas*

METAMORPHOSIS: change of form or character. In this chapter I want to speculate about the possibility, the likelihood, that the profession of marketing will move away from its image of being the last resort of hucksters, carpetbaggers, snake-oil salesmen and second-hand car dealers, to the status of a profession, with acknowledged standards of conduct, even its own equivalent of the Hippocratic oath.

I am going to examine matters that must exercise the minds of all management professionals and especially management educators. Educators must speculate continuously about how management can be made to function more effectively and more efficiently. The world is metamorphosizing as we speak. Current changes in the balance of world economic power, instantaneous global communications, and global terrorism are all developments requiring us to think about the system in which marketing management functions, namely market-driven capitalism.

We are in the midst of what Francis Fukuyama called the 'Great Disruption' (Fukuyama, 2000). Globalization is made possible by technology, worldwide systems of monetary exchange, trade and marketing. Information technology places space-time-place relations in great flux – we have yet to grasp the scope of this disruption. The Marxist view of paradise is totally discredited, we observe a world in thrall to market capitalism, but my fear is that we are all the sightless psychopaths of market forces (Ascherson, 1999). People, places, states and phenomena are all potentially interrelated and interdependent. We know that consumer choice is influenced by cultural values and life-styles, and that in the current dialogue, consumer choice is equated with human freedom. But, especially since 9/11 (the terrorist attacks on the USA), and 7/7 (the terrorist attacks on London) a dark cloud hangs over the world. It is the fundamentalist, radical challenge to the system dominated by market-driven capitalism. It represents a challenge to progress, to the very values upon which our economic world is built. This suggests to me at least three questions that need to be explored.

1. *Consumer freedom of choice is a cornerstone of the marketing philosophy upon which our empires are built. Is this concept a dishonest invention of marketers, a device merely for justifying our manipulations?*
   Probably less than one-fifth of the world's population has real discretionary income. The Pareto principle rules – 20 per cent of the world's population controls 80 per cent of the world's wealth. So, who has choice? How can the notions of consumer choice be compatible with human well-being or environmental sustainability, indeed with survival itself?
2. *Is freedom compatible with well-being?*
   This is a philosophical question beyond the scope of this chapter. However, it is an unstated principle of the market-driven economy that freedom includes the freedom to choose your life-style, the freedom to consume whatever takes your fancy and whatever you can afford. Society, acting through public policy, polices this activity, and manages it in so far as government can manage the economy. In a global market environment, its powers are circumscribed, thus the secondary mortgage market weakness in the USA brings a British bank to its knees!
3. *Who has choice?*
   Not everybody! In the United States close to half the adult population has no medical insurance, hence very little choice in matters concerning their own health management. Most of the developed countries have an underclass which often resorts to crime in order to participate in consumer society.

After this opening statement, I want first to explore a little further the subject of globalization. Then I will turn to the role of marketing managers, or market-driven professionals, as I shall call them. This will be preceded by six questions that will provide a framework for the ensuing discussion.

What is required of us if we are to become, not market-driven professionals, but civic-professionals (professionals who care about the future of civil society, and the health and well-being of its citizens) in a global market place overshadowed by fundamental questions about belief and environmental sustainability?

If we are to navigate the future, we need to understand the metamorphosis and effects of globalization. The agenda is a long one.

1. *Economies and economics – industrialization, de-industrialization, post-industrialization, the role of international institutions (WTO, World Bank), scale and its effects*
   In the world today, there are three parallel systems. Industrialization is taking place in the Far East – in particular in India, China, Taiwan, Korea, Malaysia and Thailand, with other countries, such as Vietnam, not far behind. South America is overlooked and underestimated – Brazil for example has a thriving commercial aircraft building industry. De-industrialization is occurring in North America and Europe, where manufacturing is in decline, and service industries are growing. Post-industrialization is a threshold that the United Kingdom is about to cross, an economy where services and brainwork prevail, where manufacturing and physical work are in steep decline.

   The global economy is characterized by the dominance of global corporations, and global institutions. The World Bank and the World Trade Organization effectively supervise much of the world's economic development and trade.

   Scale is measured by global reach. Future development will see the growth of global companies exploiting economies of scale, whilst innovation may flourish in small start-up companies, which, once having proved the viability of their innovation, will be gobbled up by large organizations.

2. *Politics and political economy – tyranny, despotism, Enlightenment; the establishment and the supporting and nurturing of democratic structures*
   We live in an age when the hope and trust that we in the West have placed in Enlightenment values is questioned everywhere. The global political world is awash with tyrannies, with despotic rulers, with theocracies, and indeed with failed states. The presence of mature and enlightened establishments, supported by the majority of a well-educated and nurtured middle class appears to be unattainable in much of the twenty-first century world. Yet that establishment has been the foundation of true democratic structures.

3. *Culture – the viability of local culture, and ethnic/religious tradition*
   Globalization portends the homogenization of systems of meaning, and of life-styles. Global communications are so efficient and extensive that life-styles are learnt not in the nursery of local culture and tradition but from the internet and the airwaves. Though not necessarily a bad thing, two obvious problems loom large. We will call one,

the politics of envy – those who have not now know all about the life-styles and aspirations of the haves. And two, the clash of both ethnic-ity and religious tradition portends in the near future a titanic strug-gle. The history of the world records the death and destruction wrought by religious wars – today that struggle has global reach.

4. *Social institutions – from the village to the global village; from the manor born to the global city; from central government paternalism to rampant individualism*

Social institutions, which historically have been the glue of human society are transforming dramatically. The village is hardly viable as an economic or social unit. If you live in a village in England, you commute to a city to earn a living, or else you use the village as your second home. If you live in a village in India or China, you want to get out as soon as possible to go and live in a big city. The global cities dominate the economies of the countries in which they exist.

Governing these entities is a huge task, and we have not yet invented institutions capable of so doing. The clash between central and local government can be observed around the globe.

Compounding the problem is the fact that the market-driven system puts the consumer and personal consumption in the driver's seat. Rampant individualism is lauded, diminishing the community and the sense of shared values. 'Me' is the focus, 'We' are diminished.

## Globalization and the meaning of citizenship

The push towards globalization and the accompanying decline of the nation-state leads to fundamental questions about the future of citizen-ship. We, as individuals, play out several roles in parallel, and some of those roles are in conflict.

Ideas of citizens and citizenship describe our socio-political role in society. We are members of a polity, with rights and obligations to the whole. This sense and understanding is highly developed in such coun-tries as Great Britain and the USA.

We are also consumers playing the role of buyers of goods and services in our market-driven economy. The economic welfare of the polity trad-itionally requires us to spend rather than save.

Customers and their suppliers are merely another aspect of the role of the consumer. In a modern economy we have to become someone's customer in order to consume. We produce very little ourselves, and are reliant on a supply chain to meet our requirements.

'Client' is a term applied to our role in what might be called professional relationships. We are clients of accountants, banks, insurance companies, doctors and occasionally of HM Prison Service. There is a sense of obligation in such relationships which does not characterize our relationship with the local supermarket.

'Citizen-professionals' – if we regard our obligations to the state as necessary to the future well-being of the state and its citizenry, than we would rightly be described as citizen-professionals. This term applies to our whole lives – as individuals, as householders, as job holders, as managers, as business owners, as wage-slaves, as electors.

## Management as a profession

The management profession suffers from 'epistemopathology'.

Epistemopathology is diseased, sick, and bad knowledge that is mechanically applied to contemporary (global) market systems, in self-serving ways, to identify and solve immediate problems, problems which are not well understood and without any consideration of ripple effects on society as a whole. Lindbloom (1990) calls this tendency 'impairment', suggesting that we fail to see the whole picture. Senge (1994) calls it 'organisational learning disability', the failure of the organization to understand its holistic role. The pursuit of the bottom line, the focus on shareholder value, ignoring the wider implications of the role of the corporate entity in society.

We live in a global world, a world fashioned by the machine, the factory, the assembly line, and with increasingly sophisticated information systems operating in and networking large-scale bureaucratic organizations. We have been trained and educated in industrialized, bureaucratized schools, colleges and universities. Our profession is an instrument of market-driven, industrialized, bureaucratic society. We are steeped, indeed brainwashed, in mechanical, market-driven professionalism. Our watchwords are planning, organizing, motivating, controlling, stability, conformity, predictability, regulation.

The postmodernists are threatening that world. Ambiguity, complexity, and chaos threaten our cosy self-defined world. Future shock and paradigm shifts are post-reality, the world we now inhabit.

I am going to concentrate on market-driven professionals, partly because I am a fully paid up member of the class (a Chartered Marketer, and past president of the Market Research Society), partly because I am interested in the role of the professions in our society. Another set of questions.

1. Do market-driven professionals really demonstrate social responsibility? I fear that the answer must be 'rarely' in most spheres of economic activity. However, the caring professions consistently demonstrate social responsibility. Individual managers may try to act with social responsibility, but they are governed by a corporate ethic.
2. If consumer freedom of choice epitomizes the dichotomy between the citizen-professional and the private citizen, can interdependency be re-established? If the planet is to be saved, interdependency must be understood and established. The consumer is an actor in a system that encourages him/her to aspire to the good life, and to consume is part of that aspiration. The market-driven system heretofore has shown little or no concern for the larger canvas – the well-being of a planet with finite resources. The market-driven system has had no mechanisms for calculating costs and benefits on this scale.
3. Can democracy, citizenship and socially responsible professionalism be made the hallmarks of the twenty-first century? This is the great challenge of our time.
4. Today, does mechanical, market-driven professionalism prevail? Has social trusteeship been compromised?
5. Can we invent social trusteeship in our profession? Can mutual empowerment and constituent practice theory help? I believe so.
6. Can you educate citizen-professionals, and can they contribute to the transformation of the sightless psychopath? We marketers claim to have the tools, the insights and the know-how to sell refrigerators to Eskimos (they may be needing them soon!), surely we can help transform the sightless psychopaths.

Implicit in these questions is a contrast between what I will call mechanical, market-driven professionalism, and social trustee civic professionalism. The remainder of this chapter will dwell on these two definitions, since the author's contention is that the management profession must metamorphose itself into a social trustee role if it is to survive.

## Social trustee civic professionalism

We want to propose that in the era of globalization, social trustee civic professionalism must rule. Narrow self-interest must no longer characterize our professionalism. Citizen-professionals must minister to the needs and wants of other citizens. We must not pretend, as we have, that we regard the needs and wants of consumers as grist to our mill, for the needs and wants of some consumers cannot be equated with the needs and wants of our citizens.

We envision paradise as a globally networked society, dedicated to promoting social welfare, with citizen-professionals dedicated to sustainable, integrated, equitable, social and economic development. Citizen-professionals will promote democracy and ensure social responsibility. In other words, instead of being self-serving, method-bound, narrowly-focused profession members, we will become social trustees of the common good. We will have a clear, comprehensive vision of the good and just society and its place in the world order. We will abandon our pretences about value-neutrality and objectivity (our inheritance from the philosophy of science) and focus on ethical-moral, social responsibility as it confronts the citizens of global, cosmopolitan democracies.

The most powerful criticism is directed at the changed role of global corporations. 'Corporations are much more than the purveyors of the products we all want; they are also the most powerful political forces of our time, the driving forces behind bodies such as the World Trade Organisation' (Klein, 2000).

Figure 15.1 provides a model for understanding civic professionalism in its social trustee dimension. This model may help us to explore a new approach to the role of marketing and management in civil society. In Table 15.1 I contrast market-driven professionalism (the viewpoint of

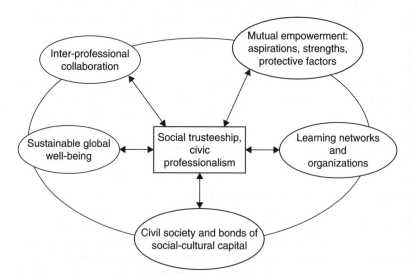

*Figure 15.1* Mutual determination with social trustee civic professionalism
*Source*: Thomas (2006).

*Table 15.1* What is it we need to do to become more professional?

| | Market-driven professionalism | Civic professionalism |
|---|---|---|
| *1. What is the current relationship between purpose and orientation in the management profession?* | | |
| a. Primary purpose | Improvement in buyer-seller relationships | Holistic improvements in better human beings, citizenship in a good society |
| b. Power orientation | Top-down professional knows best | Shared. People served have knowledge and expertise |
| c. View of customers/ clients. | Needs, problems | Aspirations, needs, wants |
| *2. What needs to be done to change attitudes toward work and behaviour? How does this impact on the management profession?* | | |
| a. Action orientation | Professional distance and emotional detachment | Empathy, advocacy, caring and strategic support |
| b. Focus of work | Individuals' behaviour and characteristics, sometimes moderated by professional norms | Individuals, groups, families in their community, social and cultural environments |
| c. Work organization | Bureaucracy | Learning organizations |
| d. Criteria for 'good' work | Units delivered, fidelity to rules and norms, specified by the organization | Improvements in shared learning goals, social trust and quality of treatment |
| e. Work orientation | Method-bound, role-taker, tendency to fit person to methods and programmes of the organization | Role-maker, tailored to persons, cultures and contacts |
| *3. What root/core metaphors and systems characterize the management professions?* | | |
| a. Organization directions | Administration and management following proper procedure so things are done right | Leadership ensuring good results because the right things are done, at the right time, for the right reasons |
| b. Career orientation | Individualistic: mobility and prestige stem from personal achievements | Collective as well as individual mutual responsibility for stewardship of the community, society and the planet |
| c. Root metaphors | Machine (assembly line) | Social ecology |
| d. Reference | Reductionistic, specialized, and categorical | Ecological, relational, and interdependent |
| e. System | Specialized compliance, adherence, reinforcement, control and regulation | Empowerment, social trust, mutual aid and assistance, reciprocity, social responsibility with reference to well-being and the just society |
| *4. Should human and societal welfare needs be served? What role does management play in this? How does this impact orientation?* | | |
| a. Cultural orientation | Assimilation, cultural diversity problems and needs for control | Mutual accommodation, referencing, social diversity as an asset |

*(Continued)*

*Table 15.1*   (Continued)

|  | Market-driven professionalism | Civic professionalism |
|---|---|---|
| b. Kind of rationality | Formal methods and goals, means may become ends | Substantive democratized social-rational practices ensuring human and social welfare needs are served |
| c. Theory of change | Simplistic restricted to psychological micro-theories | Complex theories developed to generate mutually-beneficial synergy |
| *5.   How does management theory impact on management practice?* | | |
| a. Philosophical grounding | Positivism and post-positivism | Neo-pragmatism, aspects of post-modernism |
| b. Imagery of knowledge use | Behavioural and social engineering | Participatory, democratic planning and decision-making |
| c. Theory-practice frame | Theory is constituted by facts and propositions gained through empirical observation; theory is value free | Theory begins with value referents regarding good, just, sustainable societies. Practice is an exercise in the social construction of theories in pursuit of these visions (praxis) |
| *6.   Should attitudes towards competition be supplanted by more cooperative approaches? How will this impact on organizational structure?* | | |
| a. Legitimization strategy | Conventional: keeping up with those deemed to be role models | Confidence that the future will provide a more rational and fairer society for all |
| b. Orientation towards civil society | Indifferent, perhaps ignorant, only market-focused | Committed stewardship and nurturing of freedom |
| c. Ethical-moral grounding | | |

the sightless psychopath) and civic professionalism. By comparing each column the reader may observe the metamorphosis that is required. Though focused on marketing, the metamorphosis required applies to all management activity, so that in the columns, management and marketing are interchangeable terms. As a profession we must demonstrate by our professionalism that we are crucial to the survival both of the organization we claim to serve, or are employed by, and to society in general.

Management as a culture means that management professionals have a critical role to play as advocates for customers and for the value system that puts the customer first. The customer is not defined as only the ultimate purchaser – the concept of internal and external marketing defines the customer as any downstream contact. Marketing relationships are becoming much more complex, and mutual dependency relationships, strategic alliances and network organizations require insights well beyond those traditionally associated with the marketing function, namely, the management of promotion and distribution, the management of the sales force, and some opportunities to influence pricing and product policy. The new insights will derive from such diverse disciplines as political economy, organization psychology, and cultural anthropology – to name but three.

The most important asset a business has is its ongoing relationships with its global customers. Management professionals have a legitimate claim to a profound understanding of the development and nurturing of those relationships. Though increasingly it is claimed that everyone in the corporation must be charged with this responsibility, understanding it and interpreting it should be the domain of the management professional.

The management profession has a powerful rhetoric. We do not lack ideological materials. It is more than a set of techniques for the management of external markets. Our flexible ideology, our disposition to accept change as the inevitable consequence of the interplay of market forces would however, be hijacked by others, for quite different purposes.

We must improve our reputation as knowledge generators, through strategic linkages and alliances with leading-edge knowledge generators. We must demonstrate, perhaps by benchmarking, that the most successful companies are those that are truly both market-driven *and* responsible global citizens.

More urgently perhaps, we must recognize that in addition to high standards of objectivity, integrity and technical competence, we must, in responding to the changing environment, demonstrate that we can and will serve society in general. This requires clear and articulate demonstration of our ability to be relevant in the political sense. Accountants have been successful in part because they have been so obviously servants of Anglo-American capitalism with its historical focus on finance. Though this is not the correct forum to discuss this, we could develop the argument that this historic focus has served us poorly in competition with the Japanese. In the global economy, and in the face of the competitive forces within it, it is the company and the country that delivers value to the marketplace that will survive. If we remain tied to the forces of manipulation and hype, if we are seen merely to be the servants of our capitalist masters, we will remain marginal and untrustworthy. If we can demonstrate that we have the keys to the knowledge base that will benefit society as a whole then we may prosper.

Consistent with the themes of this book, I have pursued the idea that marketing is a metaphor for the nature of the times in which we live. For most of the twentieth century it represented the means by which we became efficient consumers, it was a driver of consistently improving living standards, rarely criticized as being either too manipulative or unconcerned about profligate use of the world's resources. The twenty-first century will become increasingly preoccupied with the consequences of global warming and the clash of cultures. What new roles will marketing have to play? Can the profession, and indeed the citizenry that it claims to serve, metamorphose into civic professionalism, working to save the planet from a very unpleasant and uncomfortable end?

## References

Ascherson, N. (1999),'The indispensable Englishman', *New Statesman*, 29 January: 26.

Fukuyama, F. (2000), *The Great Disruption: Human Nature and the Reconstitution of Social Order*, London: Profile Books.

Klein, N. (2000), *No Logo*, London: Flamingo.

Lindbloom, C. (1990), *Inquiry and Change: the Troubled Attempt to Understand and Shape Society*, New Haven: Yale University Press.

Senge, P. (1994), *The Fifth Discipline Field Book*, New York: Doubleday.

Thomas, M.J. (2006), 'Management: a profession in theory', *Management Decision*, 44(3): 309–15.

# Index

Academy of Marketing 1
adolescents
  face-to-face interaction 129, 130
  mobile device use 120–30;
    psychological attachment
    to 122–3
  opinion leaders for 123, 130
  social networking 121–2, 128,
    129, 130
  as viral marketing target
    group 123–30
advertising 91–2
  case studies 107–10
  comparative 146, 147, 148–51,
    157
  credibility enhancers in 157
  hierarchy of effects model in 5,
    147–52, 156–7
  as hyperbolic 98
  metaphors, use of 18
  negative comparative 146–51
  of new products/brands 149,
    157, 159
  viral marketing 5, 102–17, 118–31
affective effects 147, 150–2, 156
  see also hierarchy of effects model
alchemy, as marketing
  metaphor 94–100
alternative reality games (ARGs) 119
ambassadors see brand ambassadors
American Marketing Association
  (AMA) 2, 45, 55
analogy, use of 197
Annan, Kofi 29
anthropological metaphors 18
Apple 186, 188, 189
Arndt, Johan 17, 57
attack advertising see negative
  comparative advertising
attitude-towards-the-advertisement/
  brand 147, 150–1, 157, 158, 160
automobile industry 31, 178–9
aviation industry 33

Baldinger, A. L. 152
Bass, Frank 170
Beck, Ulrich 40
behaviour
  buyer behaviour models 5
  emotional 105–6, 112–13, 115
  buyer response 43–4
Berger, Peter L. 38, 39
Berry, Leonard 19
biological metaphors see evolutionary
  metaphors
Bitner, M. J. 17–18, 56–7
*The Blair Witch Project* (film) 107,
  116, 119
Bongo, Omar 40
Booms, B. H. 56–7
Borden, Neil H. 45, 55
Boston Consultancy Group 6, 17
Boston (share-growth) matrix 185,
  191–2
  see also product life cycle
Bowlby, Rachel 90
Boyd, R. 14
Brahimi, Lakhdar 39, 40
brand ambassadors 88–94,
  132–45
  celebrities as 99, 134, 139; as
    damaging 139–40
  consumer typologies 88–90
  criticism of 137–40
  customers as 134, 140–1
  definition 132–4
  employees as 134–9, 142, 144
  as evangelists 142, 143
  halo effect from 142
  job advertisements for 136–7
  as a metaphor 132, 134, 135,
    141–2, 143–4; controversial use
    of 138–9
  purpose 132–9
  represented company, relationship
    with 132, 140–1
  as sales promoters 136–9, 143–4

brand awareness/relationships 18,
    118, 123, 129, 134, 136
    *see also* viral marketing
brand loyalty 156, 158, 159, 178
brand promise(s) 135
brands/branding
    global brands 26, 27, 36
    iconic brands 141
    luxury brands 99
    new/revived brands 135–6, 149
Bremer, Kristine 45–6, 53
Brown, S. and D. Turley: *Consumer
    Research ...* 15–16
Brown, Stephen 88–9
    *Writing Marketing ...* 93–4
Buckingham, Ian: *Brand
    Engagement* 198
Burger King 109–10, 119
Burrow, Sharan 38
business failure 96
business screens concept 6
buyer behaviour models 5
buyers *see* consumers; customers
buyer-seller relationship *see* customer
    relationship management
buzz
    as a metaphor 118
    in viral marketing 119, 121, 122,
    123, 130

Cacciopo, John 150
Campbell, Joseph: *The Power of
    Myth* 203–4
Carrigan, T. 118–19
Carter, Jimmy 28
celebrity endorsement 99, 134, 139
    as damaging 139–40
    *see also* brand ambassadors
Celuch, K. G. 18
change, resistance to 163–5, 168
    *see also* laggard group
change process management 135–6
Childwise 120
choice *see* customer choice
Churchill, Winston 11
Clinton, Bill 29
cognitive effects 147, 148–50, 156
    *see also* hierarchy of effects model

communication 44, 208–9
    as apt 53
    barriers to 198
    as comprehensible 53, 195–205
    importance of 180–1, 199
    internal within organizations
    195–205; key communicators
    204–5
    language, use of 195–205
    leadership issues and 200–3
    as memorable 53, 55–6
    metaphors, use of *see* marketing
    metaphors; metaphors
    storytelling 197, 203–4
communication technology 30, 37,
    102, 206
    mobile devices 120–31
comparative advertising 146, 147
    advantages 148, 149
    consumer reactions 148, 149,
    150–1
    definition 146, 147
    evaluative/factual 157
    message believability 149–50
    negative 146–61
competitive advantage 2, 19, 30
competitive strategies 142, 183–4
computer games *see* alternative reality
    games
conative effects 147, 156–7
    *see also* hierarchy of effects model
consumer consent 20–1
consumer goods 36, 183
consumer leapfrogging effect 162–3,
    166–8, 169, 170
consumer research 18, 46
consumer typologies 88–90
    *see also* brand ambassadors
consumers
    and customers, differentiation
    between 69–73
    in global markets 209–10
    as promiscuous 178
    *see also* customers
consumption/production *see* supply/
    demand
contractual relationships 177–8
conveyance metaphors 14, 19, 46
Copeland, Gary 152

core metaphors 14, 19, 46
  marketing mix as 46–7
Cornelisson, Joep P. 18, 46
corporate identity 18
corporate imperialism 28–9
cosmetics industry *see* fashion/
  cosmetics industries
cost-cutting 66
Cote, Dave 134–5
Cranfield University School of
  Management 63
credibility enhancers, in
  advertising 157
Culliton, James 45
cultural issues 30, 208–9
  organizational 199, 203–4
customer choice 66, 75, 97,
  148, 172
  freedom of choice 207, 211
  high/low level involvement 148, 158
  influences on 206
  poor choices 158
  process of 147–52, 156–7, 158
  rational/emotional 148
  transformational products 158
customer first concept 214–15
customer lists, marketing of 21
customer needs 5, 74–5, 76, 77,
  211–12
customer relationship
  management 2, 5, 18, 179–81
  buyer response 43–4
  choice of customer 179–80
  development of 174
  interpersonal relationships 21–2
  marriage metaphor in 19
  *see also* relationship marketing
customer-brand relationship 18, 134
  brand ambassadors 88–94, 132–45
customers 199–200
  buying process 3, 5
  as clients 173
  and consumers, differentiation
    between 69–73
  as critical/discerning 3, 30, 216
  critical purchase influences
    (CPIs) 80
  direct 69–70
  in global market 209–10

identification of 69, 70–1
in relationship marketing 172–3

D2 Communications 125
Day, George 176
decision-making/makers 50, 52
  critical purchase influences
    (CPIs) 85
  by customers *see* customer choice
  identification of 75, 76, 79–82, 84,
    85, 86
demand pull 66, 73
  *see also* supply/demand potential
Dennis, N. 18
designer labels *see* brand ambassadors
Dhalla, N. K. 193
Dholakia, U. M. 121
diffusion of innovation curve 65–6,
  164, 165, 166–7
  *see also* new products; product life
    cycle
distribution chain 76–9, 85
dormant/dead metaphors 17, 22, 26,
  37, 157
Doving, E. 15
Draper, Tim 119
Drucker, Peter 26
due diligence issues 2
Dunbar, Ian *see* McDonald, Malcolm
  and Ian Dunbar
Dunford, R. 15
DuPont 193
Dwyer, R. F. 174

early majority (adopters) group, in
  product diffusion 64, 65, 162, 163
e-commerce 115
  *see also* viral marketing
economic growth
  globalization and 30–1, 37, 40–1,
    208
  industrialization 208
  net present value (NPV) 170
economies of scale 185, 189
Elaboration Likelihood Model
  (ELM) 150, 151, 158
Elder, Larry 27–8
emotional language 197–8

emotional responses   105–6, 112–13, 115
   *see also* behaviour
employees   199–200
   as brand ambassadors   134–9, 142, 144
   communication between   195–205; as hierarchical   200–3
   customers, relationship with   134, 200
   employers' view of   200–3
environmental issues *see* sustainability issues
epistemopathology concept   210
ethical issues
   social responsibility   211–16
   in viral marketing   116
euphemisms, metaphors as   142–3
evolutionary metaphors   17, 184, 198
exchange conditions   43, 44, 53–4
   control of   53
   new exchange model   42–5
experience-grounded metaphors   14

fashion/cosmetics industry   123
   viral marketing campaigns   123, 125–30
FCB Grid   147–8, 158
   *see also* hierarchy of effects model
financial markets   77
financial service providers   135–6, 176, 180, 181, 195, 208
The Fine Wine Delivery Company (New Zealand)   174–5, 181
Firstdirect   176, 180, 181
Fiske, R. P.   17
Foster's Group   107–8
4Ps mnemonic   45, 54–8, 92, 172, 173, 179
   basic: product/price/place/ promotion   55, 92
   extension of   56; people/process/ physical evidence   56–7
   as over-popular (P-mania)   57–8
   *see also* marketing mix
Fowler, H. W.   11
Friedman, Thomas   37–8

Fukuyama, Francis   206
Fuller, Ronald A.   42
fundamental metaphors   13–14

Gates, Bill   27
Gelb, B. D.   150, 152, 156
General Electric   6
global brands   26, 31, 36
global citizenship concept   209–10
global corporate responsibility   212
globalization, of markets   2, 3, 5, 6, 36–41, 76
   anti-globalization   28–9, 39–40
   corporate imperialism   28–9
   definition   26
   economic growth and   30–1, 37, 40–1, 208
   future of   34, 36–7
   impact of   26–7, 29–30, 206–10
   as inevitable   29, 37
   opinions of   27–9, 37–41
   origin of concept   26
   as positive/beneficial   27–8, 29–30, 37–9
   Rule of Three theory   31–7
   social responsibility and   29–31, 37, 211–16
Godin, Seth: *Unleashing the Ideavirus*   103
Goldston, Mark   151
Grasso, Richard   41
Greider, William   39
Grewal, Dhruv   148, 149, 150, 151, 152, 157
Grey, William   157
Gronroos, Christian: *In Search of a New Logic for Marketing*   2–3

Haley, R. I.   150
Halonen, Tarja   41
*Harvard Business Review*   62, 193
Harvard Business School   43
Hensel, P. J.   147, 149, 150, 151, 152, 156
Hess, J.   18
hierarchy of effects model   5, 147–8, 158
   affective effects   147, 150–2, 156

cognitive effects   147, 148–50, 156
conative effects   147, 156–7
FCB Grid   147–8, 158
Rossiter-Percy Grid   148, 158
*see also* advertising; customer choice
Hirschman, E. C.   11, 18
home appliances industry   34
Honeywell   134–5
Horwitz, Ethan, 160
Huck, P.   104
Hunt, Shelby D.   11, 12, 19, 20, 56

Iacobucci, D.   21
Iacocca, Lee   35
IBM   187, 189
IKEA   141
imitation products   96–7
income levels   42, 183, 207
Industrial Marketing and Purchasing
    Group (IMP)   14
industrialization/
    de-industrialization   208
information *see* communication;
    product information
information technology
    services   36–7
innovation(s) *see* new products
innovation diffusion *see* diffusion of
    innovation curve
innovator group, in product
    diffusion   64, 65, 162, 163–4
    characteristics   163, 164, 166
    laggards as   163, 166, 167, 169, 170
instrumental metaphors   14
integrated marketing   2, 5
international trade   28, 30–1, 76
internet access, via mobile
    devices   124–5
interpersonal relationships   21–2
intersubjective certification   4
Ipso Insight   120

Jackson, Barbara   19
James, Karen E.   147, 149, 150, 151,
    152, 156
Jameson, Fredric   28
Japan   33, 34
    mobile devices, use of   120–1, 123–4

viral marketing   123–30
jazz, as marketing metaphor   18
Jobs, Steve   186, 188
Johnson, M. *see* Lakoff, G. and
    M. Johnson
Johnson-Cartee, Karen   152
Jordan, Bill   39
Juniper Networks   152, 155, 156
Juniper Research   120
Jurvetson, Steve   119

Kamakura, Wagner   164
Kato, Y.   122
Kerry, John F.   38
Klein, N.: *No Logo*   212
Korten, David   40
Kotler, Philip   43

laggard group, in product
    diffusion   64, 65, 162–71
    characteristics   164–6, 167–8
    consumer leapfrogging by   162–3,
        166–8, 169, 170
    definition   165–6
    economic importance   169–70
    as innovators   163, 166, 167,
        169, 170
    resistance, differentiation
        between   163–5, 168
Lakoff, G: *Fire and Dangerous
    Things . . .*   13
Lakoff, G. and M. Johnson: *Metaphors
    We Live By*   12, 13–14
language, use of   195–205
    *see also* communication; metaphors
late majority group, in product
    diffusion   64, 65
Lau, Richard   148
Lavidge, R. C.   147
leadership issues   200–3
Lee, Moonkyu   45–6, 53
legal issues
    contractual relationships   177–8
    in negative comparative
        advertising   160
Levitt, Theodore (Ted)   26, 173, 193
    *The Marketing Imagination*   6, 19
    *Thinking about Management*   96

Lindbloom, C.: *Inquiry and Change . . .* 210
literary metaphors 14, 19, 46
logical positivism 4
loyalty cards 176–7, 178

Macaulay, M. 18
MacCormac, E. R.: *A Cognitive Theory of Metaphor* 14
Maker's Mark bourbon 140–1
management *see* marketing management
management consultants 62, 62, 66, 93, 95, 195
Mandelson, Peter 40
market definition 68, 74, 75–9, 84, 85
  geographical boundaries 75–6
  importance of 86
  *see also* target markets/groups
market growth 66, 68, 71–2, 185, 206–7
market mapping 76–9, 84, 85
  leverage points 77, 80, 81
  purpose 76
market niches 33–4, 35
market segmentation 5, 62–87, 164, 165
  critical purchase influences (CPIs) 85
  definition 62, 64
  importance to success 62–3, 69–73, 84
  key discriminating features (KDFs) 85
  market mapping and 76–9, 84, 85
  market sectors, differentiation between 64
  as a metaphor 62
  objectives 74, 86
  a priori 64
  process/methodology 64–9, 75–86
  in Rule of Three theory 34–6
  target markets 64–9, 70–3, 74, 75
  viable segments 74–5, 83–6;
    micro-segments 79–82, 84, 85
market share 73–4, 185
marketing

alchemy as metaphor for 94–100
criticism of 1, 2, 3, 4–5, 7, 57, 98, 88–101
definition 1, 4, 9
as empirical 57, 59
exchange conditions in 53–4; new exchange model 42–5
future of 1, 2–3, 4, 205–16
globalization of *see* globalization
as good/bad 99–100
as a metaphor 7–8, 17–25, 49–50; *see also* marketing metaphors
sales results, effect on 191, 192
special interest groups in 99
successful 5, 63, 86
as ubiquitous 8
marketing concept *see* marketing mix
marketing history 42–5, 172, 183
marketing management 59, 157–60, 179–81, 191–3, 195
  as epistemopathological 210
  future of 206, 210–16
  planning process in 18, 185
  professionalism in 210–16
  role/purpose 212–14
  social responsibility in 211–16
marketing metaphors 5–7, 17–25, 46
  in advertising 18
  anthropological 18
  brand ambassadors as 132, 134, 135, 141–2, 143–4; controversial use of 138–9
  as constraining 10
  in consumer research 18
  evolution as 17
  market segmentation as 62
  marketing mix as 45–59
  marriage as 10, 11, 12, 19–23, 177–82
  negative comparative marketing as 157
  services oriented 17–18, 20
  servicescape metaphor 17–18
  use of 10, 11, 15, 22, 142–3; over-use 195–205
  viral marketing as 103–4, 113, 118
  warfare as 5, 6, 17, 142, 146–7, 184
marketing metamorphosis 7–8, 59, 206–16

marketing mix 4, 5, 42–61
    criticism of 48–52, 57–8
    definition 42, 45, 46, 50
    denotations of 48–52
    4Ps mnemonic 45, 54–8, 92, 172,
        173, 179
    as a metaphor 45–59
    origin of concept 42, 44–5
    over-use of 53, 55, 56, 57–9
    relationship marketing and 53–4
marketing myopia metaphor 46
marketing paradigms 3–4
marketing research 5, 97–9
markets
    financial 77, 135–6, 176, 180,
        181, 195
    mature 65, 66, 68, 72, 172
    target 64–9, 70–3, 74, 75, 110–11,
        113, 115, 116, 121, 123
marriage metaphor 54
    case studies 174–7
    in customer relationship
        management 19
    definition 19, 20
    importance of 19–20
    over-use of 11, 19, 21–3
    in relationship marketing 10, 11,
        12, 18–23, 177–82
McCarthy, Jerome: *Basic Marketing . . .*
    55, 56, 58
McCarthy, M. 146
McDonald, Malcolm and Ian Dunbar:
    *Market Segmentation . . .* 69, 86
McWilliams, David 100n1
Meat and Livestock Commission
    (UK) 175–6
Menon, A. 11, 12, 19–20
mergers and acquisitions
    (M&As) 33–7, 172
metaphors 10–17
    in advertising 18; *see also* marketing
        metaphors
    alternatives to 197
    classification/types of 13–14,
        19, 46
    as contradictory/inconsistent 144
    definition 12, 45–6, 47, 55, 196
    dormant/dead 17, 22, 26, 37, 157
    as euphemisms 142–3

    importance of 10–11, 15–16, 18,
        26, 196, 198–9
    limitations to 11, 12, 14
    in marketing *see* marketing
        metaphors
    mixed 12, 142, 195, 203
    nature/role 12–14
    as partial/selective 47, 53
    primary/secondary concepts 46,
        47–8
    product life cycle as 184–5
    use/choice of 10–11, 12–13, 15–17,
        20, 21, 144, 198; internal organi-
        zational use 195–205;
        over-use 57–8, 195–205
Michael, Bernd 149
Microsoft 187, 189
military metaphors *see* warfare
mind prints concept 2
Mirowski, P. 16
Mitchell, A. A. 150
mobile devices
    adolescent use of 120–30; psycho-
        logical attachment to 122–3
    i-mode 123–4
    internet access via 124–5
    for music 185–6
    numbers of users 120–1; in
        Japan 123–4
    QR codes 124
    short message service (SMS) 120,
        122
    in social networking 120–1
    in viral marketing 120–30
monopoly power 32
    *see also* Rule of Three theory
multinational corporations *see*
    globalization

Nader, Ralph 28
Naisbitt, John 38, 41
negative comparative
    advertising 146–61
    advantages of 148–9, 156, 157
    backlash against 151, 152, 159
    brand loyalty and 156, 158, 159
    cognitive effects 148–50
    competitor's response 160

(negative comparative advertising
  – *continued*)
  consumer reactions   147–52, 156–7
  credibility enhancers in   157
  definition   147
  Diet Pepsi   152, 154
  direct/implied   152, 156
  effectiveness   158–60
  evaluative/factual   152, 157, 160
  Juniper Networks   152, 155, 156
  legal issues   160
  managerial implications   157–60
  message believability   149–50,
    156, 160
  as a metaphor   157
  by Miller Brewing   152, 153
  product/image   152, 159
  target groups   159
  use of   147, 157–60
  *see also* comparative advertising
negativity bias concept   148–9, 150
net present value (NPV)   170
  *see also* economic growth
network marketing   2, 14, 178–9
new exchange model   42–5
new products/brands   2, 35, 42,
    135–6, 183, 192
  advertising of   149, 157, 159
  diffusion   64–6, 102, 162–71
  dominant design
    development   162, 166–7
  failure of   2, 62
  as imitation products   96–7, 184
  launch process   65
  as new technology   66, 188
  *see also* product life cycle
new technology   66, 186, 189
  in communications   30, 37, 102, 206
  technology life cycle   188
  in viral marketing   110, 112, 113,
    119; mobile devices   120–31
Norway, mobile device use   120–1

O'Neal, Shaquille   164–5
Olsen, J. C.   150
open source software   187–8
opinion-leaders   111
  for adolescents   123, 130
  in product diffusion   64, 65

organizational culture   199, 203–4
Ostrom, A.   21

Palmer, I.   15
Parasuraman, A.   19
Pareto principle   207
Parise, Jessica   160
partial metaphors   14
penetration pricing   189–90
Penrose, E. T.   184
Peters, Tom J.   63, 66
Peters, Tom J. and R. H. Waterman: *In
    Search of Excellence*   62, 66
Petty, Richard   150
planning models *see* strategic
    planning
political attack advertising *see* negative
    comparative advertising
political issues   207, 208
portfolio matrices   5, 6, 17
price competition   35, 36, 70, 71, 189
pricing strategies   44, 189–90
Proctor & Gamble   73
product classes/classification   44, 190
product information, availability
    of   3, 43, 148
product life cycle   5, 6, 14, 46, 66,
    72–3, 183–94
  Boston (share-growth) matrix   185,
    191–2
  case studies   185–8; mobile
    music   185–6, 188, 189;
    typewriters/keyboards   187,
    188–9, 190
  level playing field for   188–9
  management use of   191–3
  as a metaphor   184–5
  new products *see* new products
  shortening of   188
  standards/protocols and   189
  superseded/obsolescent
    products   187, 189, 190
  technology life cycle   188
  *see also* diffusion of innovation curve
product managers   183
production/consumption *see* supply/
    demand
protocols *see* standards/protocols

reciprocal marketing 44
referral(s) 102
  *see also* viral marketing
Reich, Robert 38
relationship marketing 2–3, 18,
    172–82, 215
  breakdown in 178, 180
  case studies 174–7
  commitment in 20–1, 22
  consumer consent 20–1
  contractual relationships 177–8
  customer-brand relationship 18
  customers in 172–4, 175, 176, 177,
    179–81
  definition 172–3
  as exclusive 178
  failure of 21
  Firstdirect 176
  importance of 172, 183
  interpersonal relationships in 21–2
  as long-term 178–9
  management of 179–81
  marketing mix and 53–4
  marriage metaphor, use of 10, 11,
    12, 18–23, 177–82
  stages in 174, 177
  Tesco 176–7
  *see also* brand ambassadors; customer
    relationship management
Remington typewriters 187
Rindfleisch, A. 11, 13–14
Rink, D. R. 191
Rogers, Everett 64–5, 66
  *Diffusion of Innovations* 164, 165
Ross, Geoff 108–9
Rossiter-Percy Grid 148, 158
  *see also* hierarchy of effects model
Rule of Three theory 31–7
  in aviation industry 33
  definition 31
  exceptions to 32, 36
  as global 32–7; *see also* globalization
  in home appliance industry 34
  monopoly power and 32
  process of 34–6
  in tyre industry 33–4

sales 66
  marketing contribution to 191, 192

value issues in 122
  *see also* consumers; customers
sales promotions 136–9, 143–4
Samuelson, Paul A. 39
Sato, N. 122
Schroeder, Gerhard 39
Schultz, D. E. 3
Schultz, H. 3
Sen, Arjun 156
Senge, P.: *The Fifth Discipline . . .* 210
service industries 172, 208
  financial 135–6, 176, 180, 181,
    195, 208
services oriented marketing 2–3, 18
  brand ambassadors and 134
  metaphors, use of 17–18, 20, 56–7
servicescape metaphor 17–18
Shakar, Alex: *The Savage Girl* 90–1
share-growth matrix 6, 17
  *see also* Boston matrix
Sheth, Jagdish N. 4–5
Sheth, Jagdish N. and Rajendra S.
    Sisodia: *The Rule of Three . . .* 32,
    41n4
Sholes, Christopher 186–7
Short, Clare 29
similes, use of 197
Sisodia, Rajendra S. *see* Sheth, Jagdish N.
    and Rajendra S. Sisodia
Sloan, Alfred 183
social issues 209
social networking 120–1
  by adolescents 121–2, 128, 129, 130
  virtual communities 121, 140
social responsibility 209–10, 211
  globalization and 29–31, 37
Sony 185–6, 189
Sorescu, A. B. 150, 152, 156
specialization/specialists *see* market
    niches
standards/protocols 189
Steiner, G. A. 147
Stern, B. B. 11
Stone, Gregory 88
Story, J. 18
storytelling 197, 203–4
  *see also* communication
strategic planning 5, 72–3
supply chains 178–9

supply/demand potential 42, 43,
44–5
demand pull 66, 73
sustainability issues 207
Swan, E. 191
Sweeney, John J. 40
systematic metaphors 14

target markets/groups 64–9, 70–3
definition 68, 74, 75
in negative comparative
advertising 159
in viral marketing 110–11, 113,
114, 115, 116, 121, 123–30
*see also* market definition
technology life cycles 188
*see also* new technology; product life
cycles
television set manufacturers 37
Tesco 176–7, 178, 180
theoretical metaphors 19
theory-constitutive metaphors 14, 46
marriage metaphor as 19
Thomas, M. 5
trade *see* international trade
transaction marketing *see* 4Ps
mnemonic
transitioning process 3
transformational products 158
trust, importance of 181
Turley, D. *see* Brown, S. and D. Turley
Twitchell, James B.: *Adcult USA* 90
Tynan, C. 174
tyre industry 33–4

UBS 135–6
United Kingdom 4, 208, 209
United States 31–2, 307, 208, 209
United States Federal Trade
Commission 147

value added chain 76–9, 85, 172
value issues 18, 122
Van den Bulte, Christophe 11, 12, 14,
15, 16, 17, 19, 22, 45, 46, 47, 48
Vaughn, R. 158
Vietnam 28, 29

viral marketing 5, 102–17, 118–31
*The Blair Witch Project* 107
brand awareness/relationships
and 118, 123, 129
Burger King's 'Subservient
Chicken' 109–10
Carlton Draught's Big Ad 107–8
case studies 107–10; in
Japan 123–30
costs 113
customer involvement 104–6;
emotional response 105–6,
112–13, 115
definition 102, 118, 119
development of 118–19
effectiveness 113–16, 120, 128–30
ethical issues 116
as exploitation 116
42 Below 108–9
Hotmail 111
inward effect 129, 130
message content 111, 115, 123
as a metaphor 103–4, 113, 118
outward effect 129, 130
process/methodology 102–3, 104,
110–15, 116, 123–30
rewards for referrals 113, 115,
122, 126
as social networking 120–1
target groups 110–11, 113, 114,
116, 121, 123; adolescents
as 123–30
technology used 110, 112, 113,
119; mobile devices 120–30
uses 102; in advertising 103–4,
107–10, 123–30
virtual communities 121, 140
*see also* social networking

Wade, Dwyane 165
Wal-Mart 73
warfare
language of 198
as a metaphor 13, 46, 184; in
marketing 5, 6, 17, 142, 146–7
Waterman, R. H. *see* Peters, Tom J. and
R. H. Waterman
Welch, Jack 27

Whitehead, A. N.: *Science and the Modern World* 15
Williams, Raymond 90
word processors 187–8
word-of-mouth effect 169, 170
World Bank 208
World Trade Organization 208, 212

young people *see* adolescents
Yuspeh, S. 193

Zaltman, G. 10, 18
Zaltman, G. at al: *Theory Construction in Marketing* 11